ENDORSEMENTS FOR
THE GOOD PASTOR BOOK

As I read Pastor Kelly's words to us, I was moved by the stark realistic description of the daily life and meaningful struggles to walk in a God-honoring manner privately, as well as to nourish and nurture the people of God to whom we have been appointed as overseers. The openness of the author to life in the "trench" of the ministry, as well as in the home provides a helpful lens to seeing ourselves in a "mirror," with the resultant realization that we who have felt the call of God to pastoral function share many of the same weaknesses of the flesh, spiritual struggles, and depression, born of disappointment, in ourselves and the work. However, thankfully, this work is more than that. It is full of wisdom and instruction from a peer who is both articulate and devoted. Through his own struggles, and the disciplines God has honed through his life and ministry, there is to be found here insight for all of us. I can highly recommend this volume.

John D. Hannah, Ph.D.
Professor of Historical Theology
Dallas Theological Seminary
Dallas, Texas

"Pastor Kelly grapples with a question that every pastor should ask themselves: What does it take to persevere in ministry? Alongside important exhortations such as confessing sin and remaining committed in the face of challenges, Pastor Kelly's daily habit of immersing himself in God's Word stands as a striking example to those who shepherd God's people. If Christian ministers hope to know the voice of the Savior and guide people toward him, we must search the Scriptures, as they remain our singular source for the words of eternal life."

John A. Adair, Ph.D.
Associate Professor of Theological Studies
Dallas Theological Seminary
Dallas, Texas

The number of pastors who actually cross the finish line in vocational ministry is depressingly small. Pastor Kelly has tackled the core issues of this tragedy with grace and hope, providing practical and yet deeply spiritual rails for us all to run on. A must-read for any pastor who aspires to stay in the race for the long-haul.

Craig A. Smith, Ph.D.
Lead Pastor
Mission Hills Church
Littleton, Colorado

Mark Twain once said, "War talk by men who have been in a war is always interesting; whereas moon talk by a poet who has not been on the moon is likely to be dull." The strength of this book is in the 25 years that Pastor Kelly has actually fought the good fight, and here reveals what it takes to faithfully persevere and overcome. It is not dull. Honest, direct, confessional, insightful. Definitely. Dull? Definitely not.

Marshall Shelley, DD
Director of the Doctor of Ministry Program
Denver Seminary
Denver, Colorado

"There are about as many ways to pastor as there are individuals, but one quality that every good pastor needs is an undying commitment to God's people. Pastor Kelly, both in his decades-long service as a minister of the Gospel, and in the writing of this book, continues to demonstrate exactly that kind of commitment. I should know—I not only served alongside him in ministry for years, but, along the way, was also shepherded by him as a member of his flock. Now more than ever, the church needs more pastors like Kelly--those who are willing to remain steadfast in their vocational commitment to the Bride of Christ, in good times and bad, for richer or for poorer, till death do us part."

Kutter Callaway, Ph.D.
Associate Professor of Theology and Culture
Fuller Theological Seminary
Pasadena, California

Marilynn,

Many blessings to you
in Jesus name!

Kelly

the good
PASTOR

Finding the disciplines,
principles and
commitments needed
to serve the Lord

KELLY M. WILLIAMS

VƆ1DЄ

Vide Press
6200 Second Street
Washington D.C. 20011
www.VidePress.com

ISBN: 978-1-954618-22-0 (Print)

Printed in the United States of America

Certification of Registration's: TXu 2-232-496, TXu 2-249-627

DEDICATION

I dedicate The Good Pastor Book to
Pastor Jon and Sandi Elsberry

Every Pastor and Pastor's wife need to be pastored.

Thank you Jon and Sandi for faithfully loving us over the past 20 plus years and serving our lives, family, and church family faithfully. We also dedicate this book to your godly moms, Elaine and Velma. Thank you for generations of faithfulness to Jesus in the pastorate.

No passage encapsulates your ministries to us and others like Hebrews 6:

*[10] For God is not unjust so as to overlook your work and the love that you have shown for his name in serving the saints, **as you still do**. [11] And we desire each one of you to show the same earnestness to have the full assurance of hope until the end, [12] so that you may not be sluggish, but imitators of those who through faith and patience inherit the promises.*

Thank you Jon and Sandi!

Thank you for pressing on!

We LOVE you!

CONTENTS

ACKNOWLEDGEMENTS

No one can accomplish anything of significance for the Kingdom of Jesus Christ on their own.

We ALL stand on the shoulders of those who have come before us and we rely on those around us who hold up our arms when they get heavy from the burdens God has called us to carry for His Kingdom.

I have had the privilege of being the recipient of both in my lifetime and in my pastoral ministry. At just the right time and in the right season, God has sent just the right person to encourage my heart to carry on in the face of great sorrow, darkness, loss, betrayal, and burden.

Yes, it is in community that we are wounded, but it is equally true it is in community that we are healed and made whole again.

God gave me a rich pastoral history when he gave me my mom and dad. They faithfully stewarded the pastoral calling God placed on their lives. They didn't quit and they didn't fornicate. Thank you, mom and dad, for giving me a pastoral heritage I can call on and a reminder I can follow.

All of us need more than one person to guide us. It is in a multitude of counselors that there is wisdom. We are not for sure what a multitude is, but we know it is more than one. Over the years I have had a plethora of faithful examples to look to for guidance in my walk with the Lord. I have had a number of pastors who have sought to help me become the person and pastor God created me to be. From my early childhood until now, even as a pastor, myself, I have had need of being pastored, guided, and directed.

Here is a list of some of the pastors who have invested in my life at various times and seasons: Larry and Linda Sue Williams (my parents and my childhood pastors), Gary Davidson (my first youth pastor), Phillip and Sharon Coomer (my second youth pastor), Ray and Linda Woodie (my pastors in my late teenage years), John and Sharon Yeats (my pastors during seminary).

These pastors and their wives have invested in me and my bride, Tosha, in our adult years: Armin Sommer, John Pauls, David Chrzan, Craig and Jeannie Whitaker, and Jon and Sandi Elsberry.

All these pastors in this list invested in me, allowed me to stand on their shoulders, have been overly generous in their own ways, and have held my arms up when I couldn't. I am eternally grateful!

I want to thank Prof John Hannah for speaking that prophetic word over me all these years ago now at Dallas Theological Seminary when I was just getting started in the ministry. His words, "Don't quit and don't fornicate" have resonated and reverberated in my life now for almost thirty years!

I want to thank Tom Freiling, Vide Press, and The Christian Post for believing in this project and giving it wings to fly.

I want to thank Vanguard Church and its leadership for believing in me as their senior pastor these twenty-five years. It takes people willing to follow you in order for you to be a shepherd to others. Thank you for your faithfulness to allow me to lead.

I want to thank my children for living in the "fishbowl" known as being a "PK." It is not easy to be "the example" when you are trying to find your own way too. Like my dad was to me, thank you for allowing me to be your dad and pastor, too. Thank you for seeing my clay feet and still allowing me to lead you.

I want to thank my bride, Tosha Lamdin Williams, I couldn't do this without you. God has used your belief in me to teach me to soar above the clouds and lead with courage even when I couldn't fully see where we were going. And even when the darkness seemed in surmountable, your companionship gave me the courage to take the next step by faith. My life and pastoring have been SO MUCH BETTER because of YOU!

I want to thank ALL the pastors out there who have decided God's calling on their life to shepherd His people matters and thus you have chosen to sacrifice for God's people regardless of what it costs you. Thank you! What we do for God matters, and in the end, it is ALL that matters.

Finally, I thank my Savior Jesus Christ who called me and appointed me to be a shepherd for Him. It is my hope that when I meet Him for the first time face to face, He will say to me, "Well done, MY good and faithful servant." I live each day to hear those words one day.

INTRODUCTION

"Do you want to be a great pastor for God?"

"Don't quit, don't fornicate, you will be the only one left and you will be great."

I was stunned by those words.

Really?

Is that all it takes to be great for God as a pastor?

I heard these words for the first time in my Historical Theology class at Dallas Theological Seminary in 1994 from Dr. John Hannah when I was a twenty-three-year-old seminary student studying for the pastorate.

I am now fifty years old and realize how difficult it is and seemingly impossible at times to do these two simple things:

Don't quit.

Don't fornicate.

You will be the only one left.

And ... well ... you'll be great.

For some of you reading this, this statement is incendiary to you. Maybe you have had a moral failure in the ministry, and have gone through the process of properly being restored, and you are serving God's people again. If that is the case, please know that this is not a book about bashing those who have quit or had moral failures. I am extremely grateful for those choice servants of the Lord who did the very difficult task of allowing others to dig deep into their hearts and help them be restored to the pastorate. I wish them nothing but the best and I cheer them on, but this book is not about that.

This is not a book about moral supremacy in the ministry. This is not a book about how "perfect" someone can be while serving God's people. This book is about very good men and women who early on in life dedicated their lives, their entire lives, to serving the Lord and His people as a pastor, but do not have the necessary disciplines, principles, and commitments in place to help them do this. Somewhere along the way, their sincere desire to serve the Lord gave way to a lesser desire in their flesh that led to devastating pain, shame, and embarrassment that they never intended to be a part of their bio for God.

This book seeks to answer the question of "how do I set out on a journey to live for God my entire life as a pastor and cross the finish line of life without having prematurely quit or fornicated along the way?"

I have now served at the same church for twenty-five years. In 1996, my wife and I traveled to Colorado Springs, CO, with the Southern Baptist Convention and started

Vanguard Church. Vanguard was one of thirty-four church plants at the north end of Colorado Springs that year. Two and half decades later, I am the only founding pastor still at the church they started. Don't quit. Don't fornicate. You will be the only one left and you will be great.

But here's the problem, I don't feel great. I pastor a church that has only averaged over 1000 people for one year and that was almost a decade ago. Matter of fact, one year, 23% of the church left in seemingly one week. I really felt "great" that week.

My professor would tell me I'm great, but my heart tells me I'm average at best. I had grandiose illusions of what the church I planted could become. I had grandiose illusions of who I could be for God. Thirteen years into this journey I was lost, discontent, deeply wounded, confused, angry, hurt, betrayed, and forced to face the reality that I too had created a church *with problems.* It was not perfect. It did not ring the bell and solve all the dilemmas the modern church is facing. Matter of fact, as I look around, most of my church is just like your church. As a church planter, I wanted to create a *unique* church, but the problem with that is the church is made up of *other people besides me* and eventually someone other than yourself has to win out or you get to do it all by yourself. And as I reflect on the church I planted twenty-plus years ago, I realize 80% or more of the church I planted is probably just like every other church. *We are not as unique as I thought we would be.*

So, the dilemma of this book is that it is a book for pastors who are pastoring churches, but it is not about how to grow a church. This book is about how to keep growing spiritually with God as a pastor *while pastoring* others to grow spiritually with God. It sounds simple and it is. But after twenty-five years, I have discovered what my teacher already knew. Simplicity doesn't equal easy.

In all of these years of church planting and pastoring, *I have discovered four D's that have anchored me along the way and have enabled me so far to remain faithful to my calling and to my Savior, Jesus.* I don't pretend to have perfected these, matter of fact, I am downright fearful to even put them in writing. I have battled the enemy and his ploys long enough to know I do not want to become more of a target for his anger and rage. I tread very cautiously on what I am going to say in this book because I know I will give an account to my God for how I attempt to lead HIS choice servants who have dedicated their entire lives to serving His people.

Please know I am not an expert. Please know I don't feel great for God. Please know I don't even feel significant, but so far, I have attempted to heed my professor's words and in the pages that follow I am going to attempt to show you how I and others are doing just that. Please take what is helpful for your ministry and life and use it to bring more glory to Jesus and, whatever you find unhelpful, remember this is not the Bible, it is just a book.

My favorite prayer to pray after I preach, teach, or counsel others is this: "Lord, whatever they have heard from me that is of you, help them never forget it. Whatever is of me, I pray they forget it the moment they walk out of the building."

I am just a servant like you. But I am more convinced than

ever that after two plus decades of ministry that these words of wisdom, which I will outline through a series of "Ds" throughout this book, have guided and protected me along my journey. More than I can emphasize with my native tongue, these four Ds have anchored me along the way and allowed me to live out the calling God has placed on my life.

It makes me nervous to say these four Ds will "make you great for God." But what I do feel comfortable saying is these four Ds can help you be a good pastor for Jesus. And with that said, I think these Ds are good enough. May they anchor you as they have me and may you be able to say at the end of your life these words:

"I didn't quit."

"I didn't fornicate."

And may you then hear from the Lord...

"Well done, good pastor."

And you, my friend, will be known as GREAT for God by your spouse, your children, and God's people in your lifetime!

CHAPTER 1

THE DISCIPLINE OF MEDITATION

Disciplines are like investing, the earlier you start, the greater the potential.

My most frequent memory of my dad in the early years of my childhood is of him sitting in his easy chair, in his tighty-whities (TMI), Bible in hand, reading God's Holy Word.

That memory has shaped my life and scarred it for life too. 😄

I went off to college at Liberty University in 1989, during the dark ages prior to the internet, cell phones, and even computers (at least for most of the people I knew).

I was like most transitioning from childhood to adulthood. I was, for the first time in my life, on my own—well, sort of. The Liberty University Way Manual was chalked full of rules that, if not obeyed, would ensure me an early exit home, but for the most part, the disciplines of my life had to become mine and I had to own who I was going to become.

Liberty didn't allow televisions, and a lot of other things, and so it created a world view I had given no consideration to before in my life. My time at Liberty showed me a more disciplined Christian worldview. As a pastor's kid, I had grown up in church: Sunday morning, Sunday evening, Wednesday night prayer meeting, and then Thursday night visitation. I did it all. Or, at least I thought I did. Along the way, I realized I was not reading the Bible as much as I should have been, along with a lot of other things I learned in these years.

I don't fully remember what triggered this decision, maybe the early image of my dad and his Bible. But, on August 16, 1989, I decided I would give up drinking Coca-Cola and I would read ten chapters of my Bible every day (that's reading through the Bible roughly three times a year). At the time I made this decision, I wasn't aware of anyone else who read through the Bible this much. However, while I was working on this chapter, I was reading a book by John Piper called, *21 Servants of Sovereign Joy: Faithful, Flawed, and Fruitful*. It is a book comprising seven books that tell the stories of people who walked faithfully with the Lord. One of those people was George Muller who lived from 1805-1898. He spent most of his life in Bristol, England, and pastored the same church there for over sixty-six years.

John Piper says, "Happiness in God comes from seeing God revealed to us in the face of Jesus Christ through the Scriptures".

When Muller was seventy-one years old, he spoke to younger believers and said,

> *"Now in brotherly love and affection I would give a few hints to my younger believers as to the way in which to keep up spiritual enjoyment. It is absolutely needful in order that happiness in the Lord may continue, that the Scriptures be **regularly read**. These are God's appointed means for the nourishment of the inner man . . . Consider it, and ponder over it . . . **Especially we should read regularly through the Scriptures, consecutively, and not pick out here and there a chapter.** If we do, we remain spiritual dwarfs. I tell you so affectionately. For the first four years after my conversion I made no progress, because I neglected the Bible. But when I regularly read on through the whole with reference to my own heart and soul, I directly made progress.*

> *When Muller was 76 years old, he wrote . . . I saw that the most important thing I had to do was to give myself to the reading of the word of God, and to **meditation** on it.*

I think the Psalmist said it best thousands of years ago:

> **Psalm 119:16** says, "I will meditate on your precepts and fix my eyes on your ways. I will delight in your statutes; I will not forget your word."

And I did just that, every day as I went through bible college and seminary. I started to learn that God's Word meditated upon every day and memorized would just pop up in my head during certain circumstances, temptations, challenges in my day or week. The reminders of God's Word in my mind kept me from wandering away from God's commands. I found that when I meditated on His Word, my eyes remembered the way and my heart then delighted in His commands. This gave me the strength to respond accordingly.

It reminds me of what the Psalmist said:

> **Psalm 119:105,** "Your word (God) is a lamp to my feet and a light to my path."

I will forever remember March 6, 1992, the day my mother was killed by a drunk driver. I was enroute home coming from Liberty. She had called me the night before to tell me she loved me. I said, "I love you too, Mom, I will see you tomorrow."

Tomorrow hasn't come yet, but it will.

I came home that night and went into her bedroom and beside her bed was her Bible. I picked it up to open it. It had a pen stuck inside of it. I opened to where the pen was placed and found the passage of Scripture she read either the night before or the day she died.

> **Ecclesiastes 9:1-3,5,12 (NIV),** "So I reflected on all this and concluded that the righteous and the wise and what they do are in God's hands, but no man knows whether love or hate awaits him. All share a common destiny ... As it is with the good man, so with the sinner ... This is the evil in everything that happens under the sun: The same destiny overtakes all. For the living know that they will die ... Moreover, no man knows when his hour

will come: As fish are caught in a cruel net, or birds are taken in a snare, so men are trapped by evil times that fall unexpectedly upon them."

My mother read these words just a few hours before she lost her life. It is as if God was preparing her for the last day of her life and for what was about to happen to her that day. Just as I believe, she called me the night before because God prompted her. He ordered her steps because that is what He does for the righteous.

However, meditation on God's Word won't necessarily change your dark circumstances, but it will guide your feet along the path to full and complete redemption in Jesus Christ. Meditation enables me to feel God in my everyday life. It enables me to see how God was at work in my mother's life, including the last day of her life. That brings great comfort to my soul for her and for me in my future with the Lord. It alerts me that God is not just with me, but is an all-around consuming presence that I can't escape from even if I wanted to.

Paul felt this way about God and described it this way to the unbelievers in the Areopagus in Athens.

> **Acts 17:27–28a,** "…that they (we) should seek God, and perhaps **feel their (our) way toward him and find him.** Yet he is actually not far from each one of us, for 'In him we live and move and have our being;'"

When we feel God, it keeps us upright and alert to the next step. It will light the path and say, "This is the way … walk here."

I know for me I hear a lot of people say, "God never speaks to me." I don't have that problem. My problem is I don't want to do what God sometimes tells me to do. I am reminded of what the Psalmist said about this.

> **Psalm 95:6-9,** "Oh come, let us worship and bow down; let us kneel before the Lord, our Maker! For he is our God, and we are the people of his pasture, and the sheep of his hand. Today, **if you hear his voice, do not harden your hearts**, as at Meribah, as on the day at Massah in the wilderness, when your fathers put me to the test and put me to the proof, though they had seen my work."

Meditation centers our attention on God's Word and His Word then speaks to our hearts. And, if we listen, He softens the calluses of our souls. Freeing us to respond to Him in softened obedience, from the grace of His Word, instead of having to be broken by the rod of His judgment. We are comforted by the guidance of His staff.

One of the things that I have observed in reading the Bible over and over again is how when God appears to people (in whatever form) He usually says something like this...

"Be not afraid."

Why? Well, I think one reason is because most of us spend the majority of our lives afraid. Twice in my devotions just this week the Lord said to me, "Be not afraid." Fear has a great effect on the decisions we make and, if not careful, we can make poor choices born out of our fears. As I age, I realize I have more fears than I thought. The life of faith is like being in a room where the lights slowly come on and you realize more and more how fear has truly impacted you all along the way.

Second, I think God says, "Be not afraid" because when God does visit us, it scares us to death. We don't expect it!

One of the people throughout history that God visited often was Joshua, the mighty warrior and commander of the nation of Israel after the leadership of Moses.

The book of Joshua opens with "Be strong and courageous" over and over again. I can only assume that like us, Joshua struggled with confidence, and fear often got the best of him. I can't tell you how many times I have almost lost hope. I can't remember how many times I was on the verge of throwing in the towel on being a pastor, maybe even a Christian, and then I went to God's Word and His Word reminded me of what I needed to hear. I wonder if the beginning of the book of Joshua was given to him on a day where fear, anxiety, and discouragement had just about got the best of Him?

The commander of God's heavenly host came to Joshua and said these words to him:

> **Joshua 1:7-9,** "**Only** be strong and very courageous, being careful to do according to the law that Moses my servant commanded you. Do not turn from it to the right hand or to the left, that you may have **good success** wherever you go. This **Book** of the law shall not depart from your mouth, but you shall **meditate** on it day and night, so that you may be careful to do according to all that is written in it. For then you will make

your way prosperous, and then you will have **good success**. Have I not commanded you? Be strong and courageous. Do not be frightened, and do not be dismayed, **for the Lord your God is with you wherever you go.**"

I believe the #1 reason why we should meditate on God's Word is because it reminds us that **"we are not alone."** God is with us wherever we go and whatever we go through.

Hudson Taylor, the great missionary to China in the 1800s, contemporary and close friend of George Muller and Charles Spurgeon, had this to say:

> *In the greatest difficulties, in the heaviest trials, in the deepest poverty and necessities, He (God) has never failed me; but, because I was enabled by His grace to trust in Him, He has always appeared for my help. I delight in speaking well of His Name.*

I remember just after my mom died, I walked out onto the back deck of our house and looked up into the sky and said, "Mom, what do you want me to preach at your funeral?" I distinctly heard the Lord say to me in my mind, "Kelly, she didn't call you, I did. If you want to know what to preach, ask me."

Immediately I was reminded that even though my mom was gone, God's presence was still with me.

Why is this important? Because as a pastor, God's presence is the game changer. I have stood and preached with God's strength and I have stood and preached just in my own strength. It ain't the same!

When Jesus came on the scene, the people said:

> **Luke 4:22,** "And all spoke well of him and marveled at the gracious words that were coming from his mouth. And they said, 'Is not this Joseph's son?'"

The Pharisees became so perplexed by Jesus's authority that they eventually asked Him:

> **Luke 20:1-2,** "One day, as Jesus was **teaching** the people in the temple and **preaching** the gospel, the chief priests and the scribes with the elders came up and said to him, 'Tell us by what authority you do these things, or **who** it is that gave you this authority.'"

They knew Jesus had something they didn't have. I know Jesus has something I don't have.

Do you know where authority as a pastor comes from? On my back deck, after my mom's death, God reminded me my authority didn't come from my mother, it came from Him. He is the one who called me to do what I do.

I have learned over the years to draw great strength from God's presence which calls me and never leaves me nor forsakes me.

I can go into a worship service and feel so depleted, discouraged, defeated, and down-right resentful that I have to get up and tell God's people how "good" God is. But the moment I start to worship and say to the Lord, "I can't do this, Lord, without you. I need your strength. I need your presence." Something starts to change.

Moses said to the Lord:

> **Exodus 33:15-16,** "If your presence will not go with me, do not bring us up from here. For how shall it be known that I have found favor in your sight, I and your people? Is it not in your going with us, so that we are distinct, I and your people, from every other people on the face of the earth."

I remember feeling this very feeling Moses felt when my wife Tosha and I came to Colorado Springs in 1996 to start Vanguard Church. We realized very quickly we couldn't do this in our strength. We realized we needed God's favor and His presence to do what He called us to do, or it just wasn't going to work. We had to become people who couldn't be apart from Him.

In Saul's day, the Bible says, the Spirit of the Lord came over Saul and he became a different man.

> **1 Samuel 10:9-11,** "When he (Saul) turned his back to leave Samuel, God gave him another heart. And all these signs came to pass that day. When they came to Gibeah behold, a group of prophets met him, and the Spirit of God rushed upon him, and he prophesied among them. And when all who knew him previously saw how he prophesied with the prophets, the people said to one another, 'What has come over the son of Kish? Is also among the prophets.'"

The presence of God is the game changer and God's Word is what reminds us, "He is with us." His presence is ever before us, around us, in us, and fills us to do His work even when we don't have the human strength to do it.

Numerous times in the past two plus decades of my pastorate, I have awakened in the night and early in the morning and before my feet even hit the floor, I have uttered the words, "I can't do this. I don't want to do this anymore. I can't do this anymore even if I wanted to."

And then through God's Word I hear Him say time and time again, "I know, but I can, through you."

I have often wondered when God's presence comes over me, "Where does the discouragement, defeat, and fear go?" And after many years, I know. It doesn't go anywhere. It just loses its effectiveness in the light of God's omnipotent presence in our lives.

Where God's presence has been given full authority, the demons of this life have to flee. God told Joshua, "Be strong and courageous, do not be frightened, do not be dismayed, for the Lord your God is with you wherever you go."

This confidence in God's presence gives us the ability like Joshua to overcome our fears and discouragement and instead be strong and courageous. We become different people when we submit our minds, feelings, and actions to the presence of God. As leaders, we begin to attract other Christ's followers because they can sense Him in us.

Over the years of doing ministry, I have been humbled many times and I am sure there are many more lessons in my future. But out of these lessons I have learned to recognized who God wants me to be as a pastor. And thus, one of my most favorite sayings is this, "If you see anything in me that is impressive, well, that's Jesus. If you see anything in me that is unimpressive, well, that's me."

I think John the Baptist said it best.

> **John 3:30,** "He (Jesus) must increase, but I must decrease."

I want people to be attracted to the presence of Christ through me. This, in my humble opinion, is the calling of every pastor and every child of God. We are to be magnets drawing people closer to Christ. The meditation of God's Word makes your magnetic force field for Christ that much greater. Paul says:

> **1 Corinthians 11:1,** "Be imitators of me, as I am of Christ."

His presence is the game changer, so much so that God promised Joshua that, if He followed His presence through meditation of His Word, He would make Him prosperous and then he would have good success.

The word "good" really stood out to me when I read this passage. God promised him "good success." Why would God need to add the word "good" to success? I get it. You get it. Success, it is what we all want. But maybe, like me, you have discovered there is "success" in this life that is not truly "good success."

I have never read an article by an organization, magazine, or person for that matter that describes the "top ten" pastors who have loved their families well, been faithful to God and their spouse the longest, served in the ministry the longest without a moral failure, read through their Bibles the most, fasted the most, or prayed the most hours.

I was taught people measure what matters to them. And like it or not, SIZE matters, until the other things don't, and then SIZE KILLS.

The world measures what matters to the world. SIZE is ALL THAT MATTERS. I call it the Brittany Spears factor. Envy sells. The world wants to build you up, take credit for your success, and then nit-pick you until they find a flaw and destroy you for it. This is the glamorous life of success. I have watched it over and over in the pastorate as well, sometimes up close and sometimes from a distance. SUCCESS SELLS BUT NEVER SUSTAINS. Living a respectful, balanced life may be boring, but it is the only thing that lasts.

And this is where the meditation of God's Word becomes extremely important because without it we may have "success" but it won't be "good success."

One of the passages that has befuddled me all my life, and every time I read it I am befuddled that much more, is when Jesus says in the Gospels:

> **Matthew 7:21-23,** "Not everyone who says to me, 'Lord, Lord,' will enter the kingdom of heaven, but the one who does the will of my Father who is in heaven. On that day many will say to me, 'Lord, Lord, did we not prophesy in your name, and cast out demons in your name, and do many

mighty works in your name?' And then will I declare to them, 'I never knew you; depart from me, you workers of lawlessness.'"

I remember when I was at Dallas Theological Seminary, my professor, Dr. Howard Hendricks, would say, "You know what scares me the most? That God would take His Spirit from me and expect me to serve Him in full-time ministry without it."

This is what happened to King Saul because of His disobedience. He wanted the success of God without being obedient to the presence of God. And even after he fell, he still wanted Samuel to bless him "in front of the people", so He could appear to still be God's man.

> **1 Samuel 15:28, 30,** "And Samuel said to him (Saul), 'The Lord has torn the kingdom of Israel from you this day and has given it to a neighbor of yours, who is better than you.' Then he (Saul) said, 'I have sinned; yet honor me now before the elders of my people and before Israel, and return with me, that I may bow before the Lord your God.'"

Did you catch that? Saul said, "So I may bow before the Lord (YOUR) GOD." Very telling. He knew God was not His Lord.

He had settled for "success" in the ministry per se. He no longer longed for "good success." What's the difference? Success is something that you can keep up on your own, at least for a while, but good success requires God's presence and our obedience to that presence.

God will not reward you for your success in the end. "Lord, have we not..." He will reward you for your "good success." He will reward you for your success that was done through His presence, born out of obedience to His voice, and submitted to His will.

Samuel told Saul,

> **1 Samuel 15:22,23,** "Has the Lord as great delight in burnt offerings and sacrifices, as in obeying the voice of the Lord? Behold, to obey is better than sacrifice, and to listen than the fat of rams. For rebellion is as the sin of divination (witchcraft, devil worship), and presumption is as iniquity and idolatry. Because you have rejected **the word of the LORD,** he has rejected you from being king."

God expects us to do what He tells us to do. This is what "good success" is.

Sometimes people ask me, where do you see yourself in twenty years? My answer, "wherever God wants me."

God told Joshua,

> **Joshua 23:6,** "Therefore, be very strong to **keep** and to **do** all that is written in the Book of the Law of Moses, turning aside from it neither to the right hand nor to the left."

It is extremely important to God that you keep and do what He has said in His Word.

God takes His Word so seriously that He ended His book with these words:

Revelation 22:14-19, 21, "Blessed are those who wash their robes, so that they may have the right to the tree of life and that they may enter the city by the gates. Outside are the dogs and sorcerers and the sexually immoral and murderers and idolaters, and everyone who loves and practices falsehood. 'I, Jesus, have sent my angel to testify to you about these things for the churches. I am the root and the descendant of David, the bright morning star.' The Spirt and the Bride say, "'Come.' And let the one who hears says, 'Come.' And let the one who is thirsty come; let the who desires take the water of life without price. I warn everyone who hears the words of the prophecy of this book: **if anyone adds** to them, God will add to him the plagues described in this book, and **if anyone takes away from the words of the book** of this prophecy, **God will take away his share in the tree of life and in the holy city**, which are described in this book. The grace of the Lord Jesus be with all. Amen."

Here is what I know: God takes His Word very seriously and, as pastors, we should as well. If we are going to be God's spokesmen, we need to remember how seriously God takes what we do. James reminds us of how serious God takes it.

James 3:1, "**NOT** many of you should become teachers, my brothers, for you know that we who teach will be judged with greater strictness."

David Seamands, the late Methodist missionary, pastor, and teacher at Asbury College in Wilmore, Kentucky said this:

"Answering the call to the pastorate most assuredly guarantees half of us won't even make it to heaven."

Years later, I learned the tragic truth of his life in the midst of this quote. The outcome of his life grieved me deeply because of the huge impact his books had on my life while I was in college. Nevertheless, the quote is telling how difficult the pastorate can be and unfortunately his life proved it in ways I am sure he wished weren't true as well.

The ministry is not easy. My choice to teach God's Word automatically brings greater strictness to my life. Because of this, I wanted to go to a seminary that took God's Word equally as serious. I went to a seminary where the motto was and is:

2 Timothy 4:2a, "Preach the Word."

I took this imperative very seriously as did the seminary. But I remember in one of my classes one of my professors was not as encouraging when it came to reading the Bible faithfully. I wrote a paper and the teacher asked us to pick a discipline we would practice in the ministry as pastors. I picked this very discipline to write about and described to my teacher in my theological paper how I was going to read ten chapters a day in my Bible. The response back was less than encouraging. He said,

"Admirable goal, but you might want to pick a more realistic goal that you can accomplish."

I consider Dallas Theological Seminary the most amazing seminary in the world, but even there some had lost sight of how seriously God takes His Word.

John Yeats, my pastor through seminary always said,

> "It is important to keep the main thing the main
> thing!"

Vince Lombardi, the great Green Bay Packers coach used to
say to his football players to get them ready for a game:

> "Men, this is a football."

We as pastors need to be reminded. "This is God's Word,
read it." It is the most fundamental element and ingredient
if you want to have "good success" in the ministry. It is
very easy to drift from this discipline because you "know
what it says." But knowing what it says, believing it, and
living it out are different things.

It's important to keep the main thing, God's Word, the
main thing.

How do we do that? In the Old Testament, a faithful priest,
Ezra, gives us the model to follow from the Old Testament.

> **Ezra 7:10,** "For Ezra had set his heart to study the
> Law of the Lord, and to do it, and to teach his
> statutes and rules in Israel."

We are to set our hearts and minds on studying God's
Word, doing what it says, and teaching others to do the
same. However, before we teach it, it's important that we
know what it says before we tell others what it says.

Before we go share God's Word with God's people, we
need to make sure we have spent time with God's Word in

our own lives. It is important that the people know that we have been with God just like Moses in his day.

> **Exodus 34:29,** "When Moses came down from Mount Sinai, with the two tablets of the testimony in his hand as he came down from the mountain, Moses did not know that the skin of his face shone because **he had been talking with God."**

He didn't know there was physical evidence he had been talking with God, but everybody else did. I find that is true for me. As the pastor, I am often the last one to realize spending time with God was worth it. Not just for me, but for everyone around me.

I remember reading one of Henri Nouwen's books. Often Nouwen would say of himself:

> "It seems like all the time I spend with God should make me a better man than I am, but I can't imagine how bad a man I would be if I spent no time with Him."

Both my dad and my mom grew up in homes where they suffered abuse at the hands of their earthly fathers. I believe it was God's Word in them that freed them from this vicious cycle of abuse. God's Word matters!

To ourselves, our time with the Lord may seem like it is not making that much of a difference and maybe even to others it might not, but in the end, like Moses, people who walk with the Lord will feel His presence through you.

If you want to go the distance in the pastorate, you must

develop your own meditations from God's Word to feed yourself independently of the sermons you prepare to feed your flock.

Did you get that? If you are going to go the distance, you have to maintain a personal relationship with God yourself independent of your sermon prep and preaching.

Without it, you are destined for failure. It is not a matter of if, just when.

Our time with God is the most important thing we do. It has to be our first priority. Jehoshaphat, King of Judah, knew this as well. He said to the king of Israel:

> **2 Chronicles 18:4,** "Inquire **first** for the word of the Lord."

I am happy to say the seminary professor's response back to me didn't discourage me. Matter of fact, it was like saying "sic 'em" to your dog who wants to chase a rabbit and I have been chasing that rabbit of meditation ever since 1989.

Thirty-two years later, I am working on my 92nd reading of the Bible. I should be on my 96th reading of the Bible now, so as you can tell I have missed a few days, 476 days to be exact. That's fifteen days a year on average. So, I have averaged reading my Bible 350 days a year out of 365 days for the past thirty-two years. Dr. Jerry Falwell used to always say, when it came to goals for our lives, "Shoot for the stars, land on the moon, no one will notice."

This discipline has single-handedly changed my life as

a pastor.

It is the most important thing I **do** as a follower of Jesus and as a pastor.

George Muller pastored the same church for sixty years and he felt the same way about the reading of God's Word. When Muller was seventy-one years old, he said,

> *Now I have been doing this (reading the Bible) for forty-seven years. I have read through the whole Bible about 100 times and I always find it fresh when I begin again. Thus my peace and joy have increased more and more.*

Muller was seventy-one, and he would live and read on for another twenty-one years. But he never changed his strategy for satisfaction in God. When he was seventy-six, he wrote the same thing he did when he was sixty, "I saw more clearly than ever, that the first great and primary business to which I ought to attend every day was, to have my soul happy in the Lord." And the means stayed the same:

> *What is the food of the inner man? Not prayer, but the word of God; and …not the simple reading of the word of God, so that it only passes through our minds, just as water runs through a pipe, but considering what we read, pondering over it, and applying it to our hearts.*

The aim of George Muller's life was to glorify God by helping people take God at his Word. To that end, he saturated his soul with the Word of God. At one point, he said that **he read the Bible five or ten times more than he read any other books.**

Muller's friend, Hudson Taylor, took the Bible equally as seriously in his life. His life was saturated with the Bible, and his interpretation of his experience was chastened by the Bible. In Taylor's own words: "Communion with Christ requires our coming to Him. Meditation upon His person and His work requires the diligent use of the means of grace, and especially the prayerful reading of God's Word. **Many fail to abide because they habitually fast instead of feed.**"

Taylor's new pattern was to go to bed earlier and then rise at five a.m. "to give time to Bible study and prayer (often two hours) before the work of the day began".

I had no idea personally until now that Muller and Taylor committed themselves to reading the Bible like this. It gives great courage in knowing this in light of the fruit that came from these men's lives for the glory of Jesus.

Moses reminded the people of what Muller and Taylor knew, when it came to God's Word.

> **Deuteronomy 4:9,** "**ONLY** take care, and keep your soul **diligently**, lest you forget the things that your eyes have seen, and lest they depart from your heart all the days of your life. Make them known to your children and your children's children."

Jesus tells us,

> **Matthew 10:24,** "A disciple is not above his teacher, nor a servant above his master."

> **John 8:31b,32** "If you abide in my word, you are

truly my disciple, and you will know the truth, and the truth will set you free."

Free from what? The lies the Devil tells you every day of your life. It is your best chance to be freed from the "success" syndrome as well. American pastors are especially preoccupied with the question, "how can I be successful?" Good success originates from taking God's Word seriously for a lifetime.

I quickly learned reading through the Bible that I was not the first person to take reading His Word seriously. God takes the reading and applying of His Word to our lives VERY seriously. God was looking at ALL of His creation and said this to Isaiah:

> **Isaiah 66:2,** "All these things my hand has made, and so all these things came to be, declares the Lord. But this is the one to whom I will look: he who is humble and contrite in spirit and **trembles at my Word.**"

The Word of God is God's Word. God's Word matters. God's Words are the only Words that matter.

Charles Spurgeon's pastorate was anchored by God's Word and especially during times when the storms of this life blew his way. Spurgeon said regarding the Bible:

> *"These words are God's . . . Thou book of vast authority, thou art a proclamation from the Emperor of Heaven; far be it from me to exercise my reason in contradicting thee . . . This is the book untainted by any error; but it is pure unalloyed, perfect truth. Why? Because God*

wrote it".

John Piper said,

> *"There is a difference in the hearts of preachers and people where this allegiance holds sway"*.

John, the Beloved, tells us,

> **John 1:1,** "In the beginning was the Word and the Word was with God and **the Word was God."**

The Bible is God's physical presence to us like Jesus was to the disciples when He walked this earth. When you abide in it, spend time in it, it makes a difference.

Being in His Word is that important. If you want God to be real to you, in the physical presence of your life, you have to read His Word.

It has made all the difference in the "good success" of my life and pastorate and it will in yours too.

> **Psalm 119:105,** "Your word is a lamp to my feet and a light to my path."

> **Psalm 119:11,** "I have stored up your word in my heart that I might not sin against you."

Without a stored-up reserve of His Word in my heart, during the darkest valleys of the pastorate, I would have failed already. I don't read the Word every day and expect it to have an immediate impact on me every day. However,

I do expect the discipline to yield the fruit of perseverance over time through the darkest valleys.

> **Psalm 23:4,** "Even though I walk through the valley of the shadow of death, I will fear no evil, for you are with me; your rod and your staff they comfort me."

That's "good success."

It carried the disciples, it carried George Muller, Hudson Taylor, Charles Spurgeon, and countless others through the ages.

It will carry you and me too.

READ AND OBEY THE WORD, it's the game changer, good pastor!

CHAPTER 2

THE DISCIPLINE OF CONFESSION

Waiting to confess sin is like waiting to pull weeds from your garden. The longer you wait, the more difficult they are to get rid of later. Proverbs confirms this.

> **Proverbs 28:13,14,** "Whoever conceals his transgressions will not prosper, but he who confesses and forsakes them will obtain mercy. Blessed is the one who fears the Lord always but whoever hardens his heart will fall into calamity."

I was seventeen years old and I was angry at God. I felt like I had given God my best and He hadn't returned the favor. Job was my favorite book during this season of my life. I walked with the Lord as a teenager. I kept myself free from the contaminants of sexual sin. I expected God to bless me for it.

I didn't perceive He did. So, I took matters into my own hands. I started dating a girl younger than me. I was seventeen, she was fifteen. She looked up to me and I liked it. She was a Mormon. I was a Christian. I knew better, but I dated her anyway. All of my friends kept asking me, "What are you doing?"

I didn't listen. I was angry at God and tired of giving Him my best when He didn't seem to return the favor, at least, so I thought.

One night, I decided I was tired of being a virgin. I was tired of being the "good ole preacher boy." I wanted to live a little and I wanted to give God a reason not to bless me, so I thought. I decided, if she was willing, I was going to lose my virginity that night.

We went parking. I was able to clearly articulate with my actions what I was looking for from her and for a while we were headed that direction and then, in a moment of awareness, she stopped me.

The next morning, I remember thinking to myself, "Maybe it will be tonight." We had planned to go on another date and I was planning on going parking again. She seemed okay with it. Before I could get to my date, my mom stopped me in the living room of our house and took my hand. She looked up at me with that ugly-momma-face-cry with her lip quivering and her eyes filled with compassionate tears. It was all I could do to stand there and experience it. I kept a stone face, but on the inside, her tears were shaving away the calluses of my hard heart and God's voice got through one more time. I heard God's words in my head in the midst of her compassionate tears.

"Kelly, if you lose your virginity tonight, your life and ministry will never be the same. I will use your life, but it won't be like I had planned."

You may not agree with this sort of theology or that God would speak this sort of way, listen to what Paul told young Timothy, the pastor:

> **2 Timothy 3:19-21,** "But God's truth stands firm like a foundation stone with this inscription. 'The Lord knows those who are his,' and 'All who belong to the Lord must turn away from evil.' In a wealthy home some utensils are made of gold and silver, and some are made of wood and clay. The expensive utensils are used for special occasions, and the cheap ones are for everyday use. **If you keep yourself pure, you will be a special utensil for honorable use.** Your life will be clean, and you will be ready for the Master to use you for every good work."

God's words to me sobered me momentarily and I heard my mom say to me, "Kelly, I am praying for you."

God's words and my godly momma's words broke me internally, although I held my composure on the outside and acted as if I was the Cool-hand Luke. I said to her, "Yeah, yeah, I know what I am doing. I will be fine."

That moment may have very well saved my virginity, my ministry, and God's specific calling on my life. That night I was gonna go for it. She was ready and so was I. In the heat of the moment, I heard the Lord say again, "You can do this, but your life will never be the same again." Scripture supports this claim.

> **Proverbs 6:32,33,** "He who commits adultery lacks sense; he who does it destroys himself. He will get wounds and dishonor, and his disgrace will not be wiped away."

Consequence is real and sometimes permanent, at least for the remainder of our physical lives on planet earth.

I stopped. She was surprised, so was I. I said, "I can't do this. I need to take you home."

I took her home and I immediately called my youth pastor. I confessed it to him. I then met him at my home church's pastor's house and confessed it to him. Confession to God is important, but it is equally important to confess it to those you are accountable to as well. James, Jesus's brother, tells us this as well.

> **James 5:16,** "Therefore, confess your sins to one another and pray for one another, that you may be healed."

I realized I had to make a change if I wanted to avoid going down this road again. About nine months later, I went off to college. I knew I needed to make some changes in my habits and disciplines. My mind and actions were not where I needed them to be if I was going to be the man God had created me to be.

I met a couple of older guys, Darren and Chuck. They were very serious about their personal holiness and their walk with the Lord. I met a young lady named Tosha. She was a sweetheart. She was pretty and had a life in her eyes that drew me to her. As I got to know Darren and Chuck,

I realized I had some work to do on what I would now call, "renewing my mind." I had walked with the Lord externally through my actions, but my thoughts were not yet submitted to His will.

I learned a lot from these guys, the Apostle Paul tells us:

> **2 Corinthians 10:6,** "We are to take every thought captive to obey Christ being ready to punish every disobedience."

Honestly, I wasn't there, yet.

I joined an accountability group. I had no idea what it was. I had never heard of an accountability group. But in 1990, my friends told me I needed it if I wanted to grow in my walk with God. I agreed to go, reluctantly.

In the meantime, my roommate, Joel, had decided he was no longer interested in Tosha and that cleared the way for me to get to know her. Somewhere along the way, I learned a few details about Tosha's story. I learned she had never kissed a guy. What? See, that kind of info travels fast, at least at college. I was awed by this, intimidated, and motivated to grow in my real relationship with Jesus in my thoughts.

I went to the accountability group, and man, I didn't see that coming. They went around the circle and asked one question, "What sin do you struggle with?" I wasn't ready for that! The guy next to me started talking about his ongoing battle with masturbation. Whoa! I couldn't even look at him. I just looked down because for me it had been a battle since I was twelve years old. See, when

I was twelve, my older brother introduced me to the only pornographic movie I have ever watched from start to finish. I was introduced to a world that I previously had no idea existed. And six years later, here I was, smack dab in the middle of an accountability group at college. I was extremely uncomfortable. I wanted to crawl under my chair and leave the room.

Finally, it was my time to "confess." The guys said to me, "What do you struggle with?" I reluctantly and sheepishly pointed at the guy who had just confessed and said, "I guess I struggle with what he said he struggles with."

I was hoping that was it. They followed it up with, "How long has it been?" I wasn't ready for that and so I did what any fearful bible student studying for the ministry would do.

I lied.

I said, "Oh, I can't remember, it's been so long." (It had just been the night before.) At that point, they kept asking me questions, but my mind zoned out.

And then I heard them say, "Well, how about . . ." they had moved on to the next guy and I had survived this extremely shameful moment, or at least I thought I had until I heard this voice in my head say,

"Kelly, what are you doing? You just lied for your sin."

It is one thing to choose not to tell the truth, it is another to lie when asked. Sin, unfortunately, is inevitable for all of us, but covering it up is always optional. Cover up only delays the inevitable consequences of sin and, like weeds, it actually increases the consequences and difficulty of ridding ourselves of it as time goes on.

In every situation we have two options when it comes to sin: 1) Confession or 2) Cover-up

We choose the option; God chooses the outcome. Paul tells us:

Romans 3:23, "The wages of sin is **death.**"

The consequence for sin is physical death in some way, whether it be emotional issues, mental issues, relational separation or complication, sexual dysfunction or disease, financial crisis, friendship absolved, health issues or some other form of physical death or separation. We have all experienced the consequences of sin more than once in our lives.

And leaders are no exception. Moses shows us this.

> **Leviticus 4:22-26,** "When a leader sins, doing unintentionally any one of all the things that by the commandments of the Lord his God ought not to be done, and realizes his guilt, or the sin which he has committed is made known to him, he shall bring as his offering a goat, a male without blemish, and shall lay his hand on the head of the goat and kill it in the place where they kill the burnt offering before the Lord; it is a **sin offering**. Then the priest shall take some of the blood of the sin offering with his finger and put it on the horns of the altar of burnt offering and pour out the

rest of its blood at the base of the altar of burnt offering. And all its fat he shall burn on the altar, like the fat of the sacrifice of peace offerings. So the priest shall make atonement for him for his sin, and he shall be **forgiven.**"

Confession does **NOT** erase consequence. Ask Moses.

Moses sinned by hitting the rock with the staff God gave to him to get water to come out of the rock.

> **Numbers 20:11,12,** "And Moses lifted up his hand and struck the rock with his staff twice, and water came out abundantly, and the congregation drank, and their livestock. And the Lord said to Moses and Aaron, 'Because you did not believe in me, to uphold me as holy in the eyes of the people of Israel, therefore you shall not bring this assembly into the land that I have given them.'"

God forgave him, but his consequence was, "You can see the land but you can't enter it."

> **Deuteronomy 34:4,5,7,10** "And the Lord said to him, 'This is the land of which I swore to Abraham, to Isaac, and to Jacob, 'I will give it to your offspring.' I have let you see it with your eyes, but you shall not go over there.' So Moses the servant of the Lord died there in the land of Moab, according to the word of the Lord, Moses was 120 years old when he died. His eye was undimmed, and his vigor unabated. And there has not arisen a prophet since in Israel like Moses, whom the Lord knew face to face."

The greatest prophet of God to ever live suffered consequence for his sin too.

So will you.

So will I.

My sin issues consequence and requires action. In the Old Testament, it required the action of a sin offering. In the New Testament, it required Christ's blood as the sacrifice for my sin. But, neither sacrifice annuls my consequences. However, it can lessen it or change it in some way. King David should have died for his indiscretion with Bathsheba, but because of his confession, God granted him a reprieve. But he still had to suffer the consequences God spelled out for him in Scripture. Samuel records these for us.

> **2 Samuel 12:13,14,** "David said to Nathan, 'I have sinned against the Lord.' And Nathan said to David, 'The Lord also has put away your sin; you shall not die. Nevertheless, because by this deed you have utterly scorned the Lord, the child who is born to you shall **die.**'"

As a dad, I believe this consequence would be greater than dying myself. God chose to change the consequence spelled out in the law of Moses to spare David's life by taking his child in place of his sin. God won't change the natural laws of sin and consequence, but He can give a modified reprieve so that His will for Creation can be accomplished.

After the fall of humanity, through Adam and Eve, consequence became a natural result determined by God. For example, they could tell God they were sorry, but this did not change the permanent reality of physical death. "Sorry" does not change the fact that we must all face the consequences caused by their disobedience and ours as well.

King David repented, but repentance does not erase the consequences we all must face.

As Paul describes in the book of Romans:

> **Romans 6:23,** "For **ALL** have sinned and come short of the glory of God."

So, maybe you are thinking, like me, if confession does not necessarily erase consequence, then why confess? Well, because confession leads to forgiveness and cleansing from the contaminants of sin, such as guilt, shame, condemnation, and so forth and so on. Thus, confession enables us to be restored to the right relationship with God and hopefully others, so we can fulfill His purpose for our existence.

John the Beloved tells us:

> **1 John 1:9,** "If you **confess** your sins to God, He is faithful and just to **forgive** you, and **cleanse** you of all unrighteousness."

Confession to God doesn't erase consequence. It erases condemnation. Confession ALWAYS leads to forgiveness and forgiveness erases condemnation and shame. That encourages me and I hope it does you as well. People may not forgive, but God ALWAYS forgives when we confess.

Cover-up, on the other hand, leads to more severe consequences and greater shame, guilt, condemnation, judgment, unneeded humiliation, and ultimately destruction. You can either confess and receive forgiveness or cover up sin and receive humiliation for harbored secrets.

There are no secrets with God, only things He hasn't yet exposed. Moses reminds us of this.

> **Numbers 32:23,** "...be sure your sin will find you out."

This is the inevitable end of all sin not confessed. And it is far more painful for your sin to find you than for you to confess it to God and forsake it. The weeds of sin take deeper roots into sensitive parts of our souls the longer we ignore the promptings of honest confession.

I find the longer I wait to confess, the more likely I am to lie about it, and deepen the sinful activity. However, going back to discipline number one, meditation on God's Word naturally leads us to confession.

In August of 1989, I had started reading ten chapters a day in my Bible. Six months later, I found myself in this accountability group, and even though I initially lied to the group, God used this practice to bring me into a deeper awareness of my own sinful depravity.

And while I sat there, in that accountability group, the Spirit of God began to move over my heart. I felt the conviction of the Holy Spirit and God's Word began to work in me. The writer of the book of Hebrews said it best.

Hebrews 4:12-16, "For the word of God is **living** and **active**, sharper than any two-edged sword, piercing to the division of soul and of spirit, of joints and of marrow, and discerning the thoughts and intentions of the heart. And no creature is **hidden** from his sight, but all are **naked** and **exposed** to the eyes of him to whom we must give an account. Since then we have a great high priest who has passed through the heavens, Jesus, the Son of God, let us hold fast our confession. For we do not have a high priest who is unable to sympathize with our weaknesses, but one who in every respect has been **tempted as we are, yet without sin. Let us then with confidence draw near to the throne of grace, that we may receive mercy and find grace to help in time of need.**"

I don't know this for a fact, but I don't believe, had I not been reading my Bible like I was, I would have done what I did next.

With my heart beating fast, I raised my hand.

They said, "Yes, Kelly."

I don't fully remember what I said, but I said something like this.

"Guys, I lied FOR my sin. You asked, 'How long has it been?' I said, 'Can't remember it has been so long ago.' The truth is, it was just last night, because it is every night, sometimes multiple times a day."

There, I said it. I confessed it. I was free forever, right?

WRONG!

But, I was free like I had never been before in my life.
I made a commitment that night to abandon this practice
and begin to learn how to take every thought captive in
obedience to Christ.

I started dating Tosha on January 27, 1990.

I was not worthy of her presence or relationship, but I was
extremely grateful. What I didn't know then that I know
now is God saw my teenage years and He had someone for
me. She had decided to go into the ministry and believed
God had called her to be a pastor's wife, but she wanted to
marry someone who was a virgin. I thought God didn't see
my sacrifice in high school, but the truth is, I couldn't see
the blessing He had in store for me in my future.

Our dating relationship has to be one of the best things
that has ever happened to me. Being with her made
me want to be a better man. Somewhere along the
way, I learned from her about journaling. She had been
journaling since she was twelve years old. I had never
heard of it. She made me a little booklet with verses in
it and suggested that I use the blank pages to record my
thoughts, feelings, and interactions with God. She opened
up a whole new dimension of real relationship with God
that I had never experienced before in my life. It has now
become a discipline that I believe has carried me through
the years of pastoral ministry.

It has been tedious over the years and at times very time
consuming with seemingly little evidence of its value, but it
has enabled me to live like Paul described in the Bible.

Acts 24:16, "So I **always** take **pains** to have a clear conscience toward both God and men."

I decided to live a life of full-disclosure with a clear conscience toward both God and men and my journaling has enabled me to do this.

No secrets!

My wife has FULL authority to read my journals at any time without my permission. I have also made a commitment to my five children that I will give them my journal that corresponds to the year of their age. I started journaling consistently when I was twenty years old.

Life is about to get real for them and me.

In preparation of writing this book, I went back and re-read my journals from the past thirty years. In a later section in the book I will talk more about accountability and friends who can hold you accountable. But for now, I want to focus on the discipline of confession through journaling.

At least twice a week, I journal. I journal before I write a message and I journal before I give that message for the first time. I want my sin to be set aside so God can use me to minister to His people, in His way, and for His glory.

Journaling forces me to put on paper what I may not otherwise have the courage to say or acknowledge to myself or others. It has proven to be my most consistent, dependable, and reliable form of accountability to keep me honest with God, others, and myself.

One of my favorite verses in the Bible is from the Psalmist.

> **Psalm 119:29 (NLT),** "Keep me from lying to myself."

One of the worst forms of deception is self-deception. I have found that if I don't lie to myself, I most likely won't lie to anyone else.

When I journal, I am freed from the deception of me. I am free to utter the words of the Psalmist, in the midst of his journaling confession, preserved for all of us to read. Through confession, I am freed to give up "performing" before God's people, and can instead lead them into the presence of God and His holiness for them.

> **Psalm 51:10-13,** "Create in me a clean heart, O God, and renew a right spirit within me. Cast me not away from your presence, and take not your Holy Spirit from me. Restore to me the joy of your salvation and uphold me with a willing spirit. Then I will teach transgressors your ways, and sinners will return to you."

Journaling before I write a sermon and before I preach does the following things inside of me:

1) It creates a clean heart in me before God.
2) It renews a right spirit within me.
3) It brings me into a deeper experience of God's presence.
4) It restores my joy.
5) It gives me a willing spirit to do what God has asked me to do.

6) It gives me the courage to teach "transgressors" His ways and challenge others to return to Him as I have.

Confession is GOOD for my preaching. It frees me from the vice of performance and a judgmental spirit toward those I lead. It is good for my congregation. It is good for my family. It helps me focus more on them.

It is good for me. The Psalmist described the result of confession best:

> **Psalm 90:8,** "You have set our iniquities before you, our secret sins in the light of your presence."

Confession, through journaling, frees me from my secrets. Not only does it free me from my secrets, it creates a control over my thoughts that benefits me. I am then able to take every thought captive and obey Christ through the discipline of prayer and Scripture memory. Whereas, if I don't confess, I cling to my sin as the Psalmist said and "cherish my sin." I find myself on an island where the success of my preaching is up to me because God withholds my ability to hear Him and have my prayers answered. My confession either withholds God's blessing on my preaching or it frees me to experience it. The Psalmist understood this.

> **Psalm 66:18-20,** "If I had cherished iniquity in my heart, the Lord would not have listened. But truly God has listened; he has attended to the voice of my prayer. Blessed be God because he has not rejected my prayer or removed his steadfast love from me!"

I have preached without the presence of God on me because of unconfessed sin and I have preached with it on me because of confession to Him.

Confession enables me to be who God has created me to be and do what God has called me to do as a pastor. The burdens of ministry get a lot lighter through confession.

Purity matters. And I am convinced that, apart from the discipline of confession through journaling, I would probably not be writing this book or still be in the pastorate. Because with purity, we are able to do what Paul challenged Pastor Tim to do:

> **2 Timothy 2:24-26,** "And the Lord's servant must not be quarrelsome but kind to everyone, able to teach, patiently enduring evil, correcting his opponents with gentleness. God may perhaps grant them repentance leading to a knowledge of the truth, and they may come to their senses and escape from the snare of the devil, after being captured by him to do his will."

Having any trouble with any of the above qualities and actions?

What are you struggling with right now?

Remember temptation is human, not sinful. Jesus was tempted in every way just like us yet, without sin. He understands what you are going through in the pastorate.

> **Hebrews 2:18,** "For because he (Jesus) himself has suffered when tempted, he is **able** to **help** those who are being tempted."

I am many years removed from that uncomfortable confession I made to that group of guys. And, thanks to my wife, I have developed a means to fulfill the discipline of confession on an ongoing basis as a pastor and follower of Jesus Christ and to her I am forever grateful.

Maybe it is time for you to grab your journal for the first time, the weeds aren't going to get any smaller, and say, "Lord, I can't be a good pastor and tend this church garden without you!"

He knows!

He won't ignore you!

JOURNAL YOUR CONFESSIONS, GOOD PASTOR, ALL OF THEM!

CHAPTER 3

THE DISCIPLINE
OF COMMITMENT

Commitment does not guarantee success, but a life void of it assures failure.

> **Joshua 11:18,** "Joshua made war a long time with all those kings."

There is no substitute for faithfulness.

In 1922, Winston Churchill, the eventual Prime Minister of England during WWII in the 1940s, was defeated at Dundee—by a Prohibitionist and a Labour candidate. For the first time since 1900, he was **without** a seat in Parliament. The new Conservative Government had no interest in finding him one or offering him a Cabinet Post; indeed, although the Liberal Party had been drastically reduced in strength, he was still determined to stand as a Liberal.

The General Election was held on December 6, 1923, a week after Churchill's forty-ninth birthday. Churchill stood at West Leicester and **failed** to get elected.

In March 1924, Churchill ran again as an Independent and lost, yet, again. It was the ninth parliamentary election of Churchill's career. As the final packet of votes was counted, Churchill was told that he had been elected with a majority of a hundred, a result that was passed by the wire services to all the London clubs. In fact, Churchill had been defeated by forty-three votes.

Certainly, the public announcement that he had won when he had in fact lost, just added insult to injury to a very dark season of Churchill's life and career. It was probably during this time that he coined the phrase, "Cats look down on you, dogs look up to you, but pigs treat you as equals."

All of us have been there. Regardless of how much "success" you have had in your life or career, eventually the gloomy dark dog of defeat bites you.

The great heavyweight boxing theologian of the world, Mike Tyson, probably said it best.

"Everyone has a plan until they get hit in the mouth."

Defeat is inevitable. You can't win forever. Matter of fact, defeat may very well overshadow more days of your life than perceived success. When I was a student at Liberty University, Dr. Jerry Falwell would often say, "If today is a good day, the next two probably won't be." He went on to explain that he had found in his life that two out of every three days he would deem difficult.

If you are discouraged by this, Dr. Falwell was more encouraging than Job. Job said,

> **Job 14:1**, "Man who is born of woman is few of days and full of trouble."

Churchill put a little different spin on this. His most frequent response to the "defeats" and struggles of his life was to say, "KBO."

Keep buggering on!

And yes, I understand, the original meaning of this word was very derogatory, but like many words they morph over time and come to mean something very different.

The Apostle Paul would have said it a little better:

Keep pressing on!

God has called us to KPO! Keep pressing on! Paul said it best:

> **Philippians 3:13,14**, "Brothers, I do not consider that I have made it my own. But one thing I do: forgetting what lies behind and straining forward to what lies ahead, I **press on** toward the goal for the prize of the upward call of God in Christ Jesus."

The past can be the greatest enemy of the future, especially if you have faced great tragedy or trial or even success for that matter. In the midst of WWII, England was consumed with comparing the past WWI with the present WWII with Germany. In an attempt to inspire England, Prime Minister Churchill said,

"If we open a quarrel between the past and the present, we shall find that we have lost the future."

I have been there and I am sure you have as well. We set out with great dreams and ambitions, but along the way our dreams are dashed against the rocks of life. What we imagined this becoming, it is anything but. The disillusionment sets in and fear begins to take over. The courage to stand is lost and the will to press in is paralyzed by the night terrors that haunt your day thoughts.

Maybe you are saying right now, "How does he know me so well?" Because I have been there, many times and unfortunately, you and I, if we stay engaged, will be there again. The one universal language in the world that every human being understands is pain, regardless of their success, we all feel the pain of this fallen world we are surrounded by. Pastors are no exception. You can't ride your bike and never skin your knee regardless of how good you are at riding your bike.

Commitment does not make us immune to defeat, nor does it guarantee success, but it does assure us that we can keep pressing on.

KPO.

I love the game of basketball and especially love shooting three pointers and if you are a shooter, you know you can't win if you don't score. In basketball they have a saying, "You miss every shot you don't take." Stephen Curry of the Golden State Warriors is currently the best three-point shooter in the history of the NBA game. He shoots 44% a game and hits seven three-pointers a game. That's amazing, right?

Well, think about his failures.

That means he misses 56% of the shots he takes a game on average. What does that mean? It means he misses more than he makes. It means he fails more than he succeeds. For every seven he hits, he misses nine.

You can't win, if you can't fail.

At the age of forty-nine, after eleven terms in parliament, Churchill's career had stalled. He was out of a job, practically broke from the crash of the stock market in the 1920s with little promise in his future. Yet, at the age of sixty-five, he was elected as the Prime Minister of England to practically lead England and the entire world to defeat Hitler and Mussolini.

Did you get that? Sixty-five years old. So many of us as pastors in our forties, fifties, and sixties feel like the church world has passed us by because we are not in our twenties or thirties, being the coolest pastors on the planet. It's okay. Let the twenties and thirties be the coolest, in some ways it is needed, but don't let yourself get lost in the shuffle because you think God no longer has something for you in the ministry. You are STILL valuable to God. We all get lost in the middle.

What if Churchill had quit in his forties or fifties because of his perceived failure? Honestly, if he had, we may have never seen the light of day due to the atrocities of Herr Hitler.

Though my story is not as dramatic as Churchill's, and not as glamorous as Stephen Curry's, I had a moment of "failure" that just about paralyzed me as well. Matter of fact, I had more than one. I have many to choose from, but I distinctly remember this one because depending on my choice, I wouldn't be writing this book, because the church known as "Vanguard Church of Colorado Springs" would have never come into existence.

My seminary professor, Bill Lawrence, from the Leadership Center of Dallas Theological Seminary, had come to visit me in Colorado Springs in 1996. We had recently moved from Dallas after completing our studies to start a church with the Southern Baptist Convention. We had set up our little apartment, using the second bedroom as the church office.

Bill came by and we sat in my living room. As we sat there and talked, I told him how discouraged I was with church planting. We had hosted a weekly meeting for a few months now and the week prior NO ONE came.

I remember saying to God, "God, we came here to start a church *for people*. We can't start a church *with no people*." I said those words over twenty years ago and I still feel the desperation in those words as I write them.

I remember Bill looking at me, smiling, looking me square into my eyes, peering into my soul, and saying, "You are MORE than numbers and one day you will realize what

I mean by this."

I recently saw a statistic that said there are roughly 300,000 churches in the United States and approximately 1600 of them are over the size of 5000 people. That means 298,400 of the churches in America are pastored by people who probably don't "feel" successful and the other 1600 would give anything to be in a setting where they could let go of the success and feel the significance of God's calling on their life without the pressures of "figuring out how to grow bigger churches."

We have an epidemic problem among pastors in America, it is not a moral failure, it is not burnout. It is the feeling of insignificance regardless of the size of their church. Honestly, I wouldn't even believe these words myself except that a few years ago I went to a simulcast of the Leadership Summit Willow Creek puts on every year. At this simulcast, Bill Hybels, the founder of Willow Creek Community Church and the Willow Creek Association and the Leadership Summit, said in his talk, "I am glad I stuck around to experience this."

I thought to myself, "Why would a guy with that kind of success dating back to the 1970s need to tell me forty years later he is glad he stuck around?"

Maybe because *numbers and size of church are not enough to keep us going?* Sadly, since that statement was made by Bill we have learned again there is no substitute for integrity and holiness in our personal and private lives. Bill is yet another example of a man who started great but the ministry chewed him up and spit him out.

That's how hard ministry is. And the sooner I learn, you learn, we all learn, that we are more than the numbers, the greater significance we can have on Christ's people for *His* glory if we turn and focus on the things that really matter to the Kingdom of God, His GLORY.

I know this may surprise you, *God doesn't care how big your church is.* You want to know why? Because it's not yours, it's His.

The church is *His* bride not ours.

All of us have different skill sets, and skill attracts a crowd and the more skill and resources the bigger the crowd, but only commitment creates an army. And the last time I checked, God is more interested in the latter than the former. Don't get me wrong, there is NOTHING wrong with large churches, medium churches, or small churches. And there are MANY factors that determine the size of a church or organization. But at the end of the day, it is not about size or success, it is about service and significance.

I believe in excellence, but not primarily for the sake of success. I believe in excellence primarily for the sake of satisfaction. I want to do the best I can and take satisfaction in the work I have done. In Bible college, my professor, Dr. Paul Fink, who taught me how to preach, said this, "Do the best you can with the time you got, and move on!"

I have taken that as my mantra in all the areas of my ministry. Resources limit success. Ability limits success. Location limits success. Competition limits success. Commitment maximizes your success. Don't give up on who God has created and called you to be just because you are not as "successful" as the guy down the street, across town, or on the other side of the country or world. Be the best you and accept the fact that someone will always in some way be *"more"* successful than you.

You can't have it all, be it all, or win it all. But if you are not careful, you can *lose* it all.

You can lose who God wants you to be if you try to be somebody you are not. We live in a day and age where pastors spend more time worried about how the lights on the stage look in the livestream than on how their hearts look in the light of God's presence. I can relate. They are more concerned about relating than leading. Don't get me wrong, we need to relate, but when people look up on the stage they don't need to see themselves, they need you to show them how to be who they don't know how to be. They need an example to follow.

You are that example and your character matters more than your caricature.

It is okay to be cool, but not at the expense of being committed to the holiness of who God created us to be, and you can't develop that holiness without some bumps and bruises along the way. Paul capitalizes on this to the Romans.

> **Romans 5:3-5,** "Not only that, but we rejoice in our sufferings, knowing that suffering produces endurance, and endurance produces character, and character produces **hope**, and hope does not put us to shame, because God's love has been poured into our hearts through the Holy Spirit

who has been given to us."

I need hope to be committed to Christ's calling on me in order to be a pastor for a lifetime. Hope doesn't come through success, it originates through suffering and is cultivated through endurance, and produced through character that reflects Christ.

My hope is not in my ability to grow a big church. It is not even in my ability to stay committed. It is my belief that if I don't quit, Jesus will fulfill through me why He created me.

Like Peter in John 21, I may wish He would have given me another calling, a bigger church, more hair on the back of my head, more of whatever, especially on the bad days, but in the end, my hope is found in my ability to reflect Christ in my actions and fulfill His purpose for my life.

I can't do this if I quit.

Churchill was "fired" at forty-nine. He had to wait sixteen years to fulfill his purpose. Bill left me that day, my wife went to California to see her sister, and I sat there in my self-pity wondering how I would call the Southern Baptists and tell them I had made a mistake and I was leaving the church planting process before a church was even started.

I sat there in my "easy" chair looking for an "easy" way out. My devotions soon after that led me through John 10. It is the story of the "Good Shepherd." Jesus said,

> **John 10:11–15,** "I am the good shepherd. The good shepherd lays down his life for the sheep. He who

is a **hired hand** (working simply for the purpose of money) and not a shepherd, who does not own the sheep, sees the wolf coming and leaves the sheep and flees, and the wolf snatches them and scatters them. He flees because he is **hired hand** and **cares nothing for the sheep**. I am the good shepherd. I know my own and my own know me, just as the Father knows me and I know the Father; and I lay down my life for the sheep."

The verse that really got me was verse sixteen. You have heard of John 3:16.

> **John 3:16,** "For God (the Father) so loved the world that he gave his only begotten son..."

But have you ever learned John 10:16-18? This is God the Son's perspective on the same topic...

> **John 10:16-18,** "And I have **other sheep** that are not of this fold. I must bring them also, and they will listen to my voice. So there will be **one flock**, one shepherd. For this reason the Father loves me, because I lay down my life that I may take it up. No one takes it from me, but I lay it down of my own accord. I have authority to lay it down, and I have authority to take it up again. This charge I have received from my Father."

I got it. Jesus sent Tosha and me to Colorado Springs to reach "other" sheep that were not yet in the fold so they could be a part of the one flock of God, under the one shepherd, Jesus. And just as Jesus freely and willingly lay His life down for these "other" sheep, He could freely and

willingly take it up again if He so chose, the choice was
His. And as the choice was His, the choice was also mine,
the choice was ours. I heard the Lord say to me that day:

"Kelly, what kind of shepherd will you be? Will you
be one that abandons the sheep like a hired hand
(doing it for the money and success) or will you be
a shepherd like the one shepherd, Jesus, and lay
down your life for them like Him?"

I told the Lord that day, "Jesus, I will be a shepherd like
you. I will lay down my life for the sheep, regardless of the
number." The next week, it snowed, no one came to the
church meeting.

KPO. Keep pressing on!

Sixteen years later, on May 10, 1940, Neville Chamberlain
resigned as Prime Minister and Churchill succeeded him.
He was sixty-five years old. The events leading up to this
succession occurred on the evening of September 3, 1939,
less than eight hours after Britain's declaration of war on
Germany. The unarmed passenger liner, *Athenia*, on its way
from Liverpool to Montreal with 1,418 passengers on board,
was torpedoed by a German submarine called the U-30.
Ninety-eight passengers and nineteen crewmen were killed.

Twenty-three days later, Churchill gave the House of
Commons his first survey of the war at sea. The Leader of
the Labour Opposition, Clement Attlee, complimented him
on his robust, vigorous statement. Churchill had spoken
for twenty minutes. The National Labour MP, Harold
Nicolson, noted in his diary that evening: "In those twenty
minutes Churchill brought himself nearer the post of

Prime Minister than he has ever been before. In the lobbies afterwards parliament members were saying, 'we have now found our leader.'"

His sixteen-year drought was soon to come to an end and his leadership was to come to the forefront of a nation not unlike Joseph in Egypt during his time in the book of Genesis. He was created for "such a time as this."

Churchill penned these words about the turn of fortunate events.

> "I felt as if I were walking with destiny; and that all my past life had been but a preparation for this hour and for this trial. Ten years in the political wilderness had freed me from ordinary party antagonisms. My warnings over the last six years had been so numerous, so detailed, and were now so terribly vindicated, that no one could gainsay me. I could not be reproached either for making the war or with want of preparation for it. I thought I knew a good deal about it all, and I was sure I should not fail. Therefore, although impatient for the morning, I slept soundly and had no need for cheering dreams. **Facts are better than dreams."** Yes, they are. Dreams fulfilled are sweet to the palate of the soul stung by the rejection and defeat of past failure repeat.

You miss every shot you don't take.

KPO. Keep pressing on!

Churchill once said, "I write 2000 words a day and lay 200

bricks a day, this is how I stay sane."

It is not enough to just keep pressing on toward the ultimate goal. You must occupy your time with something that enables you to create what needs to be created in the meantime.

One of the greatest challenges of a pastor is preaching, even if you are great at it. It is challenging to deal with the weekly grind of coming up with something fresh every week to feed your flock so they can grow and become who God has created them to be. Yes, I know the sheep at some point need to learn how to graze on their own, but still the undershepherd must guide this process and show them what the good grasses look like, taste like, and produce in the life of the sheep, not to mention all the other daily struggles that come with the life of a church regardless of its size.

The size of the congregation has no bearing over the difficulty or ease of sermon preparation. It requires the same, every week. Did you catch that? Every week! That's the hard part of sermon writing. You write a sermon, you labor over it, you prepare to give it, you give it. Within days you have to begin the process all over again. And eventually, it wears you down. It wears you out. It exhausts you beyond measure. Preaching would be easy if it didn't require your heart or a willingness to share your life with others.

Dr. Howard Hendricks would say all the time in seminary, "Relevant preaching is easy. Exegetical preaching is easy. But relevant exegetical preaching every week, well, that seems impossible."

There is nothing more demanding on the lead pastor or teacher than preaching, or in my opinion more important. If you miss this part the church gets everything else wrong eventually.

In twenty-five years, we have prepared roughly 1300 messages at Vanguard. I have prepared about 90% of those messages. So, in twenty-five years I have written almost 1200 sermons. Early on in my ministry, I knew I needed to develop some sort of discipline that would enable me to stay committed to sermon writing, the church, my wife, my kids, my job, my staff, my integrity, my purity, and yes, my sanity.

For Churchill, it was 2000 words and 200 bricks a day. For me, it was and is, reading ten chapters a day in my Bible, journaling before I prepare a sermon and before I deliver it, and third, it is fasting on a weekly basis when I write my messages.

Somewhere along the way the phrase came to me, "I want to hear God's voice over all the other screaming voices in my head, including the one in my gut." And so, I made a commitment to fast every time I write a message. I write messages on Tuesdays four weeks in advance of when I give them. I have done this now for twenty-five years.

Yes, creativity is challenging and fasting makes it that much harder. But my solution to dealing with difficult things is to figure out a way to take the "control" out of my hands and put as much as possible into His hands.

I take hearing from God, for God's people, very seriously and I am sure you do too.

I fast from food, starting after dinner on Monday night and I go until Tuesday night. In that 24 hour period, I write my message. 9/11 happened on a Tuesday. I thought when I got up that morning I was just fasting for a sermon for our church, but before the day was over, I had fasted for our entire nation that was grieving the greatest loss of life we have ever experienced in one national tragedy. I won't ever forget that day of fasting.

What does it mean to fast?

It means this: "go without food."

Why in the world would anyone want to do this? Because that is what Jesus did before He began His public ministry to the world and if it is good enough for Jesus then it is good enough for us. The Gospels record this experience after Jesus was baptized.

> **Matthew 4:1,** "Then Jesus was led by the Spirit into the wilderness to be tempted by the devil."

I don't know about you, but that is what sermon preparation feels like every week. It is a willingness to go into a wilderness for Christ's sake and be tempted by the Devil in all the areas of our lives while trying to discern God's voice to hear what He has for the sheep He has entrusted to us to lead.

> **Matthew 4:2,** "And after **fasting forty days and forty nights,** he was hungry."

Now that's an understatement! How many times have I said, "I'm starving!" I have no idea!

> **Matthew 4:3,** "And the tempter came and said to him, 'If you are the Son of God ... command these stones to become loaves of bread.'"

The Enemy will never quit attacking our identity and he will use **food** and a myriad of other things to do it. Ever wonder why a lot of pastors struggle with their weight, their sexuality, and a spectrum of other desires?

When you start eating spiritually for more than one, like a pregnant mom, you gain weight but sometimes the wrong type of weight. The truths of God's Word can't be gleaned apart from temptation playing a role in our souls.

Look at Jesus's response.

> **Matthew 4:4,** "But He answered, 'It is written, 'Man shall NOT live by bread alone, but by every word that comes from the mouth of God.'"

When I fast, I am giving up physical food to gain spiritual food for myself and others. It also gives me the BEST chance to hear EVERY word God has for me and the flock I lead. However, the Devil won't give up that easy.

> **Matthew 4:5,6,** "Then the devil took him to the holy city and set him on the pinnacle of the temple and said to him, 'If you are the son of God, throw yourself down, for it is written, 'He will command his angels concerning you, and 'On their hands they will bear you up, lest you strike your foot against a stone.'"

Don't let it be lost on you. Satan is one arrogant dude. He tried to tempt JESUS by quoting Scripture. The Devil will use anything to get you to believe His lies and do what He wants you to do and when you Fast it gets a lot clearer.

Ministry can make you dumb in your thinking if you are not careful because of the pressure mount and your heart desperately wanting some relief from the tension. It is in these moments the Devil will say things like "kill yourself," "call her on the phone," "go over to her house, her husband isn't there," "look at that stuff on the internet, it will make you feel better, you deserve it, given how hard you are working for the Lord," "they're really not paying you enough to do this every week," "you don't have time to devote this much of your week to preparing this message, you better skip it and help the staff figure out…"

It is in these times that the Enemy tempts me to take matters "into my own hands." My greatest temptations come DURING sermon writing without fail.

Look at Jesus's response.

> **Matthew 4:7,** "Jesus said to him, 'Again it is written, 'You shall not put the Lord your God to the test.'"

I am the servant. He is the master. I can't misuse my authority to get what I want even if it is in my power to do it. I believe one of the biggest reasons pastors fall in the ministry is because they can. Being a pastor is a very influential position, a very powerful position. And it is easy, over time, to think the power flows *from* you not just through you. Even Jesus Himself was tempted in this way by the Devil. We are ALL tempted to misuse our authority and when I fast, I see this more clearly as I prepare a message. The most powerful and influential thing I do every week is prepare a message. Like it or not, whoever is on stage preaching is perceived as the most powerful person in the room. Preaching is power over people's lives, and the Devil knows that too.

So, before you go out into your public preaching ministry, don't you think it is important that you fast like Jesus, so the Spirit can speak louder to you than your own selfish urges and ambitions? I do.

Again the Devil comes back to Jesus, and rest assured, he will again to you.

> **Matthew 4:8,9,** "Again, the devil took him to a very high mountain and showed him all the kingdoms of the world and their glory. And he said to him, 'All these I will give you, if you will fall down and worship me.'"

The Devil has authority to make you a successful pastor in this life. He could have made Jesus a successful Savior. He has the authority to give you what you want: 1) urges fulfilled, 2) control, and 3) fame and fortune. It is at his fingertips, if you will just bow down, he will make you a successful pastor. But look at how Jesus responded:

> **Matthew 4:10,** "Then Jesus said to him, 'Be gone, Satan! For it is written, 'You shall worship the Lord your God and him only shall you serve.'"

We are not here as pastors to worship ourselves or to have our congregations worship us. We are here to worship Jesus. Fasting enables me to say no to the urges screaming in my head and gut, it helps me realize I am not invincible and I need God to get through this life, and last, it helps me realize I am weak and I am here not to point people to me, but to Him.

If every sermon I write can be written with this environment and foundation, then the flock of God entrusted to me has the best possible chance to hear through me what He wants them to hear, and to grow and become who He has created them to be. If I can fulfill this, then I have been a good pastor to my sheep. I have given them the best of me. I have "laid down my life" for the sheep freely and willingly, knowing I have the authority to take it, yet choosing that if Christ died for them, the least I can do is fast for them when I write a message.

Fasting is what has shaped my spiritual nose to be like a bulldog's nose. Did you know a bull dog's nose enables him to keep fighting while continuing to breathe? Here are some of the things I have learned through fasting while preparing sermons:

1) It has taught me how to breathe spiritually, while fighting for my congregation, through sermon preparation.

2) It creates in me a clear conscience which enables me to bear my responsibility for sermon preparation and preaching with composure.

3) It keeps me focused on the goal: victory for others through Jesus no matter the cost.

4) It reminds me I have a part to play in the sermon, it's just not a very big one.

5) It encourages me that nothing worth doing is easy.

6) It reminds me that all I have to do is my part and God will do the rest through me.

7) It allows me to see firsthand that greater is He that is in me than he that is in the world.

8) It transforms my office into an altar.

9) It grows my personal resistance against the temptations and attacks of the Evil One.

And last, before I give you #10, look at verse eleven:…

> **Matthew 4:11,** "Then the devil left him, and behold, angels came and were ministering to him."

10) It reminds me that, through the ministering spirits God sends my way, I am not alone in the pastorate.

Churchill may have said it best in reference to winning WWII:

> "If you hold out alone long enough, there always comes a time when the tyrant makes some ghastly mistake which alters the whole balance of the struggle."

And the mistake that Satan makes over and over again is how he underestimates the power of Christ in a person who is fully surrendered to His work through them.

You are NOT alone!

Fast when you prepare your sermons, and after the temptations, the Enemy will flee and you will feel God's ministering angels for you.

Lay down your life for His sheep.

Commitment doesn't guarantee success, but a life void of it assures failure.

Don't quit!

FAST, GOOD PASTOR, and you will KPO! I guarantee it.

CHAPTER 4

THE DISCIPLINE
OF LISTENING

Listening to God is costly, but it is certainly cheaper than ignoring Him and going it alone.

Amos, the shepherd turned prophet, seemed to agree. The people had decided they didn't need to hear what God had to say, that is, until He stopped talking.

> **Amos 8:11,12,** "Behold, **the days are coming,**" declares the Lord God, "when I will send a **famine** on the land—not a famine of bread, nor a thirst for water, but **of hearing the words of the Lord.** They shall wander from sea to sea, and from north to east; they shall run to and fro, to seek the word of the Lord, **but they shall not find it.**"

One of my favorite verses in the Bible is:

> **Isaiah 55:6,** "Seek the Lord while He may be found. Call on Him while he is near"

I believe the MOST important work of a pastor is listening to God.

I believe the primary purpose of a pastor is to help their sheep hear their God speak to them too.

Do you remember the first time God ever spoke to you?

I do.

But, do you remember the first time you decided to intentionally listen for God?

I actually do, thanks to my childhood pastor, my dad.

The first time God speaks, it is startling, confusing, and can be gravely misinterpreted. To me, this is the main reason why God gave us teachers and pastors.

I will be the first to admit, it is not normal to hear God speak to us and it is even more unnatural for us to develop a process by which we intentionally listen for His voice. But that is what this chapter is about. If you are going to go the distance in the ministry as a pastor, you are going to have to learn how to live a life that intentionally listens to God and shares what you hear from Him with the people He has entrusted to you.

Winston Churchill often said during his illustrious political career, "It takes courage to speak and then it takes more courage to sit down and listen."

I believe this is the hardest work and truest work of a pastor. We stand and speak what we hear from Him and then we return, sit down in our studies, and wait courageously, through studying His Word, for Him to speak again to us for His people.

You know as well as I do, if you have preached for any length of the time, one of the scariest thoughts and recurring nightmares we all have as pastors is us standing in front of our congregation with NOTHING to say because God didn't speak. But when He does, we're different pastors.

When I listen for God, my imagination is ignited by the unlimited possibilities of the One who is speaking. But when I stop listening, or for some reason can't hear Him, I am left to figure it out through my own limited self on how to deal with all the problems of my life and those I pastor. Most of the time, in these moments, I conclude, it's not possible. Or, if it is, it's probably not worth it. My fear, anxiety, and selfishness often get the best of me.

This is why listening to God is so vital to being able to go the distance in the pastorate and the longer you wait to develop this discipline the more difficult it becomes.

Learning to listen, not just as a pastor, but as a human being, starts early and if someone doesn't help you develop the ability to listen, you are then forced through the circumstances and relationships of your life to learn lessons that would have been a lot cheaper in your youth.

I remember the first time God ever spoke to me. I wasn't trying to listen, He just spoke. I didn't initially know who it was, but I will certainly never forget it. It was April 30, 1980. I was eight years old. The reason why I remember this is because two days later I gave my life to Jesus Christ. The very next day, my mom took me and bought me my very first Bible. She wrote in it the date I gave my life to Christ.

I gave my life to Christ on May 2, 1980. This just so happens to be my last born's, Journey Grace, physical birthdate as well. I love how God connects all the dots in our lives between the physical and the spiritual.

On April 30, 1980, in Knob Lick, Kentucky, at Antioch Baptist Church, we were having a revival service. I don't remember the song. I don't even remember the sermon. But I will never forget the invitation. I was standing in the second row and I heard someone say my name. I turned, looked and said,

"Yes?"

They all shrugged their shoulders, confused by my question.

I turned around and felt super-confused. What just happened to me?

On the way home from church that night, I told my mom and dad what happened. My dad said, "Kelly, that is the Holy Spirit speaking to your heart and calling you to be His." My dad said, "The next time you hear it, just respond by coming down and I will pray with you to receive Christ."

There it is. My Dad introduced me at eight years old to the first step to living an intentional life of listening to God's voice.

He said, "The next time you hear it."

Do you expect God to speak to you?

It's not arrogant, it's simply the evidence that you are Jesus's sheep, His child.

Jesus said it best:

> **John 10:27,** "My sheep hear my voice, and I know them, and they follow me."

Expect God to speak to you.

I know, but what if He doesn't? One of my heroes of the faith is Oswald Chambers. He lived 1874–1917. He was a Brit. He is most known for the devotional book, *My Utmost For His Highest*. His wife published it after his death. It has never been out of print since 1935. It is one of the most popular Christian books ever published. Early on in Oswald's life, he thought he would be an artist, a painter. However, God got a hold of his heart and he felt the tug toward pastoral ministry. He anguished deeply over this and at one point had only heard the Lord speak personally to him three times in a four-year period.

Oswald expected God to speak. Job expected God to speak. I expect God to speak. You should expect God to speak to you.

But what if He doesn't? That is not your part to play in the equation, it's God's.

He tells us in His Word in Hebrews,

Hebrews 13:5a, "I will never leave you nor forsake you."

God doesn't expect you to do His part, but He does expect you to do yours.

The discipline of listening to God requires you to actively expect God to speak to you. Expecting Him to speak means you set aside intentional time to listen to Him. If He doesn't, that's okay. Your intentional time demonstrates you expect Him to speak and eventually He will. You have to combat your fears with action. This is why the disciplines of Bible reading, journaling, fasting, and prayer are vital to the process. I do these disciplines not to make myself "holy," though hopefully, it is a by-product of the process. I do these things primarily to position myself to have the best chance possible to hear God speak to me.

Time set aside to engage these disciplines demonstrates my love and affection for God's words and presence to me. Sometimes the experiences are good and sometimes, well, I can't tell any difference.

One time a pastor was getting ready to retire after forty years of preaching and teaching. One of his congregants came up to him and said, "Pastor, I have listened to you for forty years. I have heard almost every one of your sermons and with the exception of a few, I can't remember any of them. How does that make you feel?"

The Pastor smiled back at the congregant and said, "Do you remember everything you ate in the last forty years for breakfast, lunch, and dinner?" The congregant said back to him, "Very little." The pastor said, "Do you think you would still be alive today if you hadn't eaten?" The congregant smiled. He got it.

You and I don't have to remember everything God says to us nor does the experience need to be all that amazing. But in the end, without it, our souls die. Pastors especially will not go the distance for God if we don't dedicate time to hear from God and expect Him to speak.

Jesus told us in John 10 that we hear His voice and we follow Him. What does it mean to follow Him?

Remember what my dad told me when I asked him about the voice I heard? He said, "The next time you hear His voice . . . come down." In essence, when you hear His voice, respond.

Follow Him. Do what He tells you to do. Expect Him to speak and when He does,

Respond To What God Says To You.

I know, "But what if I am wrong?"

Your ability to hear and respond to God is not based on your accuracy, but your willingness to listen, and God's faithfulness to speak.

Charles Stanley says it well:

> "Yieldedness is vital in listening to what He has to say."

Are you willing? Are you sincerely trying to do what you think God said to you?

The Bible says,

> **Hebrews 11:6b,** "He (God) rewards those who diligently seek Him."

Remember the story of the talents in the Gospels? There were three people. They each were given a certain number of talents. The only one God rebuked and judged was the one who did nothing at all with the talent God had given him.

We have to put ourselves in a consistent and intentional position to hear from God, but once we have, it is God's job to speak and our job to respond.

Don't get hung up on what He said, how He said it, or how you can know for sure He said it. At least for now, just assume you will know and simply say to Him, "When you speak, I will listen and I will obey regardless."

I find God often uses the voices of those I trust to repeat to me in my mind what He wants me to do and the Enemy often uses the voices of those who have wounded me to speak into my soul. Listen to the voices you trust, they will most likely be the voices of God, but you need to make sure they align with Scripture.

Rest assured, if you are walking in obedience, He rewards those who sincerely seek Him. You can't mess up His plan even if you wanted to. You don't have that much power. Look at what the Proverb says:

Proverbs 19:20, "Many are the plans in the mind of a man, but it is the purpose of the Lord that will stand."

You couldn't mess it up even if you wanted to. Relax and respond!

Do you remember little Samuel in the Old Testament? His mom wanted a baby. Hannah was so distraught that she lay on the altar praying and crying at the Temple. Eli the priest came by and saw her and thought she was drunk. She wasn't drunk, she was crying out to God and intentionally seeking Him for a son.

She told God, "If you will give me a son, I will give him back to you to serve you."

As a young boy, my mom recounted the story of my life to me over and over again. I was born with a birth defect. The nerves in my large intestines didn't work. You get the picture. It happens, but for me it didn't. After multiple surgeries in Louisville Children's Hospital, the doctors told my parents they had done all they could do for me. I had gangrene and it was spreading all throughout my body. They told my mom and dad to prepare for the worst.

Countless times during my childhood my mom would recount the story to me, she called it a miracle. She said, "I knelt by your bed and I made a promise to God and said, 'God if You would spare Kelly's life I will give him back to You to do whatever You want him to do.'" And she would smile and say, "Just like Hannah did Samuel."

God gave Hannah a son. For my mom, God gave her son back to her.

I remember when I went off to Liberty University it broke my mom's heart to see me go. She locked herself in the bathroom so she wouldn't have to watch me leave. I don't know what kind of effect it had on Hannah, but I was eighteen when I left, and Samuel was just a few years old. 1 Samuel records this experience:

> **1 Samuel 1:9-14,17,20,24,26,28,** "After they had eaten . . . Hannah rose. Now Eli the priest was sitting on the seat beside the doorpost of the temple of the Lord. She was deeply distressed and prayed to the Lord and wept bitterly. And she vowed a vow and said, 'O Lord of hosts, if you will indeed look on the affliction of your servant and remember me and not forget your servant, but will give to your servant a son, then I will give him to the Lord all the days of his life, and no razor shall touch his head.'"

As she continued praying before the Lord, Eli observed her mouth. Hannah was speaking in her heart; only her lips moved, and her voice was not heard. Therefore, Eli took her to be a drunken woman. And Eli said to her, 'How long will you go on being drunk? Put your wine away from you.' Hannah answered, 'No, my lord, I am a woman troubled in spirit.' Then Eli answered, 'Go in peace, and the God of Israel grant your petition...' And in due time Hannah conceived and bore a son, and she called his name Samuel ... And when she had weaned him, she took him up with her ... and she brought him to the house of the Lord at Shiloh. And she said (to Eli), 'Oh, my lord! As you live, my lord, I am the woman who was standing here in your presence, praying to the Lord. Therefore I have lent him to the Lord. As long as he lives, he is lent to the Lord.'"

She kept her promise and gave him back to God just like my mom did me. Samuel was given for Temple service under the guidance of Eli the priest.

As you can see, Eli's intentional life of listening for God's voice had drifted to say the least. In the midst of this, Eli sees a woman crying out to God and his first thought is, "She's drunk." We later see the same drift of his faith in his sons.

> **1 Samuel 2:12,17,** "Now the sons of Eli were worthless men. They did not know the Lord. The sin of the young men was very great in the sight of the Lord, for the men treated the offering of the Lord with contempt."

Later, when a prophet comes to Eli, we see that this is a result of Eli's faith drift as a priest. It can happen even to the best of pastors. It happened to Eli. The prophet confronted him.

> **1 Samuel 2:29,30,34,35,** "Why ... do you scorn my sacrifices and my offerings ... and honor your sons above me by fattening yourselves on the choicest parts of every offering of my people Israel? Therefore the Lord, the God of Israel, declares ... this ... shall come upon your two sons, Hophni and Phinehas, shall be the sign to

you: both of them shall die on the same day. And I will raise up for myself a faithful priest, who shall do according to what is in my heart."

And with that, God calls Samuel.

1 Samuel 3:1, "Now the boy Samuel was ministering to the Lord in the presence of Eli. And the word of the Lord was rare in those days; there was no frequent vision."

Rarity of the word unfortunately was a result of Eli's ministry of not seeking after the voice of God. He cared more for what He could get out of the ministry than what God could do through him. Sad, but it happens often in the pastorate. We drift. We lose our focus. We lose our intentionality. We settle. We imagined more, it didn't happen, so we give up and make the ministry about what we can get out of it instead of how God can use us to lead His people through intentionally seeking His voice.

Like many pastors, including myself, who have been in the ministry for a long time we can lose our disciplined intentional lifestyle of listening for God's voice, and when we see it in one of our own sheep that we pastor, we don't even recognize it and call it something as unsacred as drunkenness.

Eli had lost touch, but this supposedly drunken woman, through her lifestyle of intentional pursuit of God, delivered a young boy to Eli that would not only change his perspective on the priesthood, but would ignite the voice of God for the entire nation of Israel. Thanks to Hannah, who intentionally sought the voice of God.

However, ironically enough, as God would have it, it wasn't Hannah, but Eli who introduced Samuel to a life of intentionally listening for the voice of God. We pick up the story in 1 Samuel.

> **1 Samuel 3:4,5,** "Then the Lord called Samuel, and he said, 'Here I am!' and (Samuel) ran to Eli and said, 'Here I am, for you called me.' But he said, 'I did not call; lie down again.' So he went and lay down."

Eli didn't get it. Remember, he had drifted. It had been a while since God had spoken to this priest.

> **1 Samuel 3:6-8,** "And the Lord called again, 'Samuel!' and Samuel arose and went to Eli and said, 'Here I am, for you called me.' But he said, 'I did not call, my son; lie down again.' Now Samuel did not yet know the Lord, and the word of the Lord had not yet been revealed to him. And the Lord called Samuel again the third time. And he arose and went to Eli and said, 'Here I am, for you called me.' **Then** Eli perceived the Lord was calling the boy."

Unlike my dad, who got it the first time, it took Eli a few tries to remember what it was like for someone, including himself, to hear the voice of God. Sad, but many pastors, for various reasons, haven't heard God speak to them in years.

Eli clears out the cobwebs and instructs young Samuel on how to expect God to speak to you and how to respond.

1 Samuel 3:9,10, "Therefore Eli said to Samuel, 'Go, lie down, and if he calls you, you shall say, "Speak, Lord, for your servant hears."' So Samuel went and lay down in his place. And the Lord came and stood, calling as at other times, 'Samuel! Samuel!' And Samuel said, '**Speak, for your servant hears.'**"

In the Old Testament, only a few got to hear God's voice, but in the New Testament, because of Jesus's sacrifice and the Holy Spirit living inside of each of His children, we ALL get to hear Him speak to us. You just have to learn how to, like Samuel.

You have to expect it. You have to be taught what to say. Eli taught Samuel to say, "Speak Lord, your servant is listening." I think that's the best place for all of us to start. To simply utter the exact same words. I do it all the time.

And then, you have to listen. Just as Samuel did:

1 Samuel 3:11-13, "Then the Lord said to Samuel, 'Behold, I am about to do a thing in Israel at which the two ears of everyone who hears it will tingle. On that day I will fulfill against Eli all that I have spoken concerning his house, from beginning to end. And I declare to him that I am about to punish his house forever, for the iniquity that he knew, because his sons were blaspheming God, and he did not restrain them.'"

Talk about a difficult FIRST word to hear from God at such a young age. I can't imagine the fear Samuel must have felt from the words he heard. Maybe he, like us, said to himself, "Did I hear Him right? What if I am wrong?"

So many times people ask, "How does God speak to you?" He speaks in various ways, but for me, He primarily speaks to me through His Word and His Spirit who lives inside of me.

The third step in living an intentional life of listening to God is **to share what you hear from Him with others.**

God doesn't just speak to us as pastors for our own good. He wants us to share what He says to us through our devotions, our fasting, our prayer times, and our journaling, with others.

Samuel did just that with Eli.

> **1 Samuel 3:15-17,** "Samuel lay until morning; then he opened the doors of the house of the Lord. And Samuel was **afraid** to tell the vision to Eli. But Eli called Samuel and said, 'Samuel, my son.' And he said, 'Here I am.' And Eli said, 'What was it that he told you? Do not **hide** it from me.'"

You are not the first person that has ever been afraid to tell others what you believe God has spoken to you. Samuel can relate. Eli pressed him and told him not to hide it from him. As pastors, we are all tempted to hide the truth God has spoken to us that we are to speak to those we lead or are in relationship with.

And then Eli, the veteran priest, who was supposed to have spent his life representing God, says something very curious to Samuel, the inexperienced boy who was just getting started.

1 Samuel 3:17b, "May God do so to you and more also if you hide anything from me of all that he told you."

Did you get that? Eli tells this young boy who just heard from God for the first time in his entire life, "If you don't tell me what God said, I hope God does to you what He told you He was going to do to me."

That's motivation! If you don't tell God's people what God told you about them, then He will judge you in the way He had planned to judge them. We see this same concept in Ezekiel.

Ezekiel 33:6,7 "So you, son of man, I have made you a watchman for the house of Israel. Whenever you hear a word from my mouth, you shall give them warning from me. But if the watchman sees the sword coming and does not blow the trumpet, so that the people are not warned, and the sword comes and takes any one of them, that person is taken away in his iniquity, but his blood I will require at the watchman's hand" (reversed for emphasis).

Somewhere along the way, Eli had given up on this advice. It seems like Eli knew what God had said to Samuel. He had heard it before, probably many times, he had just stopped listening. Sad!

The most pathetic sight is a pastor who has stopped telling the people what God has said to them and starts telling them either what they want to hear or what he wants them to hear. Being a pastor is about telling others what God wants them to hear. It will not always be easy nor will it always be difficult. Like any relationship it will vary depending on the many factors involved in the relationship.

As a pastor, when it comes to speaking to His people what He has said to you about them, fear God's judgment more than your failure or their disapproval.

Samuel continues speaking to Eli:

> **1 Samuel 3:18,** "So Samuel told him everything and hid nothing from him. And he said, '**It is the Lord.**'"

Eli didn't lose his ability to hear from God, he just stopped listening. So God told Samuel, presumably, to tell Eli what he no longer was willing to hear from Him directly. And when Eli heard it, he knew it was God. Eli was still God's child and he could hear Him through Samuel, he had just decided long ago to ignore Him in his own life.

Many in our congregations may look like they are not His children, but when we speak God's Words, if they are, they hear it. They are His children and His children can hear His voice.

As the story begins to land, it says:

> **1 Samuel 4:1,** "And the word of Samuel came to all Israel."

It is extremely important that you share what God says to you to those you are responsible for, and in relationship with, as a pastor or a child of God for that matter.

How? You seek God through His Word. You journal it. You ask your prayer partner, pastoral team, elders, staff, congregation, leadership, other pastors, friends, spouse, children, and so forth and so on, to hear it, receive it, and pray over it to see what God wants to say to them. This is the work of a pastor. You fast and meditate on it.

The night God spoke to me for the first time, my dad shared with me what is often referred to as the "Romans Road to Salvation." He helped me understand I was a sinner and that I was separated from Christ and if I were to die without accepting Christ, I would die and go to hell.

I had never considered this concept before in my entire life. I never thought I would go to hell. I thought hell was just for bad people. And by the way, there are many people who think similarly.

The next night, I went to church and they gave the invitation. Nothing.

On the way home that night, my dad said to me, "Did God speak to you?" I said, "No, Dad. I didn't hear anything."

The next night was Friday night, from the start, the Holy Spirit was all over me. I couldn't wait for the invitation. When it began, I ran down and threw myself down on the floor and wept. My dad helped me pray the sinner's prayer and I began my intentional life of listening to God speak to me.

Listening to the voice of God is an art that is perfected over time through trial and error. I have had forty plus years of experience now and I have experienced a variety of things with my Lord. I wrote a book called *The Mystery of 23: God Speaks.* It outlines some of the trial-and-error issues that we face with hearing from God and how you can be assured you have heard Him speak. If you would like to dig deeper into the finer nuances of fleeces, prophetic words, comparing Scriptures to what God has spoken to you, and so forth and so on, I would encourage you to check it out.

Certainly, throughout the Scriptures, probably no one spoke with God or heard God any more clearly than Moses did. The Bible tells us:

> **Deuteronomy 34:10,** "And there has not arisen a prophet since in Israel like Moses, whom the Lord knew face to face."

If that's the case, then it seems like Moses would be a good person to pattern your intentional discipline of listening to and for God after him. Moses would go up on the mountain, hear the word of God and come back and share it with the people.

> **Exodus 34:29-32,** "When Moses came down from Mount Sinai, with the two tablets of the testimony of his hand as he came down from the mountain, Moses did not know that the skin of his face shone because he had been talking with God. Aaron and all the people of Israel saw Moses, and behold, the skin of his face shone, and they were afraid to come near him. But Moses called to them, and Aaron and all the leaders of the

congregation returned to him, and Moses talked with them. Afterward all the people of Israel came near, and he commanded them all that the Lord had spoken with him in Mount Sinai."

This is a great way to be intentional about listening for the Lord, responding to what He says, listening to it for others' benefit, and sharing it with others. But "the Moses complex" will eventually kill the strongest, godliest pastor to ever lead a church because even though it is a great way to be intentional about listening to God it is a terrible way to govern a church. It will eventually burn out any pastor, and as we will see, Moses, too!

What is the Moses complex?

> **Exodus 34:13-15,** "Moses sat to judge the people, and the people stood around Moses from morning till evening. When Moses' father-in-law saw all that he was doing for the people, he said, 'What is this that you are doing for the people? Why do you sit alone, and all the people stand around you from morning till evening?' And Moses said to his father-in-law, '**Because the people come to me to inquire of God.**'"

Moses was being very intentional about listening to God, but he was not helping anyone else learn how to do the same. He had an audience for God, but no army.

When I first started Vanguard, I would walk into a staff meeting, a church meeting, an elder meeting, and I would feel the weight of the world telling the leaders, the team, the congregation, what God had spoken for us. It was my job to tell them everything God had spoken and it was their job to do what He had told us to do.

Eventually, I burned out and so did everybody else. It was not a sustainable model in Moses's day and it isn't in our day today. I do believe vision comes through a person and not a team, but I do not believe God only speaks to the visionary about the vision. Wisdom doesn't come just from an individual. It is better served up through a team.

> **Proverbs 11:14a**, "In an abundance of counselors there is safety."

In 2010, our church crashed hard. We had to cut $500k out of our annual budget and within one week 23% of our church had left. The bulk of the decisions to that point had been governed by me through what I would later come to call "the Moses complex." It wasn't that I wanted all the glory. It wasn't that I didn't want anyone else to have a say. I genuinely thought, like Moses, I was to play that role, and like Moses, it was killing me and just about killed the church. We were not making the best possible decisions we could make because I was bottlenecking the process.

I would come into the meetings and I would give the "thus sayeth the Lord." I would then ask if God had spoken anything to anyone else. Some would speak, some would not, but eventually everybody was frustrated at me, at each other, and everything. We had accountability, but very little team when it came to decisions because our process was bad and no one knew which lane was theirs and who could speak when or where. It is a pretty common mistake made by church planters and young churches. You start off with a lot of horizontally shared leadership, but eventually it turns totally vertical and neither model is healthy. You need a bit of both depending on the topic, issue, and context.

From Moses's "almost breakdown" came the Jethro plan.

> **Exodus 34:17,18,** "Moses' father-in-law said to him, 'What you are doing is not good. You and the people with you will certainly wear yourselves out, for the thing is too heavy for you. You are not able to do it **alone.**'"

God never intends for the pastor to be the sole and only voice to help others know what He wants them to do. Yes, at first you may be the only one, but over time you must develop others to hear from God and trust them to lead as well.

> **Exodus 34:19-24,** "Now obey my voice; I will give you advice, and God be with you! You shall represent the people before God and bring their cases to God, and you shall warn them about the statutes and the laws, and make them know the way in which they must walk and what they must do. Moreover, look for able men from all the people, men who fear God, who are trustworthy and hate a bribe, and place such men over the people as chiefs of thousands, of hundreds, of fifties, and of tens. And let them judge the people at all times. Every great matter they shall bring to you, but any small matter they shall decide themselves. So it will be easier for you, and **they will bear the burden with**

you. If you do this, God will direct you, you will be able to endure, and all this people also will go to their place in peace. So Moses **listened** to the voice of his father-in-law and did all that he had said."

Moses could have said to Jethro, "I'm Moses and nobody can do what I do." That's true as the Lead Pastor of your church, but just because nobody can do what you do doesn't mean you have to do everything.

Pick some able-bodied people and let them help you carry the burden. If you do, you will be able to endure and everyone will go to their place in peace.

We all have a part to play, but human nature is to eventually play too much of a part. Moses found himself in this exact situation.

I love what Richard Foster says about this process:

"To be a leader means listening to all kinds of people and situations. Out of that listening, we are hoping to discern the mind of God the best we can."

Trust me, it will be painful to get there and it will require a lot of setbacks along with trial and error and mistakes, but in the end, you will be better for it. Trust will grow, and a stronger team will come out on the other side and you will be able to do what only you can do or should do just like Moses.

Now when I go into meetings I don't begin with "thus sayeth the Lord." I begin with:

Proverbs 19:19b, "Listen to advice and accept instruction, that you may gain wisdom in the future."

I go into meetings looking to hear what God is already doing in the hearts of His leaders who are vested, committed, and trusting me to do what I am called to do. I don't have to fight for my role. I know it. They don't have to fight for their roles either because they know them. Our decision-making process is much healthier and now we go about casting and living in vision in a much healthier and more mature way because everyone is doing their part. We have leaders at the different levels described by Jethro to Moses.

But not only that, I have also pressed into a prayer partner who speaks into my life every Tuesday when I fast and write my sermons. I bounce my personal life off of him. I bounce professional ideas off of him. He doesn't have any "voting authority" in the elder room or pastoral room, but he has a ton of influence in my life and shapes how I view and approach things in the leadership of the church. I am extremely grateful for my prayer partner and pastor, Jon Elsberry. He and his wife Sandi have pastored my wife and me. Every pastor and pastor's wife needs a pastor and a pastor's wife to pastor them. We are very grateful.

I have learned along the way that I can intentionally seek after hearing the heart of God and yet, still hear Him through others as well. Matter of fact, if I am hearing Him correctly, most likely, I will hear Him in others as well. It is the rare occasion when God speaks ONLY to you in a family, organization, or church setting. If God is saying it to you, He most likely is saying it to someone else as well.

It is okay to share things as ideas first instead of mandates to your team. You can always come back at a later date and say, "God has spoken, we must..." But save those times, they will be rare and may occur once every few years, but in the meantime, part of living an intentional life of listening to God is learning to listen to others who you are accountable to, or who have a vested interest in the same organization or project.

Don't be afraid to slow the process down a bit. Don't be afraid to take it to your elders, pastoral team, staff, deacons, directors, prayer warriors, church members, congregation, the community, your spouse, your family, or your personal confidants. A leader who is seeking to live an intentional life of listening to God also **listens to others** like Moses did Jethro.

And yes, there will be that rare occasion when you have to stand up to everybody, but that is the rare exception not the rule. Be careful which hills you stand on because eventually the troops may shoot you and move on.

My professor, Dr. Howard Hendricks, used to say, "Be careful how far ahead you get from your congregation when leading them because they may mistake you for a target."

They deserve to be given the chance to intentionally seek God as well at their level of calling and responsibility and impact the organization accordingly. They have an opportunity to listen to God as well and speak into the process, and then ultimately, your matrix that you have agreed upon gives you the lanes, boundaries, and parameters you follow to make decisions because at the end of the day, we are going to have times we don't hear it from God the same way, and you need a way to move on. If it is a sin issue, I am not sure how you can hear it differently, but most things are not about sin, they are about timing, preferences, and conditions. Make sure you are dying for the right things and leading in the right areas, listening carefully where it is critical that you lead and influence, and letting go of the things others honestly can do better than you.

Moses did and he and the nation of Israel went home peacefully.

Your organization will prosper in peace when you let others be intentional in listening to God in their level of expertise.

Be intentional to practice the discipline of listening to God through scripture reading, praying, journaling, and fasting. Expect God to speak. Respond to what He says. Listen to how you can share it with others. In so doing, teach others to listen intentionally to God in their lives through these same ways. Then raise up these leaders. Listen to others who have earned the right and have been given the authority to speak into your life and what you lead, like Jethro.

Listening for God's voice and praying together is not the easiest work in the world.

Oswald Chambers captures the essence of this challenge.

"Prayer is not a preparation for the work, it is work. Prayer is not a preparation for the battle, it is the battle. Prayer is two-fold: definite asking and definite waiting to receive."

When we do this hard work together it gives us the best chance possible to discover the story for which we were created and the courage to fulfill it. Listen to how the people in Joshua's day responded to his intentional listening to God and leading them to do the same.

> **Joshua 24:24,** "And the people said to Joshua, 'The Lord our God we will serve, and his voice we will obey.'"

That is music to a pastor's ears, to hear the people they lead say they are willing to follow God and His voice, regardless.

When you and the community you pastor, listen for God and to God, you are doing the hard work of praying.

Praying is listening to God and speaking to His people, this is the essence of what the Prophet Amos was referring to at the beginning of this chapter.

And who knows, your hard work may just save the people you pastor from the worst kind of famine in their lives, a famine without hearing God speak.

GOOD PASTOR, KEEP PRAYING AND SAYING, "Speak Lord, your servant is listening!"

SECTION #2:

DREAMS

CHAPTER 5

GOD-GIVEN DREAMS

Good pastors keep dreaming God's dream for their lives.

I have always been attracted to people who want to dream, imagine, and then press into figuring out how to live out the dreams that are tied to the depths of their souls. Those who believe that they and their God-given dreams have been intrinsically created by God and for God's purposes.

Winston Churchill at age fifteen told his friend that he would one day save England in a Great War from the tyranny of the world.

At age seventy-five, Abram was visited by God and told he would leave his homeland, have a son, and become the father of many nations.

At roughly ninety years of age, Sarah was told she would have a son. She laughed.

At age seventeen, Joseph had a dream that his family would bow down to him as their leader.

At the age of eighty, Moses was told he would rescue God's people from the land of Pharaoh.

At the age of roughly seventeen, Esther was told she would save God's people from evil Haman.

At age seventeen, David was told he would become King of Israel through the Prophet Samuel's prophecy and anointing.

At the age of at least sixty, Elizabeth was told she would have a son who would be the forerunner of Jesus.

At the age of roughly fourteen, Mary was told by an angel that she would be impregnated by the Holy Spirit and give birth to the Savior of the world.

At the age of roughly thirty, Peter told Jesus he would go to death for Him.

At the age of roughly thirty-five, Paul declared he would be a witness to the Gentiles for Jesus.

At the age of twelve, I was told (I believe) by God that I would be a preacher one day.

At what age did God first speak His dream to you for your life?

I believe EVERY human being is created by God and is created to live out God's dreams for them.

Our choices in this life will indicate how those dreams from God are fulfilled in us.

Romans 9 has to be one of the most difficult and controversial chapters in the entire Bible. Regardless of where you fall theologically, it is a difficult chapter to reconcile.

The chapter is about God's Sovereign Choice. He chose Israel to be His chosen people. And since that choice, in each generation, He has continuously chosen a person, groups of people, and even a nation or two to carry forth the covenant relationship that He made with Israel. And ultimately, everything that goes on in the world is for the fulfillment of the promise He made to Israel, through Abraham. The fulfillment of which was reached through Jesus and the establishment of His Church.

And thus, every human being He creates somehow serves to help fulfill that purpose.

Whether they ever place their faith in Jesus Christ or not. That is what Romans 9 is about.

> **Romans 9:15-24,** "For he (God) says to Moses, 'I will have mercy on whom I have mercy, and I will have compassion on whom I have compassion.' So then it depends not on human will or exertion, but on God, who has mercy. For the Scripture says to Pharaoh, 'For this very purpose (Pharaoh) that I (God) might show my power in you, and that my name might be proclaimed in all the earth.' So then he has mercy on whomever he wills, and he hardens whomever

he wills. You will say to me, then, 'Why does he (God) still find fault? For who can resist his will?' But who are you, O man, to answer back to God? Will what is molded say to its molder, 'Why have you made me like this?' Has the potter no right over the clay, to make out of the same lump one vessel for honorable use and another for dishonorable use? What if God, desiring to show his wrath and to make known his power, has endured with much patience vessels of wrath prepared for destruction, **in order to make known the riches of his glory for vessels of mercy, which he has prepared beforehand for glory—** even us whom he has called, not from the Jews only but also from the Gentiles?"

Regardless of a person's bend, God still divinely uses people to further fulfill His ultimate dream: that one day His Son, Jesus, will rule the nations and be seated upon His throne in Heaven FOREVER.

There are dreams that live inside of all of us. I am not talking about vain dreams of pleasure, profit, and preservation. I am talking about dreams that ultimately move God's agenda forward through us for the generation we have been called to serve on His behalf.

The most popular Christian book ever written outside of the Bible is Rick Warren's book, *Purpose Driven Life*. It seeks to answer the question, "What on earth am I here for?"

It is the most fundamental question humanity is asking. And we as Christians should ask, **"What on earth am I here for, God?"**

Now as you have probably observed, there are many in the world who don't take this view of their lives and amass temporary success, severance, and satisfaction from the perceived "accomplishments" of their lives. They see their lives as an opportunity to fulfill their personal wanton desires, ambitions, and imaginations. But as we see in Scripture over and over again:

> **Proverbs 21:1,** "The king's heart is a stream of water in the hand of the Lord; he turns it wherever he will."

> **Proverbs 19:20a,** "Many are the plans in the mind of a man, but it is the purpose of the Lord that will stand."

> **Proverbs 16:33,** "The lot is cast into the lap, but its every decision is from the Lord."

Let me say it another way. We can roll the dice, but God determines if we get snake eyes or not.

> **Psalm 127:1,** "Unless the Lord builds the house, those who build it labor in vain. Unless the Lord watches over the city, the watchman stays awake in vain."

Romans 9 simply reinforces a reality that is true throughout the entire Bible. God is in charge of everybody, and every dream that is fulfilled in this world is meant to further serve the purpose of God's promise to Abraham 5000 years ago.

Seems overwhelming, doesn't it?

At age seventeen, I accepted the call on my life that God had given to me at age twelve.

I gave my life to Christ at age eight. Four years later, I heard God speak to me again. It confused me. I thought I wasn't saved. I went home and asked my dad about it after a revival service at our church, Poplar Springs Baptist Church, in Temple Hill, Kentucky.

He asked me a few questions. I told him the experience was similar to when I gave my life to Christ. He concluded and asked, "Has God called you to be a pastor like me?"

It was the last two words of that question that got me and I immediately responded, "I don't think so."

For the next five years of my life, I knew internally what God had called me to do, but externally I fought it. I resisted it. I pretended it had never happened and lived as if I had "lots of options."

When we are younger, people say things to us like, "You have your whole life ahead of you to do whatever you want to do with your life."

That's not true.

We do have our whole lives ahead of us, but ultimately to do what God created us to do. We can agree with that dream or calling, or we can resist it. Either way, God will (and does!) take people in each generation, from each nation and fulfills through all of us what He promised to Abraham 5000 years ago.

Your life matters to God. Your dreams matter to God. *But God is not here to help you figure out what you want to do with your life. He is here to help you figure out what He has created you to be and do.*

You were created with design and purpose. It was built into you BEFORE you were born. The Bible says in Psalm 139:16, "Before one day was, He (ALREADY) knew them all to be."

God is NOT surprised by one second of your life.

He knew I would be born with a birth defect on May 25, 1971, to Larry and Linda Sue Williams. My parents thought I was going to be a girl and had planned to name me Elisha. They didn't know I was a boy, but God did.

God knew I would spend the first three and a half years of my life in and out of Louisville Children's Hospital in Louisville, Kentucky. He knew I would almost die many times before my fourth birthday.

He knew my mom would pray and ask Him to spare me and if He did, she would give me back to Him to do whatever He called me to do with my life.

He knew I would live my childhood life in the Cave City-Glasgow, Kentucky, area. He knew at age eight I would give my life to Him.

He knew at age seventeen, after five years of battling with Him, I would surrender to the call of ministry and head to Liberty University at age eighteen to begin to study for the pastorate.

God knew. Why did He know? Because He knows everything. Now don't get hung up on whether we have a choice or not. Don't get caught up in the debate over fate or choice. Just accept what we know to be true from Scripture.

God knew.

When I went off to college at age eighteen, I had no idea how God would use Liberty University to shape my life for the pastorate. I met so many incredible people in such a short period of time and many of the people I met from eighteen to twenty-five are still in one way or another impacting the life I am living now.

Many people didn't care for Dr. Falwell and his way of going about things. But I liked the guy. I thought he was a genuine, heart-felt, caring, good man who loved God and loved his family. Yes, he was rough around the edges and he said things in ways I wouldn't, but God didn't ask me to be him or vice versa and I think it is important in life to realize we are not all created equal. We each have unique components to our existence for the purpose of fulfilling who God has created us to be.

Dr. Falwell would often say in chapel:

> "Shoot for the stars, land on the moon, no one will notice."

Dr. Falwell understood failure was a part of dreams, because we are a part of the equation, but that didn't keep him from dreaming. Matter of fact, when I was at Liberty, every month they were figuring out if the school was going to make it to the next year. It is nothing like that now.

Recently, my family and I went back to visit Liberty's growing campus.

The place is amazing now. Buildings and people everywhere. Money galore. Opportunities unheard of. The day we were there, they were tearing down the religion building where I took most of my classes because they are now going to build a beautiful tower that will house all of the religion courses.

Dr. Falwell seemingly failed a lot while I was at Liberty and it appeared the school wouldn't make it. But soon after his death, the school was stabilized financially and took off, thanks to many generous donors who believed in the dream God had given him and a life insurance policy the school had gotten on Dr. Falwell.

Dr. Falwell sat down at his desk, slumped over, and went to be with his Lord. The God dream lives on today.

So often people say, "How do you know if a dream is from God?" Here is how you will know.

It comes true.

> **Ecclesiastes 3:14,** "I perceived that whatever God does endures forever; nothing can be added to it, nor anything taken from it."

If God dreams it, and puts it in you, then He will make it come true. That doesn't mean you will be around to see it in this life. You may stand beside Him and watch it unfold from heaven like Dr. Falwell did. But if God dreamed it, you are GUARANTEED, it will eventually come true. Not on your timetable, but certainly in the perfect timing of God to fulfill what He promised to Abraham.

Hard to believe that every dream from God that humanity dreams is tied to this one promise to Abraham, but it is. And it always will be. Every generation dreams dreams that usher us one step closer to the eternal Kingdom Christ will rule over one day in the fulfillment of the Abrahamic covenant between God and His people.

All world leaders exist to fulfill God's ultimate plan and promise to Israel, through Abraham, and realized through Jesus. Remember, the King's heart is in God's hand. Once again, this is what Romans 9 is all about. That is the sacred trust given to all of us and handed down to us from generation to generation. Paul describes this sacred trust handed down to Timothy from the previous generations of his ancestry.

> **2 Timothy 1:5-11,** "I am reminded of your (Timothy's) sincere faith, a **faith that dwelt first in your grandmother Lois and your mother Eunice and now**, I am sure, dwells **in you** as well. For this reason I remind you to fan into flame the gift of God, which is in you through the laying on of hands, for God gave us a spirit not of fear but of power and love and self-control. Therefore do not be ashamed of the testimony about our Lord, nor of me his prisoner, but share in suffering for the gospel by the power of God, who saved us and **called us to a holy calling,** not because of our works but because of **his own purpose** and grace, which he gave us in Christ Jesus **before the ages began**, and which now has been manifested through the appearing of

our Savior **Christ Jesus**, who abolished death and brought life and immortality to light through the gospel, for which I was **appointed a preacher**, and apostle and teacher."

Do you know why you are a pastor?

Because that is WHO God wants you to be to fulfill His giant plan for the universe. YOU MATTER! Stop comparing yourself to said pastor, God isn't.

When I was a teenager struggling with whether or not God called me to be pastor, I turned on the television and Charles Stanley was preaching. He said, "Are you trying to figure out if you have been called to be a pastor?"

I immediately said out loud, "Yes."

He said, "Here is the best advice I can give you. **If you can do anything else instead of being a pastor, do it, but if not, then become a pastor.**"

I finally came to a place in my life where I said, "I can't do anything, but be a pastor."

We don't become pastors so people will listen to us. We don't become pastors to be popular. We don't become pastors to be seen as powerful, cool, and famous. We don't become pastors, so people will follow us. We don't become pastors, so we can sip coffee, come up with cute sayings, post on social media, and write books.

We become pastors because this is the dream God dreamed for us. **God-given dreams are just that: "given by God."**

I am a pastor because that is what God wants me to be. It has been entrusted to me like Paul says: by God and the faith that has been handed down to me by the generations before me.

Now maybe, like A.W. Tozer, you come from a home where no one else believes in Jesus. Ultimately, it doesn't matter, God will use someone from the generation before you to bring you to Himself and call you to be who He made you to be.

God used A.W. Tozer's mother-in-law, Kate Pfautz, to bestow the grace he needed on his life to become who God created him to be. She was his biggest cheerleader.

God also used Paul Daniel Radar, from Denver, Colorado, and Fred Francis Bosworth from Zion, Illinois. But the bottom line is this, God will use the generation before you, one way or another, to hand to you the faith they have, so you can carry the baton to the next generation.

King David said, "I have served my generation faithfully."

This is all God asks of us. He gives us dreams. He asks us to fulfill them and then He will use someone in the next generation to carry on that same dream, modified. It may be a relative, a friend, or a distant acquaintance, but in the end, God allows the paths of His people to cross with those they need to cross with (from the previous generations) to become who God has created them to be.

I remember when I was at Liberty, I read the journals of Jim Elliott. He wrote in the 1950s, "May God raise up a Vanguard". This is not why the church I planted is called Vanguard. My wife named the church, but Jim Elliott prayed it into existence almost fifty years before it occurred.

No dream, no purpose, no prayer, no sermon, and no energy expended by God will be lost in His dream economy. You may not know why you are doing what you are doing, saying what you are saying, going where you are going, being who you are being...

But God does.

God's dreams don't require you to understand what God has called you to be or do, they just require you to obey. They just require you to act on His behalf trusting the outcome will be as He has dreamed and orchestrated it.

But how do you know if a dream is "from God."

If it comes true, then it is from God.

Okay, but how do you know if the dream you are chasing is from God? It probably isn't, if you are chasing it. **You don't have to chase God's dreams, you just have to become them.**

It is not some illusive carrot that is dangled before your eyes as an incentive for you to keep following God with your life and become a pastor. God's dreams aren't established externally this way. You were born with them "inside you."

Yeah, okay, but this is starting to sound like a popular movie that came out in the 1980s called Karate Kid with Mr. Miyagi and "Daniel son."

So, how does God let you *know* the dreams He has for your life as a pastor?

Now, that's the question, isn't it?

Here is how? **He uses MANY means to do so. Here is a list of some of those means:**

Dreams in your sleep, dreams in your daytime, visions, animals, the stars, moon, sun, and galaxies, mountains, rivers, lots, draw straws, rolling of the dice, light in burning bushes, voices from the sky, whispers to our souls that only you can see and hear and no one else, fleeces, prophets, preachers, teachers, civil leaders, family members, friends, strangers, politicians, military officials, acquaintances, world leaders, spiritual leaders, moms and dads, mentors, world events, local events, angels, miracles, health issues, and ultimately His Word and Spirit.

How does He let us know? By whatever means He chooses.

God will let you know, trust me.

My dad wasn't a Christian when I was younger and sick. He thought he was, but he realized through my sickness he wasn't. He didn't have a real faith like my mom at the time.

He gave his life to Jesus sometime after I was miraculously healed by God through my mother's prayers. He eventually became a deacon in our local Baptist church, Coral Hill Baptist Church. Sometime after this, he started feeling the tug to become a pastor. Like me, he resisted. And for good reason. We all want to make sure we don't choose this calling for the wrong reason. But at a certain point, it goes from fear to pride pretty quickly, and our resistance is born more out of our selfishness than our selfless concern as to whether He has actually called us.

In 1976, when I was about five years old, my dad was resisting the call and had entered this selfish resistance, believing that being a faithful deacon and farmer was all God had asked him to do. In this season of resisting, he was harvesting corn and putting it into the barn for the winter months.

Back then, we used grain elevators and ran the corn through the open door of the loft and dropped the corn into a large pile in the middle of the barn for access in the winter time. We used a tractor to power the grain elevator from a PTO shaft that ran from the back of the tractor to the side of the elevator. You could adjust the speed of the elevator with the throttle of the tractor. My dad opened the throttle to high and released the corn out of the door on the side of the bed wagon. He walked around to check on it, and stepped in between the elevator and the tractor. When he did this, the PTO shaft that was running at thousands of RMPs in a circular motion accidentally grabbed the sleeve of his shirt that he had wrapped around his waist because of the heat of the morning.

It began to pull his body down into the PTO shaft that was spinning at thousands of RPMs per minute. Eventually it pulled him close enough into it that it began to eat the flesh away right out from under his right arm. In the midst of this, my dad said out loud, "I will become a pastor if you spare my life."

Somehow, my dad gathered the strength to smother the engine on the tractor and killed the power that kept the shaft running. He was just seconds away from it picking up his body and literally beating him to death.

They told my dad he would never use his right arm again, they were wrong. Thank you, Lord!

Now hopefully your call to the pastorate was NOT that severe or will be that severe, but here is what I know.

God will let you know what He wants you to do. If He has the power to create you, I am sure He has the power to let you know why.

The question is, "Will you obey?"

There are other "God dreams" that come to us differently. These are dreams we "hope" are true.

The disciples spent a good bit of time arguing over who was the greatest. They didn't want to be great for God, they wanted to be the greatest for God. Don't we all.

Matter of fact, at one point, Jesus had a conversation with James and John, the sons of Thunder recorded in the Gospels:

> **Mark 10:35,** "And James and John, the sons of Zebedee, came up to him (Jesus) and said to him,

"Teacher, we want you to do for us whatever we ask of you."

Don't we all want this, but that is not how God operates in our lives. Look at Jesus's response.

> **Mark 10:36-39,** "And he said to them, 'What do you want me to do for you?' And they said to him, 'Grant us to sit, one at your right hand and one at your left, in your glory.' Jesus said to them, 'You don't know what you are asking. Are you able to drink the cup that I drink, or to be baptized with the baptism with which I am baptized?' And they said, '**We are able**.'"

I remember when I used to think like that. Jesus responds to them:

> **Mark 10:39a,40,** "And Jesus said to them, 'The cup that I drink you will drink, and with the baptism with which I am baptized, you will be baptized, but to sit at my right hand or at my left is not mine to grant, but **it is for those for whom it has been prepared**.'"

You can ask God for dreams, but He will only give you the ones He has planned for you. He won't give you the ones He has planned for others.

In another place in the Gospels, this story is recorded, but it is from the perspective of the mother.

> **Matthew 20:20-22,** "Then the mother of the sons of Zebedee came up to him with her sons, and

kneeling before him she asked him for something. And he said to her, 'What do you want?' She said to him, 'Say that those two sons of mine are to sit, one at your right hand and one at your left, in your kingdom.' Jesus answered (her), 'You do not know what you are asking.'"

I tell you this part of the story, because some of you are like me. Someone wants something to be true of your life and you are trying to figure out if it is their desire for your life or if God is using them to let you know what He has created you to do and be.

God miraculously spared my life as a child. My mom recounted that story over and over and over again to me as a boy. She would tell me I was like Samuel because she gave me back to God through her prayer by my bed that night and God spared me. She would tell me I was like Jeremiah because she knew when she was pregnant with me that God had called me from the womb. She would tell me I was a miracle and that God had a plan for my life. Well, this did two things to me. It made me feel special and it made me feel pressure.

It made me feel special in that I have never doubted that I am here for a special reason. It made me feel pressure in that I felt like the purpose for my life had to be so grand that reality can't match it and that causes me to sometimes live with my head in the clouds making decisions that can even be unwise at times because I am searching for that elusive "big calling" God has on my life.

All my life I have wrestled with specific words my mother spoke over my life and I have wondered in my journals, to those closest to me, and out loud to myself, "Lord, was this from you or are these just the words of a proud mom?"

Paul told Timothy to fulfill the calling that was given to Him by the words spoken over Him by the laying on of hands (**2 Timothy 1:6**).

I believe in this sort of process. I believe it is biblical. I believe God uses whatever means necessary to let you know who He has created you to be. And I believe it is possible God used my mom to do just that. But at times, God's call and my mom's words have been seemingly in opposition to one another and have prompted different things in my heart depending on the season of my life.

My mom's words have caused me at times to "grasp" for who I think God has made me to be, only to leave me battered, bruised, and more confused than before I took the said actions. Whereas when I follow God's calling on my life, it seems at times effortless.

I have been at this long enough to know when I am striving to fulfill God's calling on my life and when I am simply stepping into the next step He has for my life. This doesn't make the striving wrong because it is a part of figuring out who God has called us to be. Proverbs alludes to this:

> **Proverbs 25:2,** "It is the glory of God to conceal things, but the glory of kings is to search things out."

I think **we have to work at becoming who God has created us to be,** but I don't think we can become who

God has not created us to be. So, what I am saying is this, "My striving is only helpful when it gets me to where He intended for me to go all along."

How do we strive effectively?

Now, I don't bat a thousand and you won't either. As A.W. Tozer said, "We don't make a beeline to God, we all zigzag in this life to God."

I live in Colorado, the ski capital of the world. I can't ski to save my life. My wife is great at it. I am not. I have tried. I genuinely have and I have the marks to prove it. To be a good skier you have to learn to zigzag down the slope. I hate zigzagging. I want to go straight down and so I do, but then I can't stop and I crash and burn, painfully crash and burn. So, you say to me, "**zigzag.**" I just can't, it's too boring. I just don't enjoy it.

But here is what I have learned. Figuring out God's dreams for our lives is like skiing, healthy skiing. You have to **zigzag to figure out who He has called you to be** and what He has called you to do. It is like learning to ride a bike. You can't learn it in a book, you have to get on the bike. The more you ride, the more you zigzag, the better you get. Ecclesiastes emphasizes this:

> **Ecclesiastes 11:6,** "Plant your seed in the morning and keep busy all afternoon (zigzagging) for you don't know if profit will come from one activity or another—or maybe both."

Living out God's dreams for your life is the same. The more you dream and put into practice what you think He has called you to do the better you will get at discovering exactly who He has made you to be.

But you need to know this, the world around you, even the Christian world, won't applaud who God has made you to be if it doesn't fit the "success" motif they have created and asked you to buy, so you can be successful like them.

If you go off road and chart the course you believe God has created you to do, you can rest assured they won't pay for it, applaud it, or even acknowledge it, if it doesn't fit how they perceive the world is to go.

A.W. Tozer, C.S. Lewis, Oswald Chambers, and the list goes on and on, were not recognized in life like they were in death. These pastors, teachers, authors, are acclaimed now, but in their time, they were shunned.

Many years ago, I had a God dream. It cost me greatly. I put it on paper and asked numerous Christian publishers to publish it. I finally got one to tell me what I assume the rest were thinking. They said, "We wouldn't publish this." I asked, "Why?" They said, "Because we wouldn't want the Christian community to think you are a kook."

I said, "Well, here's the problem. It happened. What is in this book occurred. It is real and it is a part of my life story."

They said, "Yeah, and nobody wants to read it."

If it doesn't make dollars, it doesn't make sense.

I got it.

I said to that same publisher, "If a guy named C.S. Lewis asked you to publish his material today and you knew nothing about him, would you?" He honestly said, "No, because he didn't have a platform."

I said, "Okay, thanks for your honesty. Let me ask you one more question, If a guy named Jesus, whom you had never heard of before called you up and asked you to publish his book, The Bible, and it told how He would be the Savior of the world, would you publish it?"

He said (and I appreciated his honesty), "Probably not."

Briefly, I felt in good company.

Here is the point, "If God has called you to do it, you don't need anyone but Him to believe that you can do it. Go do it for God."

Now you might say, "But what if you turn out to be wrong?"

I got news for you, you will at times. But don't let that keep you from doing what you sincerely believe God has called you to do.

The perceived outcome doesn't determine the success of the dream, God does.

> **Hebrews 11:1,2,** "Now faith is the assurance of things hoped for, the conviction of things not seen. For by it the people of old received their commendation."

The eleventh chapter of Hebrews describes a long grocery list of names of people from the Bible that, during their generation, were faithful to living out their calling, that is, without seeing the fulfillment of God's dream for their life. We pick up the story again in verse 13:

> **Hebrews 11:13,39,40,** "These all died **in faith, not having received the things promised**, but having seen them and greeted them from afar, And all these, though commended through their faith, did not receive what was promised, since God had provided something better **for us, that apart from us they should not be made perfect.**"

Hebrews 11 tells us there were giants of the faith in every generation that didn't see the fulfillment of the promise they were given for their lives. Then it says, "That's why they need us." God's purpose and dreams for your life are not limited by the perceived premature failures at the end of your life. We are living their dream as followers of Jesus because they were living His dream.

When you can admit lack of success in areas of your life, it gives you the best chance to find and experience true significance in this life and gives you the freedom to live His dream for your life.

I am encouraged by this passage. You and I only have to be faithful and serve our purpose for our generation. My dad never pastored a church bigger than 150 people in his lifetime. I pastored that many the first year of my pastorate.

Show me someone who is "successful for a lifetime" and I will show you someone who is standing on the shoulders of people in immediate generations who removed debris and cleared the way for them. The Gospel was largely unheard of in the 1950s in and around Ecuador. Thanks to the life of Jim and Elizabeth Elliott and many others, it is now one of the Christian epi-centers of the world.

Have you ever heard of Everett Swanson? Be honest.

He started, in the 1950s, what is now the largest para-church organization in the world.

The Gospel was unheard of in South Korea during WWII, but thanks to Everett, the founder of Compassion International, it now has a higher percentage of Christians in it than even the United States of America.

I hope that this chapter has challenged your heart to dream, or maybe dream God's dreams for your life, again. The world doesn't follow the crazy dreamers of God until His dreams come true through you. And when they come true, sadly, they try to reproduce the dream through the masses. By then, God's on to the next generation.

It is my hope that this book prepares a new generation of pastors to dream God's dreams for their generation.

Keep in step with the Spirit for your life and you will find significance in your days.

But here is an important reminder: **God doesn't need your generation to applaud your life or give you popular accolades for you to fulfill ALL the reasons for your**

existence here. But, if you need the praise of man to give you the courage to do what only God can do through you, you will be miserable all your life.

Ecclesiastes says if you are waiting for the conditions to be perfect you won't ever do anything with your life.

> **Ecclesiastes 11:4,** "Farmers who wait for perfect weather never plant. If they watch every cloud, they never harvest."

At some point you have to close your eyes and take a risk with your life.

How do we discover our God-given dream?

Here is a list of characteristics I have found to be a part of God-given dreams to help you decipher:

How do we discover our God-given dream?

1) **Be assured He has a dream for you.**
2) **Trust God to bring it true.**
3) **Ask God continually what it is.**
4) **Trust Him to use any means possible to reveal it to you.**
5) **Zigzag until you find it.**
6) **Don't chase it, become it.**
7) **Don't let the perceived premature outcome dictate the authenticity.**
8) **Be you, regardless of how the world receives you and it.**

Come to terms as best you can with who God has created you to be, and be the best you, by leaning into the dreams that you believe God has given you for a lifetime. The ancestors in your history have prepared you for this moment. The future is dependent upon your courage to keep dreaming.

In your present, today,

"Shoot for the stars, land on the moon, nobody will notice, good pastor."

CHAPTER 6

GOD-REALIZED DREAMS

When you wish upon a star, makes no difference who you are, anything your heart desires will come to you.

> **If your heart is in your dream**, no request is too extreme,
> When you wish upon a star as dreamers do, fate is kind,
> She brings to those who love,
> the sweet fulfillment of their secret longing,
> Like a bolt out of the blue, fate steps in and sees you through,
> When you wish upon a star, **your dreams come true**.

The song states, "If your heart is in your dream . . . your dreams come true."

Everybody loves a good book or movie where the dream comes TRUE.

I hate to break it to you, though. It makes for warm fuzziness at Disney, but it's NOT true.

It takes more than desire for a dream to come true, especially God-given dreams.

It takes God.

Corrie Ten Boom, a Dutch Christian who helped many Jews escape the Nazi Holocaust in WWII, knew it took God to live the life He had dreamed for her. Her remarkable story of living God's dream for her life is told in the book, *The Hiding Place.*

Corrie was once quoted as saying:

"When I try, I fail. When I trust, He succeeds."

Moses knew this when he was called by God to lead His people out of bondage in Egypt and into the Promise Land. We see part of his conversation with God:

> **Exodus 33:12,** "Moses said to the Lord, 'See, you say to me, 'Bring up this people,' but you have not let me know whom you will send with me. Yet you have said, 'I know you by name, and you have also found favor in my sight.'"

When God gives us a dream, He is giving us His favor. Moses understood this. For those of us in the pastorate, we feel called by God to do something, but ill-equipped to do so. Moses felt the same way when God placed a God dream on his life, saying, "Bring up this people *out of Egypt.*"

Moses agreed, but then began to struggle with fulfilling the God dream he had been given, just like we all do.

To combat this, we must realize that God has specifically called us. Not only that, we must also recognize that God must equip us for the dream and task He has given to us. Moses knew that he needed God's help in order to realize the God dream that had been placed on His life. So, Moses says to Almighty God:

> **Exodus 33:13,** "Now therefore, if I have found favor in your sight, please show me now your ways, that I may know you in order to find favor in your sight. Consider too that this nation is your people."

Moses states three very important things to God here. First, he says, "IF I have found favor in your sight." He is not assuming anything here, but simply reiterating what God previously told him at the burning bush in Midian on the back side of the desert. In essence he is saying, "God, if you have given me this dream. If this dream is a God-given dream. Then, I need your favor to do this."

Second, he says, "If this is your God-given dream for me, then 'show me your ways.'" We can't do what God has asked us to do if He doesn't tell us how to do it. Moses got this.

Third, Moses also understood that these people were not HIS. They belonged to God. As pastors, the people (regardless of the size of your church) are not ours. They belong to God. So many pastors are tempted to take ownership of the people who come to their church, seeing their congregation as an extension of themselves, rather than viewing their leadership role as one of stewardship over God's people.

We didn't die for people. Jesus did. And more importantly, even if we die for them, we still can't save them through our righteousness. It takes Christ. Moses understood this. He understood the people "belonged" to God not him. He was one of God's children, just like they were, but He had been given the task to lead the people to where God wanted them to go.

If you and I are going to realize the God-given dream He has for our lives, like Moses, we must:

1. Proclaim God's dream for us.

For example, "God has called me to pastor His people and if He doesn't show me how to do this, I won't be able to."

This is what it looks like to proclaim what God has dreamed for you to do, but still acknowledge that you need His ability to do it, and the people you lead belong to Him, not you. I hate to say it this way, but the people who go to church with you, they are God's children, you are just the head baby-sitter. ☺

Look at how God responds to Moses's request for favor and direction to lead His people.

> **Exodus 33: 14,** "And he said, 'My presence will go with you, and I will give you rest.'"

2. Prepare to live it out.

Moses said to God, "Show me your ways."

There are a myriad of methods God can use to show us His ways. For me, God used my youth pastor in Kentucky to convince me to go to Liberty University to be trained for the ministry. While at Liberty University, God used a number of my professors, who were graduates of Dallas Theological Seminary, to convince me that I needed to go to Dallas to prepare for the ministry God had called me to. My upbringing was in the Southern Baptist denomination. In 1996, Tosha and I went to a convention in New Orleans where God used Dr. Bob Reccord and Rick Warren to help us figure out where to plant a church. Then, He used Charlie Aiken, Bill Lighty, and Greg Cole. At each step of the way, God uses various people to prepare us to do what He has called us to do.

A.W. Tozer never went to college and didn't finish his high school degree, but he self taught himself and God brought along people to train him. My dad only had an eighth-grade education when he was called to the pastorate, but he self taught himself how to read God's Word. We all need a preparation process. It will look different for everyone and the preparation process should be ongoing throughout our lives. However, there are a few keys things during this initial time of preparation that will remain true throughout the rest of your life.

How can you know if God has called you to do something? He will go with you and He will give you rest along the way.

Regardless of your formal preparation process, whether it looks like mine, my dad's, A.W. Tozer's, or someone else's, there are two constants that are necessary to keep you going in the pastorate for God. You need to be prepared to know how to discern God's presence for your life and you need to know when you need to rest.

If God is not going with you, don't go. And if you are not getting rest, don't stay.

Fatigue eventually makes cowards of us all and cowardice eventually inflames our passions for the lesser things of this life. This is when we find ourselves in compromising positions where we are indulging in sins we would normally give no thought to if we were healthy in our minds and hearts. I am convinced a lot of moral failure in the ministry is not because people want to go that route, but because they lose hope and believe the lie that it is the only way out. You don't have to self-destruct to get rest (In the last part of this book, we will talk about living a life of dependence on God through rhythms of rest in the pastorate.).

Proclaim to God what you believe He has called you to do. If He has called you to do it, He will send His presence with you, and He will sustain you with rest along the way.

You may be in a desert season of your life. Don't just push through it. Say to the Lord, "If you don't go with me, I can't go." He will send His presence and rest with you if He has called you to do it. Success isn't that important. Your soul is.

If you are going to go the distance in the pastorate, at some point you have to rest and trust that God is Sovereign over the dream He has given you. And after a season of rest, He will go with you to lead His people again.

A few years ago, I completed a nine-week sabbatical for twenty years of pastoring at Vanguard. I had many "panic attacks" along the way and at times was consumed by fear that it was all going to fall apart—even after twenty years of pastoring the same church. What is keeping you from God's presence and resting?

Your preparation, regardless of your formal training early on, is ongoing through His presence and His rest. Are you finding it in the pastorate today? How long will you wait? Moses understood this very valuable lesson. "I can't do this without you, God, your presence and your rest."

These two aspects prepare you to go and be, and go and do, what God has called you to do. Without them, failure is inevitable.

Moses continued to focus on the presence of Almighty God.

> **Exodus 33:15,16,** "And he said to him, 'If your presence will not go with me, do not bring us up from here. For how shall it be known that I have found favor in your sight, I and your people? **Is it not in your going with us, so that we are distinct, I and your people**, from every other people on the face of the earth?'"

Moses understood maybe the most important thing about being a leader for God and living out the God-given dream. If we are going to experience a God-realized dream, it is going to require God to be present.

If you can fulfill a dream without God's presence, it is NOT a God-given dream. God-realized dreams are discovered in our life through His presence going with us. It is what makes us distinct. It is what makes the dream distinct.

After you proclaim the God-given dream, realize the preparation process (both formal and ongoing), and discern His presence, finding rest when needed. Then, it is time to:

3. Play it out in your real life.

God-realized dreams don't just stay in your head. Moses understood they become a part of your "going." Moses was concerned, and rightfully so, that if his God-given dream was to play out in his real life, he needed to be sure the presence of God was going to be with him in the midst of what God had asked him to do.

No dream will ever feel as good in reality as it does in your head. Dreams can't be touched by pain in your head. However, the moment they leave your head and move into real life, pain touches every part of them and disillusionment at times becomes your only friend.

Moses understood what real life was like. He understood how difficult it was to live in the real world, not to mention believing in and living out what seemed to be an impossible dream of freeing the people from Egypt and leading them into the Promise Land.

As a pastor, I don't know if you realize it or not, but what you have chosen to do with your life is impossible apart from Christ. Pastoring is an honorable calling and purpose that demands God's presence to fulfill.

But some pastors never get to reality. They dream ...
dream ... and dream some more.

I remember when I was in seminary in Dallas, I lived at the
Seminary. I was in my apartment and noticed my neighbor
out in the apartment complex courtyard area. This was
in a season in my life where I was barely making it in
seminary. I had a job as a youth pastor of a church and
Tosha was working full-time as well while taking classes.
Life was crazy.

I noticed my neighbor standing outside for a really long
time looking up in the large tree that was beside the
swimming pool at the student housing. I finally walked
outside and asked him, "What are you doing?" He turned to
me and said, "I was just wondering how I could tie a rope
in that tree and from my second-story apartment window
swing out over the pool and cannonball into the pool."

This was a full-grown man who then told me he only had
time to take three seminary classes because it made him
too busy.

It seems like we all have time to dream, but God-realized
dreams have to be played out in your life if you want
them to come true. They will require something of you,
especially your time, energy, and yes, your emotion.

I have watched so many people over the years become
professional students and get degree after degree to "prepare
for the ministry." At some point, you have to say, "Let's go."
It is time to live out the calling. It is time to realize the dream
in your everyday life. It is time to say to the Lord, "As we go
in our everyday lives, Lord, go with us."

Some of us are afraid. Good! But don't let your fear keep you from playing it out in your life. Moses was afraid, so He asked for God's presence to go with Him and His people. Look at how God responds:

> **Exodus 33:17-23,** "And the Lord said to Moses, 'This very thing that you have spoken I will do, for you have found favor in my sight, and I know you by name.' Moses said, '**Please show me your glory**.' And he said, 'I will make all my goodness pass before you and will proclaim before you my name 'The Lord.' And I will be gracious to whom I will be gracious, and **will show mercy on whom I will show mercy**. But,' he said, '**you cannot see my face**, for man shall not see me and live.' And the Lord said, 'Behold, there is a place by me where you shall stand on the rock, and while my glory passes by I will put you in a cleft of the rock, and I will cover you with my hand until I have passed by. Then I will take away my hand, and **you shall see my back**, but my face shall not be seen.'"

This was a VERY bold request by Moses. No one up to this time had ever seen God's glory with their own physical eyes. Moses asked for something that took great courage.

A.W. Tozer in his book, *The Pursuit of God*, said this about Moses:

> "Come near to the holy men and women of the past and you will soon feel the heat of their desire after God. They mourned for Him, they prayed and wrestled and sought for Him day and night,

in season and out, and when they had found Him the finding was all the sweeter for the long seeking. Moses used the fact that he knew God as an argument for knowing Him better.

Now, therefore, I pray thee, if I have found grace in thy sight, show me now the way, that I may know thee, that I may find grace in thy sight"; and from there he arose to make the daring request, 'I beseech thee, show me thy glory.' God was frankly pleased by this display of ardor, and the next day called Moses into the mount, and there in solemn procession made all His glory pass before him."

A little later A.W. Tozer says about Moses and other faithful saints of the Lord:

"They want to taste, to touch with their hearts, to see with their inner eyes the wonder that is God."

If you are going to see a God-realized dream in your life, you will have to:

4. Persist in it regardless.

And experiencing God will ultimately determine whether you stay at it or not. There is no God-given dream worth it if you don't experience God in it.

Pain will kill the God-given dream in you, but persistence to experience God in the dream will eventually lead to the fulfillment of it. God wants us to know Him in the dream, and He will then fulfill the dream He gave us, through us.

It is not about the dream. It is about the relationship between us and God. The dream is just an excuse to get together.

God doesn't want people to be impressed with the dreams we fulfill with Him. He wants them to be drawn to the relationship we share with Him in the midst of the dream coming true. He wants us to share in His glory. He wants us to enjoy the benefits that come from His glory, but He does not want us to take credit for His glory in our lives.

I have watched a lot of guys be hugely successful "for God" and burn out, self-destruct, and completely fall apart. I have found talent in the pastorate, talent determines initial success. But realizing you are a steward of God's people, and acting accordingly over a long period of time, determines sustained success. It is difficult to have both in one. Human nature is to dream, create, and then expect others to worship you for it. God expects you to turn and enjoy the success, but not take credit. We often forget in pastoral success that although the power does flow through us, it is NOT from us. It is from God's presence.

When a dream is realized, it is primarily realized to bring glory to God, and to serve the needs of others, as opposed to establishing the importance of the dreamer.

When we persist in the God-given dream, eventually it will be realized. But ultimately, the goal is not the dream, but the deepened relationship we now share with God through working out His dream in our lives.

The God-realized dream He has for everyone's life is the same. He wants us to know Him as Paul describes.

Philippians 3:10,11, "That I may know him and the power of his resurrection, and may share his sufferings, becoming like him in his death that by any means possible I may attain the resurrection of the dead."

God gives us dreams to teach us who He is. Stop worrying about whether or not the dream will come true and persist in it. You will get to know God through it, and eventually, He will fulfill the dream in you.

Contrary to the Disney song (not trying to hate on Disney), it won't be because you wished upon a star or because all of your heart was in it. Ultimately, it won't even be because of you. It will be because God brought it to fulfillment through you, and you made His presence the focus of your life.

Success from God is a platform to share how God turned your weaknesses into strengths and your almost-failures into successes through His power. However, the problem with a dream realized is that success can also be used to hide our weaknesses if we are not careful. Human nature is fearful and success gives a person an "acceptable" cloak to cover up with. Unshared or unchecked, this leads to the fruit of a narcissistic, flesh-driven pastor. This is sadly why "successful" people tend to self-destruct. We feel the pressure to take credit and God will share His glory with no one.

You need to remember success becomes a blessing or a curse depending on how you handle it.

And when you have success, people will want to worship you instead of God. So, how do you keep success, good success. How do remain a good pastor?

This brings us to the final point on How to realize a God dream:

5. Pray God realizes it through you.

Say to the Lord,

"God, do through me what I can't do without you."

And when He fulfills dreams in you, say to Him again, "Lord, do through me again what I can't do without you."

As Moses said, "If you don't go with us, we can't go. We can't do this."

Ask God for His glory. Ask Him for supernatural experiences that confirm He is with you. IF you do this, you will persist and God will realize it through you. Then, you must remember where your strength comes from.

Moses asked for this in Exodus 33, and then, from chapter 33 to chapter 40, God instructed Moses on how to create a tabernacle so that His presence could be seen and go with them. It would become the physical symbol of God's presence that would direct their journeys. It was Moses's answer to prayer. He had personally experienced God's glory so he would be able to see and detect it for the people of God on their way to the Promise Land. The same is true for us as pastors. We must experience God before we can have confidence to lead His people to do the same.

God answered Moses's request to give the people a sign that He was with them and then He instructed them on the way that they should go. The God dream Moses had been given was beginning to take form, but there was much that went into leading up to this moment.

God may ask you to do a lot of things like build a building, hire staff, manage a budget, fire staff, deal with a million little details of people's lives and desires that drive you crazy. Take the time to read Exodus 34–40. Wow, if you do, you'll see how crazy the details are, but you'll also see how the plan comes together in Exodus 40. Moses didn't just experience God and lead the people. He gave attention to the millions of required ministerial details in the house of God so that the people could recognize the presence of God just like he did.

In Exodus 40:16, we see the culmination of Moses's God-given dream coming true and being realized through the practical everyday instructions God had given him through Exodus 34–40. It is good to dream and experience God, but at some point, you have to put into play what God has told you to do. And at times, this will feel very unspiritual. Much of my pastoral job feels very unspiritual, as I am sure the instructions God gave to Moses may have felt, but look at how Moses responds:

> **Exodus 40:16-21,33-38,** "This **Moses did;** **according to all that the Lord commanded him,** **so he did**. In the first month in the second year, on the first day of the month, the tabernacle was erected. **Moses erected the tabernacle. He laid its bases**, and set up its frames, and put in its poles, and raised up its pillars. And **he spread the tent** over the tabernacle and put the covering

of the tent over it, as the Lord had commanded
Moses. **He took the testimony** and put it into
the ark, and put the poles on the ark and set the
mercy seat above on the ark. **And he brought the
ark** into the tabernacle and set up the veil of the
screen, and screened the ark of the testimony, as
the Lord had commanded Moses.

And he erected the court around the tabernacle
and the altar, and set up the screen of the gate
of the court. **So Moses finished the work.** Then
**the cloud covered the tent of meeting, and the
glory of the Lord filled the tabernacle.** And
Moses was not able to enter the tent of meeting
because the cloud settled on it, and **the glory of
the Lord filled the tabernacle. Throughout all
their journeys,** whenever the cloud was taken
up from over the tabernacle, the people of Israel
would set out. But if the cloud was not taken up,
then they did not set out till the day that it was
taken up. For **the cloud of the Lord was on the
tabernacle by day,** and **fire was in it by night, in
the sight of all the house of Israel throughout
all their journeys."**

God answered Moses's request. God showed the people
His daily glory and showed them how to know when they
were to go and when they were to stop in His presence.
Because of it, Moses was able to lead the people of Israel
to realize the dream God had for the entire nation. No,
Moses did not get to physically lead them into the Promise
Land (because He got angry at God and struck the rock
at Meribah). But ultimately, God brought the Israelites

out of bondage and into freedom in the Promise Land by entrusting Joshua to lead them.

I love Moses's final words to Israel. Before he went to be with the eternal presence of God, who had led him for forty years in leading God's people, he said:

> **Deuteronomy 34:1,4,5,9-12,** "Then Moses went up from the plains of Moab to Mount Nebo, to the top of Pisgah, which is opposite Jericho. And the Lord showed him all the land, Gilead as far as Dan, And the Lord said to him, 'This is the land of which I swore to Abraham, to Isaac, and to Jacob, **'I will give it to your offspring.'** I have let you see it with your eyes, but shall not go over there. So Moses the servant of the Lord died there in the land of Moab . . . And Joshua the son of Nun was full of the spirit of wisdom for Moses had laid his hands on him. So the people of Israel obeyed him and did as the Lord had commanded Moses. **And there has not arisen a prophet since in Israel like Moses, whom the Lord knew face to face**, none like him for all the signs and wonders that the Lord sent him to do in the land of Egypt, to Pharaoh and to all his servants and to all his land, and for all the mighty power and all the great deeds of terror that Moses did in the sight of all Israel."

It is not a perfect ending. But neither will the God-realized dreams in your life be either. We will mess them up. As my friend, Vance told me a long time ago, "You won't pull it off perfectly." That's just the way it is, but if you make God's presence the focus on how you lead and pastor His people, you will see promises fulfilled through your life for the next generation.

And remember this book is NOT about being a PERFECT pastor, but a Good Pastor. And Moses, was good enough to get the job done. And so are you, if God's presence is your focus. You don't have to bat a 1000 to be faithful.

As Dr. Falwell said often at Liberty University, "Shoot for the stars, land on the moon, nobody will notice."

Winston Churchill, waited fifty years to fulfill his promise to his friend that he would one day save England in a Great War from the tyranny of the world.

Abraham, after twenty-five years, became the Father of many nations when Isaac was born.

Sarah became the Mother of Isaac at age ninety.

Joseph, after twenty-three years, became second-in-command in Egypt and saved His family from the famine, just as he dreamed.

Esther, after some unknown time, rescued Israel from the evil hand of Haman.

David, after thirteen years, became King of Israel.

Elizabeth, one year after the prophecy, gave birth to John the Baptist who became the forerunner of Jesus.

Mary, one year after the prophecy, gave birth to Jesus, the Savior of the world.

Moses, after forty years, led the people of Israel out of bondage in Egypt and to the Promised Land.

I, thirteen years later, planted a church and became its pastor after God told me I would be a pastor one day.

What about you? I don't know how long it will take for God to realize His dream in you, but I do know He will.

And WHEN He does, turn and say to the people like Moses:

> **Deuteronomy 8:2,4,6,7,10,** "And **you shall remember the whole way that the Lord your God has led you** these forty years in the wilderness, that he might humble you, testing you to know what was in your heart ...Your clothing did not wear out on you and your foot did not swell these forty years. So you shall keep the commandments of the Lord ... for the Lord your God is bringing you into a **good land** ... And you shall eat and be full, and you shall bless the Lord your God for the **good land** he has given you."

Never forget, with God, dreams do come true.

Keep dreaming God-given dreams. You will realize them in His time and in His way. And when you do, don't forget God.

> **Deuteronomy 8:11,18-20,** "Take care **lest you forget the Lord your God** ... You shall remember the Lord your God, **for it is he who gives you power to get wealth**, that he may confirm his covenant that he swore to your fathers ... If you forget the Lord your God and go after other gods

and serve them and worship them, I solemnly warn you today that you shall surely perish. Like the nations that the Lord makes to perish before you, so shall you perish, because you would not obey the voice of the Lord your God."

Regardless of how successful you become in the world's eyes for God, always remember it is not about the success, it is about obeying God's voice and seeking His presence over all the other gods of this world. This is what "good success" is in the pastorate. As Scripture reminds us:

> **Deuteronomy 11:26-28,** "See, I am setting before you today a blessing and a curse: the blessing, if you obey ... the curse, if you do not."

Success becomes a blessing or a curse depending on how you handle it. It can be good or bad.

Your dreams realized may just be the greatest test of your character, Good Pastor.

Paul says it best when it comes to success in our ministry:

> **2 Corinthians 10:17,18,** "Let the one who boasts, boast in the Lord. For it is not the one who commends himself who is approved, but the one whom the Lord commends."

Instead of worshipping your success, turn and give God the glory and worship Him for the dreams realized.

Bow down and thank Him today for His glory. For He will share it with no other. Isaiah tells us this:

Isaiah 42:8, "I am the Lord; that is my name; my glory I give to no other nor my praise to carved idols."

God is not impressed with our success. He gave it to us.

1 Corinthians 4:7a, "What do you have that you did not receive (from God)? If then you receive it, why do you boast as if you did not receive it?"

He is the One who gave us the dreams and fulfilled them through us. What He desires from us is our worship. This is the one thing we can give that didn't come from Him.

The next time you are tempted to wish upon star, look up in the heavens and remember:

Isaiah 40:26, "Lift up your eyes on high and see who has created these stars."

We don't need to wish upon the stars for our future to come true, we just need to worship the ONE who created them. Trust Him to bring His dreams for you to realization in His time and in His way just like Moses and all the other faithful saints of the past.

Corrie Ten Boom said it best:

"It is not my ability, but my response to God's ability that counts."

This, Good Pastor, is what "good success" looks like when God realizes His dreams for you, through you. Stop wishing upon a star and worship the ONE who MADE the stars!

CHAPTER 7

GOD-ALTERED DREAMS

Sometimes life is about risking everything for a God-given dream no one can see, including you.

God dreams require us to walk by faith not by sight. My heart can feel what God has planned for my life long before my eyes can see it.

In the Bible, I see this as true in Abraham and Sarah's life regarding God's promise to them through their future son, Isaac.

When I read the story of Abraham and Sarah in the book of Genesis, I wonder, "Why would God give a couple a dream, let them agonize over it for two and a half decades, then when it comes true, ask for it back?"

I am convinced it will be easier to live the life you have dreamed for yourself than the one God has dreamed for you. However, your "good success" in God's eyes, has no comparison.

Has God given you a dream? Has He made it seemingly impossible to come true? Are you in a season where He has asked for it back?

Corrie Ten Boom once said:

"Hold everything in your hands lightly, otherwise it hurts when God pries your fingers open."

God gave Abraham and Sarah a dream, but He made them wait twenty-five years for it to come true, and then, when it did, He asked for it back. Why does God alter the dreams He gives us and make it seemingly so hard for them to come true?

To answer this question, we have to go back to the story before the story. Just like for you to understand the story of your life you have to go back and study the story that has existed for thousands of years prior to your arrival. That is, the story of God's redemptive plan for humanity.

We pick up the story in Genesis 11 (which is after the magnificent creation of the world, the fall of humanity, the murder of Abel, the increase of wickedness in the world, the descendants from Adam to Noah, the great flood that destroyed the earth minus Noah and seven of his family members, and the nations that came from Noah in Genesis 10).

In just one chapter removed from the great flood, humanity was back at it again, trying to rebuild a devastated world, establish some order, and along the way maybe even make a name for themselves.

Can you blame them?

I can relate. If I am honest, I want to make a name for myself. I want to be remembered after I am gone from this world. Don't we all? Don't we all want to know our being here has made a difference in the future?

Genesis 11 tells us the whole earth had the same words and one language. From this, the people of the earth decided to build what is known as the tower of Babel. We pick up the story in verse 4.

> **Genesis 11:4,5,** "Then they said, 'Come, let us build ourselves a city and a tower with its top in the heavens, and **let us make a name for ourselves.'** And the Lord came down to see the city and the tower, which the children of man had built."

Humanity has always wanted to make a name for itself.

> **Genesis 11:6,** "And the Lord said, 'Behold, they are **one** people, and they have all one language, and **this is only the beginning of what they will do. And nothing that they propose to do will now be impossible for them.'**"

God understands how powerful humanity has been created to be. We are fashioned in His image, unlike any other creature or thing on this earth. We bear in our bodies the ability to recreate, not just ourselves, but this world. And through time, we discover that humanity gives little thought to why God put them here and instead efforts to **make a name for themselves.**

Being a Christian doesn't exempt you from this battle. Being a pastor doesn't exempt you from this battle. God knows this about every human being He has created. We are ALL tempted to make a name for ourselves at the expense of who and what He has created us to be and do.

If you can accept that about yourself, you will be able to embrace the alterations God will make to the God-given dreams He has placed inside of you.

So, God goes down to the earth and begins the alteration process of the redemptive story of Abraham and Sarah (and truly all of Israel) prior to them even being on the scene.

> **Genesis 11:7-9,** "'Come, let us go down and there **confuse** their language, so that they may not understand one another's speech.' So the Lord dispersed them ... and they left off building the city. Therefore its name was called Babel, because there the Lord confused the language of all the earth. And from there the Lord dispersed them over the face of the earth."

So, this was a season in history that was rote with confusion. Sound familiar?

Two-hundred-and-twenty-two years after the flood, Genesis 11 tells us:

> **Genesis 11:24,** "When Nahor had lived 29 years, he fathered Terah."

Who is Terah?

> **Genesis 11:26,** "When Terah had lived 70 years, he fathered Abram, Nahor, and Haran."

I have never noticed this before, but it would seem Abram may very well have been a triplet. Two-hundred-and-ninety-two years after the flood, Terah fathers Abram, one of three sons potentially born at the same time. Here is Abram's family tree at the time:

> **Genesis 11:27,28,** "Now these are the generations of Terah. Terah fathered Abram, Nahor, and Haran; and Haran fathered Lot. **Haran died in the presence of his father** Terah in the land of his kindred, in Ur of the Chaldeans."

They understood pain. They understood loss. They understood death in their homeland.

> **Genesis 11:29,30,** "And Abram and Nahor took wives. The name of Abram's wife was Sarai, and the name of Nahor's wife, Milcah, the daughter of Haran the father of Milcah and Iscah. **Now Sarai was barren; she had no child.**"

Here is what we know about the story of Abram so far: it occurred during a very confusing and frustrating time for humanity. The world had been dispersed by God. Abram's brother had died in their presence in their homeland. And now Abram was married unable to have children with his wife.

He was battling a world of futility, the loss of his brother, and the inability to have children.

I think he was pretty weighted down by his own life and family. I bet you can relate. I can.

It is during this very dark and painful season of Abram's family that his father decides to uproot the family and move.

> **Genesis 11:31,** "Terah took Abram his son and Lot the son of Haran, his grandson, and Sarai his daughter-in-law, his son Abram's wife, and they went forth **together** from Ur of the Chaldeans to go into the land of Canaan, but when they came to Haran, they **settled** there."

We all have had painful seasons in our lives. We lose a loved one. We battle infertility. We move together to get away from it. We settle. We try to find peace. We make a life for ourselves. And then tragedy strikes, again.

> **Genesis 11:32,** "The days of Terah (Abram's father) were 205 years, and Terah died **in Haran.**"

Terah was seventy years old when Abram was born. He lived another 135 years after Abram was born before dying in Haran, the place named after his deceased son. Why is this important? You are getting ready see as we look closer at Abram's life and the calling of the God dream God had placed on his life.

> **Genesis 12:1-4,** "Now the Lord said to Abram, '**Go** from your country and your kindred and your father's house to the land that I will show you. And I will make of you a great nation, and **I will bless you and make your name great, so**

that you will be a blessing. I will bless those who bless you, and him who dishonors you I will curse, and in you all the **families** of the earth shall be blessed.' So Abram **went**, as the Lord had told him, and Lot went with him. Abram was seventy-five years old when he **departed from Haran."**

If Abraham would do what God asked him to do, God promised to give him what many people in the world want. But, when God gave it to him, He expected Abram to use it to bless others, not simply to make a name for himself.

Seems like a good deal, right? But let's recap. Abram was possibly a triplet. My dad is a twin: Harry and Larry. They have farmed together ALL their lives and they will until death do them part. I don't think my dad has gone a day in his life without talking to his twin. They are inseparable. They may argue and fuss like cats and dogs, but they are bound to one another. My mother learned this the hard way.

Abram was potentially a triplet. Haran, one of the triplets, had Lot, and then died in his dad's presence in his kindred's homeland. This left Abram and Nahor. They married women. Abram and Sarai were barren. It was a tough deal. Terah, Abram's father, was to move them to a place named after Abram's deceased brother, Haran. And they lived happily ever after? NO!

Terah was seventy when he had Abram. Abram was seventy-five when God called him to **leave Haran.** Terah lived 135 years more after Abram was born. So what? That means when Abram was called at seventy-five to **leave Haran and his dad**, his dad still had seventy more years to live.

I remember when I was eighteen, God called me to leave Glasgow, Kentucky, and go to Lynchburg, Virginia, to study for the ministry. It was painful on my mom, that was obvious to me, but looking back, I now know it was extremely difficult on my dad as well. He offered me a sweet deal to stay on the dairy farm and he would pay for my education if I wouldn't leave. I remember saying to my dad, "I have to go to Liberty, that is where God has called me." He doesn't remember this, and that's okay, but He said to me, "If you go there, you will never amount to anything as a preacher."

We have no record of Abram's conversation with his dad, Terah. We know Terah moved them to this land called Haran named after Abram's deceased brother. We know from human experience it must have been very difficult for Terah to hear Abram tell him his "God dream." And I can't help but wonder how painful it was for Abram to know his dad wasn't going to go with him. Leaving my family at eighteen was extremely difficult. I am now fifty and have been gone from my motherland for thirty-plus years. Go Wildcats!

When God calls us, He doesn't call us to come and dine.

In the words of Bonhoeffer:

"He calls us to come and die (to ourselves)."

Something has to die inside of us for us to fulfill what God has called us to do and be with our lives.

I don't know how hard it was for Abram to leave his family, but I know how hard it was for me.

God called Abram to leave the familiar and head into the unknown.

He told him to feel with his heart what he couldn't see with his eyes.

This is the life of faith.

God first alters our lives as He gives us His dream for our lives. This was true for Abram. It was true for me. It is, and will be, true for you as well.

Abram took his deceased brother's only child, his barren wife, and headed out for a foreign land to become the father of many nations.

I can just see Terah shaking his head. I can't blame him as a father. I know I would be.

For Abram to live his dream for God, he had to cause his dad more pain. On the outside, Terah could have easily assumed Abram was self-involved and consumed by his adventures at the expense of their family that had settled together in the land named after their deceased brother.

You need to know God's dream for your life won't necessarily look holy and righteous to everyone around you looking on as you live out His purpose for your existence, but nevertheless, it is God's dream for your life.

> **Genesis 12:4-6,** "So Abram went **as the Lord told him,** ... And Abram took Sarai, his wife, and Lot his brother's son, and all their possessions that they had gathered, and the people that they had

acquired in Haran, and they set out to go to the land of Canaan. When they came to the land of Canaan. Abram passed through the land to the place at Shechem, to the oak of Moreh. At that time the Canaanites were in the land."

12:7-9, "Then the Lord **appeared** to Abram and said, 'To your offspring I will give this land.' So **he built there an altar to the Lord**, who had appeared to him. From there he moved to the hill country on the east of Bethel and pitched his tent, with Bethel on the west and Ai on the east. And **there he built an altar to the Lord and called upon the name of the Lord.** And Abram journeyed on, still going toward the Negeb."

The Lord didn't just speak to Abram this time, He appeared to him. Abram got to see some form of the Lord. I assume it was the commander of the Lord's army, one of His head angels or maybe a pre-incarnation of Christ Himself.

Regardless, Abram saw this as a sacred beginning, and built an altar to worship the Lord and call on His name. He set up a sacred reminder in the spot where God called him. Good idea. I use my journal for this. Then, I can go back and see the recorded sacred encounters because pain and time have a way of distancing me from the feelings and emotions I get when God first speaks something to me.

Doubt can often cause my confidence to drift into the abyss of uncertainty.

Abram built an altar and called on God. He then "journeyed on." He had work to do. God had altered his life. He had left his homeland. God had revealed Himself to Abram in person and now, after worshipping God in this sacred place, he was journeying on toward the Negeb, the southern portion of Israel, the desert area. How exciting! 😊

The trek had just begun and already alterations to the dream were on the way.

Do you know what an alteration is?

It is an adjustment, change, or modification. There were many on the way for Abram and Sarai.

The dark would get darker, a lot darker over the next twenty-five years, before the light of the dream would be seen in the eyes of Isaac.

As soon as Abram began the trek into the southern portion of what is now modern day Israel, Genesis 12 tells us:

> **Genesis 12:10,** "Now there was a famine in the land. So Abram went down to Egypt to sojourn there, for the famine was **severe** in the land."

Have you ever set out to do something for God that has already cost you greatly and He sends a severe famine on the land in which you are journeying to?

Abram was afraid, so he journeyed to Egypt to save his family's life.

Sometimes part of the dream is just surviving.

We all have seasons like this. Abram went down to Egypt. He was fearful that Pharaoh would kill him and take his wife from him, so he concocted a story that was a half-truth, "She is my sister." Thankfully, God spared him (because God was "with him") and Pharaoh dealt well with him. But Abram lied to protect himself at the potential expense of his wife. He still had a lot to learn about being God's man and looking out for those God had entrusted to him. Maybe he was still more caught up in "making a name for himself" than using that name to bless and protect those God had given to him. I can relate. Maybe you can too.

Abram took his family and left Egypt, thanks to God's grace, and traveled into the Negeb, which is the southern portion of Israel. They journeyed all the way to Bethel to the place where his tent had been at the beginning. It was a restart. We all have them.

Lot's herdsmen and Abram's herdsmen then had a falling out. This happens at times in families. So, Abram split the land with Lot, giving him first dibs. Lot, of course, took the "best" land.

> **Genesis 13:10,** "And Lot lifted up his eyes and saw that the Jordan Valley was well watered everywhere like the garden of the Lord."

Lot understood the principle the world understands, "He who chooses first gets the best and the leftover goes to the rest."

Abram technically loses again. He takes the second-hand hand-me-downs.

The "perfect land" also just so happened to be the land where Sodom was. The Bible tells us in Genesis:

> **Genesis 13:13,** "Now the men of Sodom were wicked, great sinners against the Lord."

I have learned "the best" of whatever something is always has its problems too. And we know, these great sinners would cost Lot greatly before it is all over.

Then God says to Abram:

> **Genesis 13:14-18,** "The Lord said to Abram, after Lot had separated from him, 'Lift up your eyes and look from the place where you are, northward and southward and eastward and westward, for the land that you see I will give to you and to your offspring forever. I will make your offspring as the dust of the earth, so that if one can count the dust of the earth, your offspring also can be counted. Arise, walk through the length and the breadth of the land, for I will give it to you.' So Abram moved his tent and came and settled by the oaks of Mamre, which are at Hebron, and **there he built an altar to the Lord.**"

What do we learn from this?

ALTERATION #1: God doesn't need the "best" to do the miraculous through you.

Don't fall into the trap, "If I just had Lot's land I could do what God has called me to do." Lift up your eyes, God has already given you, or will give you, everything you need to do what He has called you to do. Don't grasp for what isn't yours. Don't try and run ahead of someone to get what you want first.

When you feel tempted to compete, serve someone.

And that is what Abram did. He didn't get caught up in the dispute. He bent the knee and let Lot go first. God doesn't need the "best" to do the miraculous through you. He just needs you. He will add all the other needed ingredients.

Abram accepted his second class "lot" in life and focused on the land God had given him to possess. In the midst of it, Lot gets himself in trouble, which seemingly always happens to people who live their lives grasping for the "best" the world has to offer.

What do you do when you are in pursuit of who God has called you to be and hear that those who took the "best" of your life are in need because of their unwise choices and associations?

> **Genesis 14:14-16,** "When Abram heard that his kinsman had been taken captive, he led forth his trained men, born in his house, 318 of them, and went in pursuit as far as Dan (as far as you can go in modern day Israel). And he divided his forces against them and pursued them to Hobah, north of Damascus. Then he brought back all the possessions, and also brought back his kinsman Lot.

> **Genesis 14:17-21,** "After his (Abram's) return ...
> Melchizedek king of Salem brought out bread and
> wine. (He was priest of God Most High.) And
> he blessed him (Abram) and said, 'Blessed be
> Abram by God Most High, Possessor of heaven
> and earth; and blessed be God Most High, who
> has delivered your enemies into your hand.' **And
> Abram gave him a tenth of everything.** And
> the king of Sodom said to Abram, 'Give me the
> persons, but take the goods for yourself.'"

The King of Sodom represented everything God isn't. He
wanted in on the "glory" of Abram's victory. He tempted
him with "stuff."

Abram was careful to protect God's glory displayed
through him because of his successes. This is what "good
success looks like. We are stewards of it, not owners.
The success of our lives is born out of the fruit of God's
greatness through us, not from us. It is God's success.
Abram knew this. He knew it wasn't from himself or
anyone else. He knew it was from God.

Abram responds:

> **Genesis 14:22,23,** "But Abram said to the king
> of Sodom, '**I have lifted my hand to the Lord**,
> God Most High, Possessor of heaven and earth,
> that I would not take a thread or a sandal strap
> or anything that is yours, lest you should say,
> '**I have made Abram rich.**'"

Abram awarded God with a tithe for his "good success."

Alteration #2: God expects you to give Him credit for your "good success."

How do we do this? We do it in word and in deed.

Abram was the first person in the Bible to model tithing. A tithe is giving back to God 10% of what He has given you. God gives us dreams. The tithe is tied to the "good success" of the God dream. He makes us successful and He expects us to award Him with at least 10% of our spoil and earnings from following Him and His dream for our lives.

God doesn't need our money or our success, but He knows we do, and this is why a tithe is so important. It is a physical act that symbolizes thankfulness to God and acknowledges where our "good success" comes from.

As a pastor, I know you can say, "I tithe my life, I tithe my time, I tithe my family, I tithe everything." But Abram specifically modeled the tithe of your money. And Jesus followed this up in the New Testament by saying:

> **Matthew 6:21,** "Where your treasure is, there your heart will be also."

And lest you think tithing is just an Old Testament principle, Jesus also said in the New Testament:

> **Matthew 23:23,** "Woe to you, scribes and Pharisees, hypocrites! For you **tithe** mint and dill and cumin, and have neglected the weightier matters of the law: justice and mercy and faithfulness. **These you ought to have done**, without neglecting the others."

God expects us to award Him for the good success of our lives by tithing. It is biblical and it is a part of the God dream He has for your life.

It is easy to expect God to award you in His dream for you. But are you awarding Him?

God comes to Abram again after Abram awards God for his good success.

> **Genesis 15:1,** "After these things the word of the Lord came to Abram in a vision: 'Fear not, Abram, I am your shield; your reward shall be very great.'"

Look at how Abram responds to God. I can relate.

> **Genesis 15:2-5,** "But Abram said, 'O Lord God, what will you give me, for I continue childless, and the heir of my house is Eliezer of Damascus?' And Abram said, 'Behold, you have given me no offspring, and a member of my household will be my heir.' And behold, the word of the Lord came to him: 'This man shall NOT be your heir; **your very own son shall be your heir.**' And he brought him outside and said, 'Look toward heaven, and number the stars, if you are able to number them.' Then he said to him, 'So shall your offspring be.'"

Verse 6 is so VERY important to this story and the story of the God dreams in our lives.

> **Genesis 15:6,** "And he **believed** the Lord, and He counted it to him as righteousness."

Abram used something physical, like the tithe, to award God for his "good success." And God used something physical, like the stars, to remind Abram of the future reward God had for him. And Abram believed.

Because Abram believed, God keeps speaking. Our belief matters in this equation. What has God told you in the past that you are tempted to doubt in the present?

> **Genesis 15:7-11,** "And he (God) said to him, 'I am the Lord who brought you out from Ur of the Chaldeans to give you this land to possess.' But he said, 'O Lord God, how am I to know that I shall possess it?' He said to him, 'Bring me a heifer three years old, a female goat three years old, a ram three years old, a turtledove, and a young pigeon.' **And he brought him all these**, cut them in half, and laid each half over against the other. But he did not cut the birds in half. And when birds of prey came down on the carcasses, Abram drove them away.
>
> **15:12-16,** "As the sun was going down, a deep sleep fell on Abram. And behold, dreadful and great darkness fell upon him. Then the Lord said to Abram, 'Know for certain that your offspring will be sojourners in a land that is not theirs and will be servants there, and they will be afflicted for four hundred years. But I will bring judgment (through Moses's leadership) on that nation (Egypt) that they serve, and afterward they shall come out with great possessions. As for you, you shall go to your fathers in peace; you shall be buried in a good old age. And they shall come back here in the fourth generation.

15:18. "On that day the Lord made a covenant with Abram saying, 'To your offspring I give this land/'"

Alteration #3: God may reward the fulfillment of your God dream without you present.

Dr. Falwell always dreamed of 50k students attending Liberty. He died without seeing this. It has since occurred in the generation after him. I have dreamed of planting 5000 churches through Vanguard and baptizing 50k people. It probably won't happen in my lifetime, more than likely, but it will happen, someday. God doesn't need us present, or even alive for that matter, to fulfill His God dream through our lives.

Keep dreaming audacious dreams. Abram did.

However, Sarai got tired of waiting. She lost hope.

> **Genesis 16:1,2,** "Now Sarai, Abram's wife, had borne him NO children. She had a female Egyptian servant whose name was Hagar. And Sarai said to Abram, 'Behold now, **the Lord has prevented me from bearing children.** Go in to my servant; it may be that I shall obtain children by her.' And Abram listened to the voice of Sarai.'"

Sarai's diagnosis of her problem was right, but her prescription couldn't have been more wrong.

Any time we "help" God get it right, we get it wrong every time.

> **Genesis 16:3,4,15,16,** "So, after Abram had lived ten years in the land of Canaan, Sarai, Abram's

wife, took Hagar the Egyptian, her servant,
and gave her to Abram her husband **as a wife.**
And He went into Hagar, and she conceived.
And when she saw that she had conceived, she
looked with contempt on her mistress. And
Hagar bore Abram a son ... Abram was eighty-
six years old."

Abram and Sarai decided to "help" God and their decision
to do so would become not only the bane of their existence,
but lead to the creation of world tension in the Middle
East that still lives on 24/7 to this day. God doesn't need
our "help" to fulfill His plan through us regardless of how
grim it may look.

ALTERATION #4: God's plan doesn't need our "help" to come true.

He expects us to listen and trust Him. Just as He said it
would come true, so it will. We only complicate the story
by trying to "help."

Thirteen years later, God visited Abram. Those thirteen
years were dark, long, painful, and super-confusing for all
involved. I have had them. You will have them too.

> **Genesis 17:1,3-6,15,17,** "When Abram was ninety-
> nine years old the Lord appeared to Abram.
> Then Abram fell on his face. And God said to
> him, 'Behold, my covenant is with you, and you
> shall be the father of a multitude of nations. No
> longer shall your name be called Abram, but your
> name shall be Abraham, for I have **made you** the

father of multitudes of nations. **I will make you exceedingly fruitful.'** And God said to Abraham, 'As for Sarai your wife, you shall not call her name Sarai, but Sarah shall be her name. I will bless her, and moreover, I will give you a son by her.' Then Abraham fell on his face and laughed and said to himself, 'Shall a child be born to a man who is a hundred years old? Shall Sarah, who is ninety years old, bear a child?'"

Alteration #5: God will do the impossible through us.

> **Genesis 18:10,12-14,** "The Lord said, 'Will surely return to you about this time next year, and Sarah your wife **shall have a son.'** So Sarah laughed to herself. The Lord said to Abraham ... 'Is anything too hard for the Lord?'"

> **Genesis 21:1,2,** "The Lord visited Sarah as he had said, and the Lord did to Sarah as he had promised. And Sarah conceived and bore Abraham a son in his old age at the time of which God had spoken to him."

It happened just like God said it would.

Alteration #6: God will fulfill the dream just like He said He would.

God gives us dreams. He alters those dreams. He fulfills those dreams. And then, when we least expect it, He asks for them back.

> **Genesis 22:1,2,** "After these things God **tested** Abraham and said to him, 'Abraham!' And he said, 'Here I am.' He said, 'Take your son, your only son Isaac, whom you love and go to the land of Moriah, and offer him there **as a burnt offering** on one of the mountains of which I shall tell you.'"

One of the most painful alterations is:

Alteration #7: God wants us to know the dream is His, not ours.

Jesus told His disciples:

> **Luke 14:26,** "If anyone comes to me and does not hate his own father and mother and wife and children and brothers and sisters, yes, and **even his own life, he cannot be my disciple.**"

God wants us to know the dream is His, not ours. And He will ask for it back from time to time to make sure we are worshipping Him for our "good success" and not ourselves or the dream.

No one always wins. No one has it all. No one gets to go through this life unscathed by the request.

A.W. Tozer said it best when it comes to God and His dream fulfilled in Isaac for Abraham:

> "He had everything, but he possessed nothing."

Tozer goes on to say

"There is the spiritual secret. There is the sweet theology of the heart which can be learned only in the school of renunciation. After that bitter and blessed experience, I think the words *my* and *mine* never again had the same meaning for Abraham. The sense of possession which they connote was gone from his heart. There can be no doubt that this possessive clinging to things is one of the most harmful habits in this life. Because it is so natural, it is rarely recognized for the evil that it is. But its outworkings are tragic. The Christian (the pastor) who is alive enough to know himself even slightly will recognize the symptoms of this possession malady, and will grieve to find them in his own heart. If the longing after God is strong enough within him, he will want to do something about the matter."

And Abraham did.

> **Genesis 22:3,** "So Abraham rose early in the morning, saddled his donkey, and took two of his young men with him, and his son Isaac."

Alteration #8: God wants us to kill His dream in us.

How? You reach a point in your life where "striving" is counter-productive. You reach a point in your life where God realizes His dream through you and then seeks to alter it. He asks you to do what you thought He would never ask you to do.

He asks you NOT just to alter it, but...

Go kill it.

Abraham headed out to do just that.

That's trust. That's faith. That's courage.

That's a God-altered dream.

When God asks that of you, will you do the same, good pastor?

CHAPTER 8

GOD-RESTORED DREAMS

Living for God requires you to take a knife to the dreams He has for you.

He requires you to trust Him at the altar of sacrifice.

The Enemy will say to you often, "Did God really...?"

You can't live cautiously and live for God. You have to abandon the pursuit of self to find your true self. Jesus told us:

> **Matthew 10:39,** "Whoever finds his life will lose it, and whoever loses his life for my sake will find it."

The pursuit of God requires us to spend our entire lives creating something He then asks us to sacrifice for Him.

> **Romans 12:1** says, "I appeal to you, therefore, brothers, by the mercies of God, to present your

bodies as a **living sacrifice**, holy and acceptable to God, which is your spiritual worship."

You can't be a living sacrifice for God and live for self at the same time.

Something has to give.

God will always ask you to give Him what you want to keep for yourself in exchange for what He has for you.

He can't restore His dreams for your life if you can't give up your dreams for your life.

Easier said than done.

A.W. Tozer said:

> "The reason why many are still troubled, still seeking, still making little forward progress is because they haven't yet come to the end of themselves. We're still trying to give orders, and interfering with God's work within us."

Abraham spent twenty-five LONG years WAITING for God to make him a father through his wife Sarah. After the death of his brother, the departure from his homeland and family, the debacle of his nephew, Lot, the demise of his marriage due to the birth of Ishamel (because of improper means through Hagar, his wife's servant), he finally gets HIS son, Isaac.

Finally, life would be PERFECT.

This was the moment when Abraham's life finally ARRIVED. At last, everything was as he had dreamed it to be with God.

He could now be GREAT for God.

Listen to what God said to him:

> **Genesis 22:1-3,** "After these things God tested Abraham and said to him, 'Abraham!' And he said, 'Here I am.' He said, 'Take your son, your **only** son Isaac, whom you love, and go to the land of Moriah, and offer him there as a burnt offering on one of the mountains of which I shall tell you.' So Abraham arose . . . and went to the place which God had told him."

> **22:4-6,** "On the **third** day Abraham lifted up his eyes and saw the place from afar. Then Abraham said to his young men, 'Stay here with the donkey; I and the boy will go over there and worship and come again to you.' And Abraham took the wood the burnt offering and laid it **on Isaac** his son. And he took in his hand the fire and the **knife**. So they went both of them **together**"

Remember what Abraham did after his brother died? He settled **together with his family** in Haran, the place named after his deceased brother. Then he left his dad and pursued God's calling on his life.

Now, here he is with his family **together** again and he is NOT settling this time. He is going. He is going toward what God has called him to. He is going to do what God has called him to do. He is going to kill the dream God gave him over three decades earlier.

He is running toward the burning building, not away from it. Doing the right thing and the easy thing is rarely the same thing. Faith requires sacrifice. Sacrifice requires death to a dream God has given us.

It is in these moments that we get to find out if we are truly living for God or simply living for God's dreams. Are we only seeking God's hand or His face? Once a dream comes true, it is easy to worship the dream instead of the One who fulfilled the dream.

God has to periodically and repeatedly take the dream out of our hearts so that there is enough room in there for us to bow down and worship Him with our lives instead of worshipping Him just because of what He does for us.

The Devil knows this about us. The Devil said to God about Job:

> **Job 1:8-12,** "And the Lord said to Satan, 'Have you considered my servant Job, that there is none like him on the earth, a blameless and upright man, who fears God and turns away from evil?' Then Satan answered the Lord and said, 'Does Job fear God for no reason? Have you not put a hedge around him and his house and all that he has, on every side? You have blessed the work of his hands, and his possessions have increased in the land. But stretch out your hand and touch all that he has, and he will curse you to your face.' And

the Lord said to Satan, 'Behold, all that he has is in your hand. Only against him do not stretch out your hand.'"

Satan knows that many of us, if not all of us, follow God for what we can GET from Him. But God allows Satan to test us so that He and Satan can see firsthand why we follow God.

You can't know why you follow God until you lose something you want. Then you get to see your true motive.

But for Abraham, it wasn't just about losing something he wanted. Abraham willingly chose to journey alongside God and voluntarily give to Him what he had so fervently asked Him to give for so many years.

I wonder how many pastors would willingly give up ALL of the success and accolades from their thirty years in the pastorate and choose to instead go live an obscure life devoid of the "dream" God had at one time given them to fulfill?

Many times in my life God has asked me to give up the dream He gave me. I don't ever find this to be easy or even easier with time.

In 2010, our church was thirteen years old and in dire straits. We had to cut $500k out of our annual budget of 1.7 million. Vanguard was the largest it had ever been and had a budget larger than it had ever had. It was a golden time. Until it wasn't. The financial bust and crisis of our nation took down a lot of businesses and churches. We made cuts, moved out of rented facilities, and maximized our mortgaged facilities. We laid off staff. Cut ministry budgets. Moved out of our offices. It was an EXTREMELY painful three years of ministry.

During this time, I was convinced our church would no longer make it. I sat down with our finance company to figure out a plan forward. We owed two mortgage companies for two loans, one to buy the building, and one to add on to it. We also had an unsecured debt that the previous owner of the building carried for us. After negotiations, we still owed him roughly $375k.

During this season, I lost friends, elders, staff, church members, and the list goes on and on.

I lost hope.

The **Christian** finance company that we were working with told us NOT to pay the unsecured debt we owed. They said, "If you attempt to pay this, you won't make it. The church will go under and we will be forced to foreclose on you."

I couldn't believe they were saying this to us. The $375k we owed, we owed to the previous owner who was Jewish and not a believer in Jesus Christ. I wrestled hard with their suggestion. We wrestled hard with it in our elder meetings.

Finally, I realized there was ONLY one right thing to do. The Bible says:

> **Psalm 37:21,** "The wicked do not pay their bills."

I told the finance company in person we would be paying back the $375k as well. They assured me the church would not make it. I said to them, "The same integrity that pays him the $375k is the same integrity that pays you."

They didn't like that.

They felt this would be suicide to the church.

It was one of the darkest hours of my life. I had dreamed of starting a church since I was young. I went to Bible college to prepare to be a pastor. I went to seminary to prepare to be a pastor. I had eight years of education and thirteen years of pastoral experience at Vanguard. Well over two decades of my life were wrapped up in this moment.

I remember going home and sitting outside my house overlooking the cliff that led to our small farm's barnyard.

I just kept saying to myself, "God, why does it have to be this way?"

A.W. Tozer said:

> "It is doubtful whether God can bless a man greatly until He has hurt him deeply."

I called my dad and told him my predicament. I told him I would probably lose the church, my livelihood, and then my home. I said, "I may need to come home and work for you so I can pay off this enormous debt the church owes."

Life felt OVER to me.

The dream felt dead.

I remember going to an elder meeting with our pastoral leadership team and having a time of prayer. We decided we would treat the church like Abraham treated Isaac. We would put him on the altar and kill him. If God deems to raise Vanguard from the dead, we would know this was not our dream but His. We would also know God better.

I dropped into a depression and for the next three years it was DARK and I couldn't find the light switch.

How does God restore His dreams for us?

1. He asks us to kill them.

I knew God was asking us to make good on ALL our debts, but I also believed the finance company. If we tried, we would fail, and Vanguard would die.

We did it anyway, because we knew it was God's will.

God's will doesn't have to make "sense" to our logical minds. It just needs to line up with Scripture.

God asked Abraham to offer Isaac. And so, He did.

> **Genesis 22:7,8,** "And Isaac said to his father Abraham, 'My father!' And he said, 'Here I am, my son.' He said, 'Behold, the fire and the wood, but where is the lamb for a burnt offering?' Abraham said, 'God will provide for himself the lamb for a burnt offering, my son.' So they **went** both of them **together.**"

Abraham had learned to trust God more deeply than his need to satisfy himself. Sometimes it takes a lifetime to learn this. Unfortunately, some never learn it.

Abraham did.

When his brother died, he settled **together** with his family, but this time, he **went together**. He ran toward the burning building knowing it would cost him his God-given dream which had taken thirty years to gain. But if Abraham had learned anything in those three decades, he had learned the true power of sovereignty that God Almighty held over his life.

He had learned that he had everything in God, but he owned nothing. It ALL belonged to God.

How does God restore His dreams for us?

2. He asks us to trust Him with them, regardless of the sacrifice required.

Abraham said it in verse 8, "God will provide for himself a lamb, my son."

He didn't fret anymore over how God would accomplish what He said He would do, he just trusted and believed.

> **Romans 4:3,** "Abraham believed God and it was counted to him as righteousness."

The path of righteousness to God is paved with trusting God with the dreams He has given us.

What dream has God given to you that He has in turn asked you to sacrifice and trust Him with? If you hold on to it, it will become an idol and wedge you away from the very God you dedicated your entire life to loving and serving as a pastor.

Don't let the selfishness of trying to keep a God dream alive keep you from holiness. God has not called us to fulfill His dreams or be successful. He has called us to be holy.

> **1 Peter 1:16,** "You shall be holy, because I (God) am holy."

In *The Lord of the Rings* movies, every ringbearer battled the desire to keep the ring for their own selfish gain. They wrestled with refusing to fulfill their purpose, so they could selfishly hoard the benefit of that purpose, even if it cost them their lives. You can't find your life if you don't lose it for Christ. This is the paradox of following Him.

We are ALL tempted to squander God's favor because of our own selfishness. Don't buy the lie that you need to be GREAT for God. Just live a life that displays how greatly you NEED God. Make choices and decisions that keep you dependent upon His will and not "GREAT" because of it.

Your fame, success, and accomplishments are God's business. Do what He says, even if it doesn't make sense to you, because it will eventually.

Sacrificing Isaac, I am sure made no sense to Abraham, but he did it anyway.

Genesis 22:9,10,12-14, "When they came to the place of which God had told him, Abraham built the altar there and laid the wood in order and bound Isaac his son and laid him on the altar, on top of the wood. Then Abraham reached out his hand and **took the knife to slaughter his son.** But the angel of the Lord called to him from heaven and said, 'Abraham, Abraham!' And he said, 'Here I am.' He said, 'Do not lay your hand on the boy or do anything to him, for now I know that you fear God, seeing you have not withheld your son, your only son, from me.' And Abraham lifted up his eyes and looked, and behold, behind him was a ram, caught in a thicket by his horns. So Abraham called the name of that place, **'The Lord will provide'.**"

What do you fear God won't provide if you sacrifice His dream for you?

I am now years removed from those three dark years and I can look back and say now.

The Lord provided.

Just weeks after we made the decision to pay our bills, regardless of how bad it got, our facilities manager at the time, Matt Dufresne, got a word from God. He said, "Pastor, God has told me someone is going to give $100,000 to the church."

I appreciated his heart, but deep down my depression was struggling to believe him. But I felt prompted by God to let him share that with our church in the weekend services.

A few weeks later, someone gave a check for $100,000.

My dad would always say when I was boy, "If you need something from God, ask. He owns the cattle on a thousand hills. Ask Him to sell a few and give them to you."

We did.

He did.

That's a lot of cows. ☺

In the years to follow, we would get not one $100k gift, but three. And then just a few months ago, we got another. We have now gotten four $100k gifts since making that commitment to sacrifice God's dream, and kill it if need be. Before then, we had never gotten any.

God showed up and provided the sacrifice like He did for Abraham.

We are now doing the BEST financially than the church has EVER done.

We NEVER missed a payment, not ONE.

God showed up the moment we gave up the dream and sacrificed it to obey Him. He did the same for Abraham.

> **Genesis 22:15,16,** "And the angel of the Lord called to Abraham a **second** time from heaven and said, '**By myself** I have sworn, declares the Lord, because you have done this and have not withheld your son, your only son."

How does God restore His dream for us?

3. He does it by Himself.

Tozer said:

> "God must do everything for us. Our part is to yield and trust."

He doesn't need our help, but He does want our obedience and our trust.

As the old hymn says:

> "Trust and obey for there is no other way to be happy in Jesus than to trust and obey."

How does God restore His dream for us?

4. He makes it better than it was before.

> **Genesis 22:17, "I will surely bless you, and I will surely multiply** your offspring as the stars of heaven and as the sand that is on the seashore."

On October 22, 2017, Vanguard launched its third location. God surely blessed us and, yes, literally multiplied our efforts. We are so grateful that He sovereignly kept the dream alive. In 2010, He asked us to kill it. He asked us to sacrifice it on the altar of worship to Him. And by the way, since that dreadful day, we have partnered through the Frontline Church Planting Center to plant seventy-three other churches as well and counting!

We obeyed.

God did it.

I became a different person because of this.

Not only did I become a different person, our church became a different church because of this. Abraham became a different person because of his experience. You will become a different person as well. We see this in the closing chapter of Abraham's life.

> **Genesis 24:1-4,** "Now Abraham was old, well advanced in years. And the Lord had blessed Abraham in all things. And Abraham said to his servant, the oldest of his household, who had charge of all that he had, 'Put your hand under my thigh, that I may MAKE you swear by the Lord, the God of heaven and God of the earth, that you will NOT take a wife for my son from the daughters of the Canaanites, among whom I dwell, but will go to my country and to my kindred, and take a wife for my son Isaac.'"

> **24:5-8,** "The servant said to him, 'Perhaps the woman may not be willing to follow me to this land. Must I then take your son back to the land from which you came?' Abraham said to him, 'See to it that you do not take my son back there. The Lord, the God of heaven, who took me from my father's house and from the land of my kindred, and who spoke to me and swore to me, 'To your offspring I will give this land,' he will send his angel before you, and you shall take a wife for my

son from there. But if the woman is not willing to follow you, then you will be free from this oath of mine; **only you must not take my son back there.**'"

You know what Abraham was saying?

"Don't take my son back to where I came from. I am not that man anymore and I don't want my son to become him either."

Abraham didn't know how it would turn out, but he knew God didn't want him to go back to his old life. He had sojourned to a new land and his son was a result of that journey. He was committed to stewarding his son based on the promise God had given him. Not based on the dreams he had once held for his own life.

Abraham had changed. He was no longer here to just fulfill God's dream for his life. He was here to steward God's dream and then pass it on to Isaac, so that God's will for generations to come could be fulfilled.

It was no longer about him.

He had died to self. His ambition was on God's will for his son: the chosen, future, seed of Israel.

How does God restore his dreams in us?

5. He restores them *before* us. Never behind us.

He meets us in the "I Am" of our lives. He meets us in the present tense.

I am not that person anymore and neither are you.

I have stepped into God's dream for my life and so have you. We can't go back. We can't take our children back there. We must go forward and live out God's restored dream in us for generations to come.

If you are following God's restored dream for your life, your best days are always in front of you, and never behind you.

I watch so many pastors flame out in their forties because they just can't handle the pressure and stress of ministry and the pastorate. The grind of sermons, meetings, stress, spiritual attack, miscommunication, financial woes, pressure to succeed, and many other things take their toll on the pastor.

Then God asks you to sacrifice your Isaac and you lose it.

You can't take another sacrifice, request, or injustice. Your ego is too fragile and your hopes too great. And so, you are tempted to cling to what you have created instead of offering it as a sacrifice of worship to God.

God is meeting you right now in the present tense of your life. He is not ashamed of you or the fact that you aren't as far down the road of life as you would like to be at this point. He knew this day would come. He knew this would be an important day in your life. He is meeting you right now on the mountain where He has asked you to sacrifice what matters most to you. He knows you don't understand. He knows you hurt.

He knows.

Trust gives way to faith. Faith gives way to action. Action gives you more of God. And isn't that what this is all about?

> **Mark 8:36,** "What shall it profit a man to gain the whole world and lose his own soul."

Don't run from this moment. Don't pretend it doesn't exist. Don't try and put a positive spin on it to your loved ones and congregation.

Just trust God to meet you in your present tense. How does God restore the dream to us?

6. He meets us in our present tense.

You do what's right and God will do the rest.

Abraham's servant was able to bring back a wife for Isaac. They married.

It was time for Abraham to die.

> **Genesis 25:7,8,** "These are the days of the years of Abraham's life, 175 years. Abraham breathed his last and died in a good old age, an old man and full of years, and was gathered to his people."

Abraham was seventy-five when God called him in the land of his father. I am sure he had no idea he would live exactly 100 years from that calling. He wandered and suffered greatly for twenty-five years trying to understand the calling that God had placed on his life. It was at best, confusing to him. But those days are a faint memory to Abraham in his latter years. The last seventy-five years of his life he knew every time he looked into the eyes of Isaac that God had been faithful to fulfill the promise He gave him so many years ago.

All of us have things we worry about from time to time. We even become paranoid about them if we are not careful. Often, we fear we won't fulfill our purpose for being here.

I remember a number of years ago I got invited to speak for the Billy Graham Evangelistic Association. I spoke for them for a couple of years. I remember one time I flew to the Cove to speak at a gathering at the Billy Graham headquarters. Before speaking, I got to sit in the green room with Cliff Barrows, George Beverly Shay, and Tom Bledsoe. Wow, that was amazing! It was wonderful to listen to them reminisce about their years of ministry with Billy Graham. They had traveled the globe multiple times over, sharing the gospel with Billy Graham.

They told story after story, after story, and I was mesmerized by their stories, engulfed in them like a little boy waiting for Christmas. And then, George Beverly told a story about Billy Graham and how he battled various illnesses through the years, often visiting the Mayo Clinic concerned that he would die a premature death.

That was fifty years ago.

Billy Graham went to be with the Lord in 2018 at the ripe old age of ninety-nine just a few months shy of his 100th birthday.

We all have fears, even the godliest, but God's got us.

Sometimes I sit around and wonder if how I handled that situation years ago took away my influence and upward trajectory. I fear my best days have passed me and that what lies before me pales in comparison to "what could have been."

These are lies. We all hear them in our heads. At some point, we have to choose to believe that God's "got it", just like He had it all under control for Abraham. He walked him through those twenty-five years of darkness and confusion and blessed him with a son that would carry on the promise of the chosen seed of Israel.

You and I are now looking back on the realization of that chosen seed coming through Isaac and ultimately being realized in the coming of Jesus Christ. He was born, lived, bled, died, and was resurrected thus taking away the penalty of sin for all humanity.

We are now stewards not of the coming of the chosen seed, but of the Second Coming, the return of Jesus. And our role is just as important as Abraham's role was then. We have a responsibility to steward the truth of God's Word and to share the awesome, life-changing message of Jesus Christ to our generation, passing onto them the faithful witness of God's ultimate promise that He will one day take us all to live in His eternal Kingdom with Christ forever.

It is easy to get lost in the darkness and forget the purpose of our existence. It is easy to cling to the God-given dreams He has given us for fear that they will never be realized.

It is easy to give up hope, lose sight of eternity, and start living for the accomplishments of the flesh.

It is easy, but the easy thing and the right thing are seldom, if ever, the same thing.

God has asked you to sacrifice like Abraham. But can you look at Abraham, at the end of his life, and see how he lived a FULL life?

In the end, he didn't want to go back. He wanted to go forth. He wanted his life to be paid forward to a new generation of people who would carry on the torch of God's hope to a new generation.

> **Genesis 25:11,** "After the death of Abraham, God blessed Isaac his son."

Abraham wanted people AFTER him to be blessed. This is HOW you know God has restored His dream for your life.

How do we know God has restored the dream in us?

7. We want to bless those who come after us.

The measure of a person's godly life is not in their life, but in their legacy, that exists long after they are dead and gone.

A.W. Tozer was one of those people. In *A Passion For God*, author Lyle Dorsett described Tozer's life like this:

> "Herein lies Tozer's enduring legacy. His passion to know God is still contagious. A Pauline mystic

with both feet firmly on earth and both eyes riveted in the Holy Scriptures, and a heart given to Christ, he wrote these words in 1948, in the preface to *The Pursuit of God*: "Others before me have gone much farther into holy mysteries than I have done, but if my fire is not large it is yet real, and there may be those who can light their candle at its flame."

Many continue to catch the fire of Tozer's love for God. His books still sell well, and *The Pursuit of God* and *The Knowledge of the Holy* are read by more people who hunger for 'something more' than during his lifetime. Only eternity will reveal the full extent and effect of Tozer's 'Society of the Burning Heart.'

Remember, we are not here primarily to fulfill God's dreams with our lives. We are here to pass them on.

How does God restore His dream for us?

8. He passes it on through us.

The dream doesn't die with us. May generations long after we are dead and gone be affected by the faithfulness in our generation. And whether or not they know our names, may God pass His restored, redemptive dreams through us. May we pay them forward to the generations to come just like Abraham, Sarah, Isaac, Rebekah, Jacob, Rachel, David, Bathsheba, Solomon, Mary, Jesus, Peter, Tozer, and you and me.

> **Psalm 78:4,6,** "We will not hide them from their (our) children, but tell to the coming generation

the glorious deeds of the Lord, and his might, and the wonders that he has done. that the next generation might know them, the children yet unborn, and arise and tell them to their children so that they should set their hope in God and not forget the works of God."

Passing on God's restored dreams for us to our OWN children, good pastor, is where we start. Don't serve the world in Jesus's name and forget to teach those same things to your own child or the children in your own home. The legacy starts there.

Abraham did.

We will too.

It is the faithful work of God for EACH generation.

Future generations are counting on you, and all past generations are cheering you on.

God will meet you in the present tense.

You can do it.

Pay the restored dreams forward.

That's what good success looks like when it comes to God's dreams for you in the pastorate.

Live your God-restored dreams, good pastor, for future generations.

SECTION 3:

DETERMINATION

CHAPTER 9:

DETERMINED TO PASTOR THROUGH REJECTION AND BETRAYAL

"It's funny how sometimes the people you'd take a bullet for ... are the ones behind the trigger" (Author Unknown).

In the pastorate, betrayal and rejection are never easy and always painful.

Persecution is not a possibility, it is an inevitability, as a pastor. You can't live for God and others not pain you for it.

Paul told the young pastor Timothy:

> **2 Timothy 3:12,** "Indeed **ALL** who desire to live a godly life in Christ Jesus will be persecuted."

The dream to lead God's people as a good pastor can quickly turn into the desperate plea of a prophet asking God to judge those same people when they hurt you deeply.

The one constant in ministry is criticism. You can't escape it.

There will **always** be someone in the church who is critical of you, but they will cloak it in "holier than thou language." It will be subtle, very hurtful, and may even cause you to second guess your efforts.

Even the great pastor/preacher, Charles Spurgeon, in the height of his pastoral success, was not immune to it.

In addition to the physical suffering, Spurgeon had to endure a lifetime of public ridicule and slander, sometimes of the most vicious kind. His wife kept a scrapbook of such criticisms, from the years of 1855 to 1856. Some of it was easy to brush off. Mostly, it wasn't. In 1857, he wrote, "Down on my knees have I often fallen, with the hot sweat rising from my brow under some fresh slander poured upon me; in an agony of grief my heart has been well-nigh broken."

At another low moment in Spurgeon's life, he had said:

> "Men cannot say anything worse of me than they have said. I have been belied from head to foot, and misrepresented to the last degree. My good looks are gone, and none can damage me much now."

The receiving of criticism for doing the Lord's work does not come naturally. I have had a lot of years to learn this lesson over and over again.

I grew up a pastor's kid. I have been either a pastor or a pastor's kid all my life with the exception of five years. So, I am speaking from forty-five years of experience here.

Going all the way back to my childhood, I remember my dad being criticized, ridiculed, almost fired, and on the verge of literally going to physical blows with the song leader of our church behind the church after a week of "revival" services.

I guess the spirit moved that night, just not the Holy Spirit. My dad endured deacon fights, backbiting, gossip, hurtful comments, little-to-no pay (he was bi-vocational), was told he didn't deserve what little he made, had a deacon board that wanted to fire him (but didn't get the chance because he resigned upon God's prompting without any foreknowledge of their plans), and had a head deacon/song leader who refused to let anyone lead the church, even Jesus.

I remember, on more than one occasion, our family driving home from church and sobs filling the car from my mom, my sister, and even once my dad because of the hate, betrayal, hurt, and rejection the people of God caused our family.

No one can prepare you for how painful the pastorate will be for you and your family, especially your spouse. You might say to yourself, "I will be the exception."

The greatest leader to ever live, Jesus, was criticized, rejected, betrayed, and abandoned. They rejected and left Jesus's ministry. They will reject and leave your ministry too.

Jesus was no doubt a perfect leader, yet see how Judas responds to Him:

> **John 12:3-5,** "Mary therefore took a pound of expensive ointment made from pure nard, and anointed the feet of Jesus wiped his feet with her hair. But Judas Iscariot, one of his disciples (he who was about to betray him), said 'Why was this ointment not sold for three hundred denarii and given to the poor?'"

I remember when I bought the property that I now own. It is a farm in the middle of town. I had a leader in the church that took exception with it and said so. I asked him what his concern was. His response, "I just have a check in my spirit." He couldn't tell me anymore than that.

I suggested he cash it. I could use it for the down payment.

He didn't find the humor in it. 😊

He left the church soon after that.

Criticism as a pastor is a guarantee. And though you will need to make changes over the years to lead better, you can NEVER lead good enough to get the criticism to completely stop.

The question is not, "Is anyone leaving the church I pastor?" The question is, "How many will leave?"

In the Gospel of John, we see what ministry looks like, even for Jesus:

John 6:66,67, "After this many of his disciples turned back and no longer walked with him. So Jesus said to the twelve, 'Do you want to go away as well?'"

The pastorate is painful. Sheep are unruly and tend to wander off even when you attempt to shepherd them. They leave for a myriad of reasons.

You will either be too godly or not godly enough. You will be too much a dictator or too wishy-washy when it comes to making decisions. You will either spend too much time on your sermon or not enough. You will either be holier than thou or, well, not holy enough. You will either not be good with handling the church's money or you could use a less corporate approach to the pastorate. I even had a key guy leave the church because the speed bumps in the parking lot were too high for his car. That's a true story.

A.W. Tozer was an incredible man of God and he pastored for years. Listen to what people said about him:

"To the ultra-traditionalists, Tozer was, at best, becoming an odd duck. And at worst, he was turning into some sort of 'mystic' who could not be fully trusted. When he preached too prophetically in the tradition of Jeremiah or Amos, some people were offended and they worried that he would repel seekers and drive away many sensitive people."

Here's the point:

They criticized Tozer. They will criticize you.

They criticized Jesus. They will criticize you.

People rejected and left Jesus's ministry. They will reject and leave your ministry too, but knowing that as a fact doesn't make it any easier to endure.

Spurgeon said to the students of his pastor's college: "One crushing stroke has sometimes laid the minister very low. The brother most relied upon becomes a traitor ... Ten years of toil do not take so much life out of us as we lose in a few hours by Ahithophel the traitor, or Demas the apostate." Rejection and betrayal cause us to question everything about ourselves and our pastorate.

John Piper describes this struggle well:

> "What begins as a searching introspection for the sake of holiness and humility gradually leaves your soul, for various reasons, in a hall of mirrors. You look into one and you're short and fat; you look into another and you're tall and lanky; you look into another and you're upside down. Then the horrible feelings begin to break over you that you don't know who you are anymore. The center is not holding. If the center doesn't hold—if there is no fixed 'I' able to relate to the fixed 'thou' (namely God), who is supposed to preach next Sunday?"

After twenty plus years of pastoring, little shocks me now.

Jesus, of all people, understands rejection and betrayal. Within His relationships with the twelve disciples that He chose, He experienced both. Judas obviously betrayed Him. Peter and the other disciples deserted Him. Eventually, Peter rejected and denied Him. One of the most painful things about the pastorate is getting up weekend and week out, sharing the real stories of your life, the real pain, and being vulnerable with an audience that inevitably has someone in it that rejects you, betrays you, and maybe even hates you. It is extremely difficult to keep your heart soft while toughing your skin. Over time your skin gets soft, and if you are not careful, your heart gets hard.

I am grateful that Jesus understood abandonment in the ministry. There are few things in the ministry more painful for a pastor and his family than when those they are close to leave the church. They are left to figure out how to deal with the social component and loss of those relationships.

I have read the Bible over and over again searching for the formula that makes you immune from this sort of behavior. Unfortunately, I can't find it in the text. So, I am left to ask a very important question. *How do we remain determined to pastor through rejection and betrayal?*

Thousands of years ago, God called a man named Moses. He wasn't a pastor, but in some ways he was Israel's first leader, first pastor, first president, first prophet, and first sucker. ☺

It took him a while to be convinced.

But God made it pretty obvious when He visited Moses from a burning bush.

I wonder how many times over the course of forty years Moses reminisced about that burning bush experience in order to give him the strength to remain the prophet of God and lead the people of God to the promised land.

And by the way, that is what a pastor does. They lead the people of God towards the promises of God.

We can't fix people. We can't even fix ourselves, but God can. And He will through us.

The burning bush gave Moses the courage to rise up and lead like God asked him.

He agreed to leave a comfortable life and head into Egypt to save over 600,000 people from slavery at the hands of Pharaoh.

That's a big church!

He gave God every excuse he could think of, like we do from time to time, and God combatted all his excuses. In the end, the burning bush won out. Moses left his comfy life with a few sheep in Midian and headed to the metro-mess of Egypt. He saddled up his camel and hit the dusty trails.

He marched into Egypt like a warrior-poet and threw down the gauntlet on the most powerful leader in the world. God told him ahead of time that Pharaoh would resist, but the resistance would be futile and Moses was to keep chanting, "God says, 'Let my people go.'"

It was effective and before Moses knew it, the nation of Israel was rising up to leave the land of bondage for the

Passover lamb had provided a way of escape. What 600,000 people couldn't do for themselves, God did for them through one man, Moses.

Leadership matters.

Your pastorship matters!

Moses and 600,000 of his closest friends hadn't much more than left Egypt than they faced one of the greatest trials of their life.

How would they cross the Red Sea? They were doomed to die. Exodus records this dramatic moment:

> **Exodus 14:10,11,** "When Pharaoh drew near, the people of Israel lifted up their eyes and behold, the Egyptians were marching after them, and they **feared** greatly. And the people of Israel cried out to the Lord. They said to Moses, 'Is it because there are no graves in Egypt that **you have taken us away to die in the wilderness**?'"

Leadership/pastoring often results in you being blamed by God's people for what God has told them to do through you.

You may have gotten to the party late, but you still get to foot the entire bill.

You are the designated driver.

The people continued to complain to Moses:

> **Exodus 14:12a-14,** "'For it would have been **better** for us to serve the Egyptians than to die in the wilderness.' And Moses said to the people, '**Fear not, stand firm,** and **see the salvation of the Lord**, which he will work for you **today**. The Lord will fight for you, and you have only to be silent.'"

We, as pastors, have to lead with confidence, even when we know the people have none in us.

How?

Do what God tells you to do in the face of criticism, knowing it will probably get worse before it gets better.

Moses did:

> **Exodus 14:21,26,27,30,31,** "Then Moses stretched out his hand over the sea, and the Lord drove the sea back . . . and the waters were divided. Then the Lord said to Moses, 'Stretch out your hand over the sea, that the water may come back upon the Egyptians' . . . So Moses stretched out his hand over the sea, and the sea returned. Thus the Lord saved Israel that day . . . Israel saw the great power that the Lord used . . . so the people feared the Lord, and **they believed in the Lord and in his servant Moses.**"

Oh, isn't victory sweet?

Exodus 15 records a song Israel wrote in honor of God and Moses for the victory.

And they lived happily ever after.

Right?

Wrong!

You know what early victory in the pastorate assures you?

Nothing.

> **Exodus 15:22,24,** "Then Moses made Israel set out from the Red Sea, and they went into the wilderness of Shur. They went three days in the wilderness and found no water. And the people grumbled against Moses."

Happy days in ministry are short-lived memories.

Yesterday's victories are not sufficient for the challenges of today.

The only thing shorter than happy days in the ministry is the people of God's memory of them.

But I guess one encouraging thing about trials is that, if you are patient, they pass. Because before you know it people are onto the next thing that bothers them about you.

With time, you learn to build an immunity from this, like a vaccine. Trust me. (Later in the chapter I will talk to you about how to do this.)

But back to the betrayals and criticisms first:

> **Exodus 16:1-3,** "They set out from Elim, and all the congregation of the people of Israel came to the wilderness of Sin ... And the **whole** congregation of the people of Israel grumbled **against** Moses and Aaron in the wilderness, and the people of Israel said to them, 'Would that we had died by the hand of the Lord in the land of Egypt, when we sat by the meat pots and ate bread to the full, for you have brought us out into this wilderness to kill this **whole** assembly with hunger.'"

Moses responds to their criticism beautifully:

> **Exodus 16:8,** "And Moses said, 'When the Lord gives you in the evening meat to eat and in the morning bread to the full, because the Lord has heard your grumblings that you grumble against him—what are we? Your grumbling is NOT against **us** but against the Lord.'"

You have to learn not to take the criticism of God's people personally when you are simply directing them to do what God has already told them to do. Easier said than done though. How do you learn to do this?

How do you learn to not take criticism personally when God's people criticize you for leading them to do what God has directed you to do with them?

Jesus talked about this with His disciples:

> **John 15:18,26,27,** "If the world hates you, know that it has hated me before it hated you. But when

the Helper comes, whom I will send to you from the Father, the Spirit of truth, who proceeds from the Father, he will bear witness about me. And **you also will bear witness"**

How do we remain determined to pastor through rejection and betrayal?

1. Realize God never wants us to quit the ministry because someone doesn't like us.

I have had people accuse me of just about everything imaginable. I have a number of people who don't like me. I have tried to reconcile this as best as I can, even if they leave the church I pastor, but still I am forced to have the awkward moments at the grocery store, a restaurant, a department store, or a coffee shop, and the list goes on. You can't pastor in the same city for twenty-plus years and never cross paths with people who may just down right hate you as a pastor.

It's part of the job.

However, the Enemy loves to function in shadows and exaggerations. He likes to make it bigger than it is. He likes to make you feel like everybody who dislikes you gets together every week to discuss you and how they can hate you better. You begin to feel like everyone who has "left you" is out there teaming up against you. But here's the truth: the average pastor ends up leaving a church because of three to five people, regardless of the size of the church.

How do you move forward as a pastor when you know this is the constant reality of the pastorate? You can't escape pain, rejection, and betrayal.

Job knew a little something about rejection and betrayal. After all, his wife even came to him and said, "Why don't you curse God and die?"

He responded to His wife:

> **Job 2:9a,** "You speak as one of the foolish women would speak. Shall we receive good from God, and shall we not receive evil?"

Job had a keen ability to see his life's success and pain as ALL ultimately from the hand of God. Whether it is allowed or caused, it doesn't matter. It is approved.

People can't treat you in a way that God doesn't allow them to. This is so important to remember.

This does not mean God approves of how everyone treats us in the sense that He thinks they are going about it the right way. But it does mean this: God has authorized it.

Nothing can pass into your life that doesn't first pass through the throne room of God and receive His permission. We see this in Job's life. He understood this even though he didn't know what we know about his story. By faith, he believed God was sovereign over the good and the bad.

This is an amazing way to view life, especially in the pastorate.

How do we remain determined to pastor through the betrayal and rejection?

2. Accept the betrayal and rejection as equally from the hand of God.

Jesus had the ability to say to Judas in His hour of trial:

> **Matthew 26:49,50,** "And he (Judas) came up to Jesus at once and said, 'Greetings, Rabbi!' And he kissed him. Jesus said to him, 'Friend, do what you came to do.'"

When you understand your purpose from God, you can accept the pain people cause you that comes with it.

It doesn't make it easy. Matter a fact, there are times that I get downright angry after someone hurts me or my family, even more so when a friend betrays me like Jesus was betrayed by His friend.

I have been in the pastorate for long enough that I now have multiple seasons of long-term friends who have left me, betraying me with a kiss. That's just the way it is.

They left me and never told me why.

That doesn't get easier with time.

During these times, my journals have become a source and an outlet for me, along with my retired pastor friend, Jon. The only people in the world that understand the pain of pastors is pastors.

I have had so many friends say to me, "I can leave 'your' church and we can be friends. Just like someone can leave my company or business and we can still be friends."

It is NOT the same.

I have a beef business. My wife teaches piano. We have had people no longer want to buy beef or be taught piano from her. It is not the same.

The pastorate is a unique calling that requires ALL of your heart, calling, purpose, emotion, relationships, friendships, intelligence, social life and time, and the list goes on. It places demands on your family in ways that NO OTHER JOB DOES.

It hurts your family in ways NO OTHER JOB DOES.

You NEVER get used to people leaving your church and if you do, you should quit. It should always matter to you.

Judas betrayed Jesus. It provoked the disciples and one of them attacked with a sword.

Jesus responds:

> **Matthew 26:52-54,** "Put your sword back into its place. For all who take the sword will perish by the sword. Do you think that I cannot appeal to my Father, and he will at once send me more than twelve legions of angels? But how then should the Scriptures be fulfilled, that it must be so?"

Jesus understood the purpose of betrayal. It serves the same purpose in our lives.

You could do something about it. Maybe not as much as Jesus could do about it, but that doesn't matter. We have to choose to overlook the pain for the sake of the purpose. We let go of our need for justice and cling to our desire to fulfill His reason for our existence on this earth. It is what got Jesus through the hard times, and it will be what gets us through the hard times.

How do you remain determined to pastor through betrayal and rejection?

Have you ever thought about determination and what it is?

The primary definition is:

Firmness of purpose.

When you know what you are called to do, you can do it. This is how you remain determined to pastor through betrayal and rejection.

3. Remember your purpose.

I have remained a pastor for twenty-plus years because I know it is my calling. It is my purpose.

You will remain for no reason except, you know this is your God-given purpose for a lifetime.

You have to be determined to remain, regardless.

I am convinced the pastorate is 90% will and 10% skill.

If I know God wants me to do something, then I have to do it.

Jesus didn't want to go the cross. He even said to God the Father:

> **Matthew 26:39a,** "Let this cup pass from me."

But then He says,

> **Matthew 26:39b,** "But not my will but yours be done."

No sane pastor wants to be betrayed or rejected by those they love and serve in the pastorate. But just as it was a part of God's plan for Jesus, so it is for us.

He learned obedience through suffering and as pastors we will too.

Judas didn't deserve to live. Jesus didn't deserve to die. But here is what I have learned as a pastor: it is easier for people to judge you than for them to deal with the sin of their own lives.

I can't tell you the scores of people who have judged, betrayed, and rejected me only to then watch their own lives, marriages, and families fall completely apart.

This grieves me deeply. It doesn't bring satisfaction to my heart. If it did I should either get help or quit.

Jesus, on the cross, said:

> "Father, forgive them for they know NOT what they do."

I learned a long time ago, "Hurting people hurt people."

During some of the lowest times in the pastorate, people have come into our lives and have served us greatly, deeply, kindly, and very generously. It has been like a cup of cold water in a hot and dry desert land.

People in these times seem to go to the extreme measures to help us and then, in a moment's notice (it seems), they turn on us for telling them the truth about their own lives. Whether in word or deed, it happens. You feel them pull away. You feel them begin to criticize where they used to praise, you feel them make excuses for why they can't get together, and then out of nowhere a third party (usually) has to inform you "they no longer go to the church."

Paul describes this sort of relationship with the Galatians. They had a special place in his heart.

> **Galatians 4:13-16,** "You know it was because of a bodily ailment that I preached the gospel to you at first, and though my condition was a trial to you, you did not scorn or despise me, but received me as an angel of God, as Christ Jesus. **What then has become of your blessedness**? For I testify to you that, if possible, you would have gouged out your eyes and given them to me. **Have I then become your enemy by telling you the truth?**"

What do you do with these people? They are not like Judas, they are friends. Not friends that intended from the beginning to harm you, but friends, like Peter, who overestimated what they could handle when they became your friends. And I mean that. Jesus was betrayed not just vindictively by Judas, but also by friends that ended up overestimating their ability to hang in there for Jesus.

Matthew 26:33-35, "Peter answered him (Jesus), 'Though they all fall away because of you, I will never fall away.' Jesus said to him, 'Truly, I tell you, this very night, before the rooster crows, you will deny me three times.' Peter said to him, 'Even if I must die with you, I will not deny you!'"

I have watched the Devil chew up and spit out more friends of mine than I care to even mention. They are close. They care. They listen. They understand. But somewhere along the way they say something very similar, "It is extremely difficult to be your friend."

They get on the inside and feel the pressures, the attacks, and the daily grind that comes with being the pastor and their family. They hold your arms up for a season, but eventually your arms get too heavy for them. They also feel judged by you without you even knowing it. They begin to withdraw. Even if they don't want to hurt you, and do everything in their power not to, they wound you deeply. The gushing geyser of your soul screams "Never again will I allow someone to get that close to me in the pastorate."

How do you come back from the depths of despair and rejection that come from a friend who never intended to betray you, but in the end, did?

Jesus predicted His friend's betrayal. He saw it coming from a long way off. His friend, Peter, initially denied that he would abandon Him, but before it was over, he would go from denying it to denying his personal friendship to Jesus.

> **Matthew 26:69,70,74,** "Now Peter was sitting outside in the courtyard. And a servant girl came up to him and said, 'You also were with Jesus the Galilean.' But he denied it before them all . . . (he denied him three times). Then he began to invoke a curse on himself and to swear, 'I do not know the man.'"

How do you keep pastoring future parishioners when you feel the sting and betrayal of those in your past?

How do you remain determined to pastor through rejection and betrayal?

4. You remember their kindness as sincere.

Don't assume they intended to do to you what Judas did to Jesus. Yes, there may be one or two in your lifetime that will be that ruthless, but most of the betrayals and rejections will come from sincere people who can no longer handle the spiritual warfare and attack that which your life and family brings into their life and family. They need out. They need relief. They need to be "normal" again. They need to "not show up at church if they want to." They need the freedom not to be seen as your first choice when you are in a bind.

Just like in *The Lord of the Rings*, the ring was hard on the Ring Bearer. It was also really hard on the friends that were closest to the Ring Bearer.

The power that comes from the pastorate from God is intoxicating to other people. At first, it is stimulating and makes one feel alive, free, and important. People are drawn to that type of emotion. But over time, it takes a tremendous amount of understanding and maturity for someone to go to your church and simply be your best friend.

Many have tried it, few have succeeded.

The pastorate requires you to be the friend of all. It requires you to not play favorites. It requires you to not display these friendships as special in the congregation. Pastors may very well have the loneliest job on the planet and yet be the most sought-after people in a vocation to walk the face of the earth.

The conundrum and dichotomy are remarkable to explain, but I have watched it first hand in at least three families' lives who got close to my family and then just couldn't handle it anymore. They still loved us. They still cared for us. But honestly, they couldn't go to the church we pastor anymore for the sake of their own sanity.

So, what do you do? As you remember their kindness as sincere, where do you go from there?

How do you remain determined to pastor through this "kind" of betrayal?

5. You release them.

They are Christ's sheep. They belong to His kingdom. They belong to His Church and it meets at different locations and is pastored by other pastors besides yourself.

I have watched some of my closest friends become close friends with other pastors of other churches in the same city.

I find it almost impossible to discuss with other pastors. I have had it done to me and I have had it done for me.

It is very important at some point to come to terms with this and see it as not unique to you, but as a reality for the pastorate and the parishioner relationship.

How do you pastor through the rejection and betrayal?

6. Accept this as a reality and part of the pastor/parishioner relationship.

In the midst of all of the criticism, if you are not careful, you can lose your awareness of the authority that Jesus Christ has given you.

Jesus said to His apostles:

> **Luke 10:16,** "The one who hears you hears me, and the who rejects me, and the one who rejects me rejects him who sent me."

As a pastor, you have been given authority by God to lead and represent God to His people.

Now, if we are not careful, these words can be used to control people, be defensive, and not handle true criticism well.

> **Proverbs 27:6,** "Faithful are the wounds of a friend."

What I am about to say shouldn't be applied to agreed-upon accountability or in a formal group leadership structure for a pastor, but here it is.

Jesus takes it PERSONALLY when people criticize you as a pastor. Jesus takes your authority seriously, whether certain people do or not, so don't let them dictate your view of who God has called you to be.

I believe the best way to deal with betrayal and rejection is to:

7. Remember the authority Jesus has entrusted to you and complete the great work He has called you to.

Nehemiah says it best:

> **Nehemiah 6:1-4,** "Now when Sanballat and Tobiah and Geshem the Arab and the rest of our enemies heard that I had built the wall and that there was no breach left in it, Sanballat and Geshem sent to me, saying, 'Come and let us meet together at Hakkephirim in the plain of Ono.' **But they intended to do me harm**. And I sent messengers to them, saying, 'I am doing a great work and I cannot come down. **Why should the work stop while I leave it and come down to you?'** And **they sent to me four times** in this way, and **I answered them in the same manner**."

Keep pressing into who God has called you to be and do. IF you stop to tend to your critics, you may never start again. We need you, Pastor.

Don't stop the work to tend to critics. The only people you should submit yourself to are those who continue to do the work of the Lord with you.

> **Nehemiah 6:5-8,** "In the same way Sanballat for the fifth time sent his servant to me with an open letter in his hand. In it was written, 'It is reported among the nations, and Geshem also says it, that you and the Jews intend to rebel; that is why you are building the wall. And according to these reports you wish to become their king. And you have also set up prophets to proclaim concerning you in Jerusalem, 'There is a king in Judah.' And now the king will hear of these reports. So now come and let us take counsel together.' Then I sent to him, saying, '**No such things as you say have been done, for you are inventing them out of your own mind.**'

Don't focus on your critics, but address their lies for what they are, at least in your own mind. God never wants criticism to cause us to quit doing what He has asked us to do. He is NEVER in that:

> **Nehemiah 6:9b,** "For they all wanted to frighten us, thinking, 'Their hands will drop from the work, and it will not be done.'"

God is *never* in that!

Look at Nehemiah's prayer, this is what determination to pastor through opposition, betrayal, and rejection looks like:

Nehemiah 6:9a,10-13, "But now, O God, strengthen my hands. Now when I went into the house of Shemaiah the son of Delaiah, son of Mehetabel, who was confined to his home, he said, 'Let us meet together in the house of God, within the temple. Let us close the doors of the temple, for they are coming to kill you. They are coming to kill you by night.'

But I said, '**Should such a man as I run away?** And what man such as I could go into the temple and live? I will not go in.' And **I understood and saw that God had not sent him**, but he had pronounced the prophecy against me because Tobiah and Sanballat had hired him.

For this purpose he was hired, that I should be afraid and act in this way and sin, and so they could give me a bad name in order to taunt me."

Some criticism is legit and some isn't. You have to learn to differentiate between the two. God's critique is NEVER for you to quit what He has called you to, but to do it with greater effectiveness and holiness.

All godly critiques come with support of the work God has called you to. The other does not. It is trying to knock you out.

Nehemiah 6:14, "Remember Tobiah and Sanballat, O my God, according to these things that they did, and also the prophetess Noadiah and the rest of the prophets who wanted to make me afraid."

Ask God to take them out. You stay focused on His calling for your life.

> 6:15,16, "So **the wall was finished** on the twenty-fifth day of the month Elul, in fifty-two days. And **when all our enemies heard of it, all the nations around us were afraid** and fell greatly in their own esteem, for **they perceived that this work had been accomplished with the help of our God.**"

If the work you are doing is of the Lord, NO ONE can stop you. NO ONE!

Good Pastor, remember the authority Jesus has entrusted to you and complete the great work He has called you to.

This is how you remain determined to pastor through betrayal, rejection, and criticism.

Nehemiah models what **good** success in the pastorate looks like.

I love the prayer Nehemiah often prayed which is recorded in the book of Nehemiah.

Ask God to remember you and the work you do for Him.

Nehemiah closes his book with these words to God:

> **Nehemiah 13:31a** "Remember me, O my God, for **good.**"

For **good.**

From God.

For you, **Good Pastor!**

CHAPTER 10

DETERMINED TO PASTOR THROUGH DISAPPOINTMENTS AND HARDSHIPS

The pastorate is lonely. It always has been, and it always will be.

Paul touched on this when he wrote to the young pastor, Timothy.

> **2 Timothy 4:16,17,** "At my first defense no one came to stand by me, but **all deserted me. May it not be charged against them! But the Lord stood by me and strengthened me,** so that through me the message might be fully proclaimed ... So I was **rescued from the lion's mouth.**"

Here is what I get from that: everyone will abandon you, but don't hold it against them. Ultimately, it is not up to you or them. God will prevail through you, the message will be fully proclaimed, and you will be rescued.

You don't have to read too far into the Epistles of Paul to pick up on the hardships and disappointment that come with the ministry. Specifically, in regards to pastoring God's sheep. The disappointments and hardships are as plentiful as the blessings that come from shepherding Christ's sheep.

Over time, our enthusiasm is weakened and we can lose heart. We can lose sight of the point and the purpose of the pain. It is easy to fall into the "Job syndrome" or the "Jeremiah syndrome" and begin to feel the effects of "no good deed goes unpunished" in this life. Especially, in the pastorate.

Every pastor faces his or her own challenges personally, and then their family faces equally as much.

I have always said, "One of the hardest things about the pastorate is, helping others with their problems while trying to help your family navigate through their challenges as well.

Charles Spurgeon's ministry, life, and family were hard. His wife, Susannah Thompson became an invalid twelve years into their thirty-six-year marriage. He bore this burden with her with great faith and character that only a man of God could measure, live, and endure as he pastored the congregation God entrusted to him.

Spurgeon stood before his people for the last time on June 7, 1891, and died the following January 31 from a painful combination of rheumatism, gout, and Bright's disease. He was fifty-seven. George Muller and Hudson Taylor laid two wives in their graves because of illness. They both lost children. All three of these men and their families understood their confidence was not that God would prevent sickness and death, but that God would give them all they needed to do His will and give him glory in life and death. Even as a good pastor, it is not possible to eliminate the hardships and disappointments. But we can grow through these challenges regardless of how devastating they may be at the time. God does not waste any of our pain, especially those who pastor in Christ's name.

One of the most painful hardships of the pastorate is being compared to another pastor who is perceived as "more successful than you."

It happens in the world.

It happens in the church world.

No one really wants you to be you.

They want you to be the you they want you to be. And at times they will say so.

Spurgeon experienced this in his pastorate.

In comparing one ministerial identity with another, he reminded other pastors that as Jesus's Last Supper, there was a chalice for drinking the wine and there was a basin for washing feet. Then he said:

I protest that I have no choice whether to be the chalice or the basin. Fain would I be whoever the Lord wills so long as he will but use me ... So you...

They will say things like, "I wish you preached like that guy, I wish you told stories like that guy, I wish you hung out with people more like that guy, I wish you weren't so serious, I wish you ... you can fill in the blank.

You have felt it.

You have been it.

You are living it.

So, by the way, did the Apostle Paul who wrote half of the New Testament. People had their chorus of "I wish you" issues with Paul as well. The Enemy uses others' comments to discourage the authenticity of who Jesus has created us to be. Satan wants us to live a counterfeit life and try to be the said guy who is "better" than us.

HARDSHIP #1:
BEING COMPARED TO OTHER PASTORS.

The Apostle Paul dealt with comparison as well. The Corinthians were the best and the worst at it. Paul was fed up with the Corinthians comparing him to what he calls "the super-apostles." They wanted Paul to be more like them. He responds:

> **2 Corinthians 11:21,** "To my shame, I must say, we were too weak for that! But whatever anyone

else dares to boast of—I am speaking as a fool—I also dare to boast of that. Are they servants of Christ?"

Here is the implication? NO! Paul is trying to get the church of Corinth not to compare him to someone who doesn't even have a relationship with Jesus Christ. He continues:

2 Corinthians 11:23-28, "Are they servants of Christ? I am a better one—I am talking like a madman—with far greater labors, far more imprisonments, with countless beatings, and often near death. Five times I received at the hands of the Jews the forty lashes less one. Three times I was beaten with rods. Once I was stoned. (And he doesn't mean with weed like some of our pastors today) Three times I was shipwrecked; a night and a day I was adrift at sea; on frequent journeys, in danger from rivers, danger from robbers, danger from my own people, danger from Gentiles, danger in the city, danger in the wilderness, danger at sea, danger from false brothers; **in toil and hardship**, through many sleepless nights, in hunger and thirst, often without food, in cold and exposure. And, apart from other things, **there is the daily pressure on me of my anxiety for all the churches.**"

I don't know about you, but I'm already feeling better about my pastoral challenges. ☺

Ministry is difficult.

Ministry is impossible without Jesus.

Without Jesus, it won't be worth it. I often say, "Adulthood is harder than it looks."

So is the pastorate.

How many times, like Paul, have I been compared to another pastor, even in the city I pastor in? It is so painful to endure. It goes something like, "Pastor, we are gonna move on to . . . said church."

I say to them, "Why are you leaving this church?"

They say, "Well pastor, we just aren't getting fed . . . or . . . you've lost your anointing . . . or we want church to be 'more fun.'"

I had a guy who had attended our church for thirteen years tell me, "Pastor, I am moving on to another church because I don't get anything out of your messages and I haven't ever."

Patient man.

Sometimes young pastors and leaders and those they lead worry about them being "prideful" about who God created them to be in the pastorate. Or serving God for the wrong motive. I always tell leaders and pastors to not worry about their motive for serving Christ, because if you serve as a pastor long enough, trust me, the ministry will beat your selfish motivations out of you and Christ will use it to purify your walk with Him and the calling He has for your life. Be faithful. God will cleanse the motive in time. Be who God created you to be.

Spurgeon describes this tension point later in his pastorate and how he settled it.

> *Friend, be true to your own identity! One man would make a splendid preacher of downright hard-hitting Saxon; why must he ruin himself by cultivating an ornate style? . . . . Apollos has the gift of eloquence; why must he copy blunt Cephas? Everyone in his own order.*

There came a time when Spurgeon had to be what he was. Spurgeon continues:

> *I have found it utterly impossible to please, let me say or do what I will. One becomes somewhat indifferent when dealing with those whom every word offends. I notice that, when I have measured my words, and weight my sentences most carefully, I have then offended most; while some of my stronger utterances have passed unnoticed. Therefore, I am comparatively careless as to how my expressions may be received, and only anxious that they may be in themselves just and true.*

John Piper said:

> *If you are to survive and go on preaching in an atmosphere of controversy (and comparison), there comes a point where you have done your best to weight the claims of your critics and take them to heart, and must now say "By the grace of God I am what I am." We must bring an end to the deranging second-guessing that threatens to destroy your very soul.*

On top of the comparison and criticisms, Paul, in 2 Corinthians 11, alluded to the next hardship of the pastorate:

HARDSHIP #2: PHYSICAL FATIGUE AND MENTAL EXHAUSTION.

The pastorate has daily challenges. Paul called them the "daily pressure on me of my anxiety for all the churches."

You can't escape it.

In twenty-plus years of pastoring, I have experienced the following health issues. 1) Bad back, 2) multiple urinary tract infections, 3) multiple surgeries to remove plantar warts from the bottom of both of my feet, 4) shingles on my forehead, 5) chronic fatigue and an inability to sleep at night, 6) weight gain, 7) anxiety and panic attacks, 8) depression, and the list goes on and on and on.

You can't be a pastor and not deal with tremendous physical attack on your body.

I haven't experienced it all, but I have experienced my fair share of physical sorrow at the hands of the stress that comes from the daily pressure of pastoring a church.

A few years ago, once again, I had developed plantar warts on the bottom of my feet. I could feel at least five of them on my feet and when I would stand to preach over time, I would feel them more and more and more.

Finally, I broke down and went to a podiatrist to get them taken off. I walked into the doctor's office. Three hours later, they wheeled me out of the doctor's office. It was one of the most horrible experiences of my life.

The doctor looked at my feet and said, "Oh, my, how many warts did you think you had on the bottom of your feet?"

I said, "Five maybe."

She said, "Try twenty-three."

I almost passed out from the overwhelming anxiety that came over me because I had some removed a couple of years prior, and let me just tell you, it was one of the most painful experiences of my life.

They have to numb your feet by putting needles into the bottom of your feet ... and that's just the beginning of the process.

By the time she was done, I was finished.

I couldn't walk for months. And during this time, a verse from Isaiah, that is also repeated in Romans, kept repeating in my head.

> **Isaiah 52:7,** "How beautiful upon the mountains are the **feet** of him who brings good news, who publishes peace, who brings good news of happiness, who publishes salvation, who says to Zion, 'Your God reigns.'"

I don't know if it was God or the Devil reminding me of that verse, because at times it gave me hope and at other times it made me angry. I HATE being needy. But with bandages on both feet, I had to make a choice. Do I speak from a wheelchair or do I wait until I am better and can stand again?

I decided to preach from a wheelchair with shorts on because I couldn't get my pants on. With my "beautiful" feet bandaged, I had two men lift me onto stage in a wheelchair so I could bring "good news of happiness and publish salvation and let everyone know their God reigns."

It seems His power is made perfect in our weaknesses. The removal of those warts and the recovery time was one of the most painful experiences of my life. Plantar warts are caused by an autoimmune disease. They occur when your body's defenses have been compromised.

Every time I go to the doctor, they ask me, "Are you under any stress in your life?"

My standard response is, "I am a pastor."

'Nuff said!

Being a "good pastor" requires us to sacrifice and live under the daily pressure and anxiety of the pastorate. At times, we may find ourselves in positions that demonstrate our weakness. Press in to these times so people can see you are real and God is powerful. He reigns.

But also, each physical and mental attack requires you and me to consider how we can better take care of ourselves over the long haul. For example, when I get one wart on the bottom of my feet, I don't wait now, I go to the doctor and have it removed immediately. I am also learning how to manage stress better through diet, exercise, and rest. I will talk more about dependence upon God through rest later in the book. That chapter is born out of many painful and difficult situations that let me know that if I am going to be a good pastor for a lifetime, I have to learn how to take better care of my body.

However, for some, physical and mental issues lead them to conclude, "I can no longer pastor." Before you make that decision, consider this: God knew, God knows, and God reigns. His strength is made PERFECT through our plantar warts. I love Jeremiah's prayer:

> **Jeremiah 17:14-16, "Heal me, O Lord, and I shall be healed**; save me, and I shall be saved, for you are my praise. Behold, they say to me, 'Where is the word of the Lord? Let it come!' I have not run away from being your shepherd,"**

This leads to the next hardship in the pastorate. This one may be the hardest hardship of all because it comes from within. It is the fear of "wasting" our lives in the pastorate with nothing to show for it but terrible health and an early death.

HARDSHIP #3: IT FEELS THE SACRIFICE TO BE A PASTOR JUST ISN'T WORTH IT.

A few years ago, I said to myself, "I am wasting my youth, health, financial resources, life, time, energy, you name it, on being a pastor."

I said out loud to myself, during this season:

"Is the sacrifice to be a pastor worth the reward that comes with it?"

I am not the first person to feel this way.

After twenty-three years of faithful ministry, and seeing little results from his ministry, Jeremiah lost it . . . momentarily.

> **Jeremiah 20:14,** "Cursed be the day on which I was born! The day when my mother bore me, let it not be blessed!"

Been there! If you pastor God's people long enough, you will too. Jeremiah continues:

> **Jeremiah 20:15-18,** "Cursed be the man who brought the news to my father, 'A son is born to you,' making him very glad. Let that man be like the cities that the Lord overthrew without pity; let him hear a cry in the morning and an alarm at noon, **because he did not kill me in the womb**; so my mother would have been my grave, and her womb forever great. **Why did I come out from the womb to see toil and sorrow, and spend my days in shame?**"

In the book, *The Mystery of 23: God Speaks!,* I ask the question in one chapter, "Why do we often feel shame for doing what God asked us to do?"

Jeremiah could relate. He had dedicated two-plus decades of his life to being a prophet to Israel and he had nothing to show for it. He was ready to quit.

Earlier he even says to God:

Jeremiah 20:7-9, "O Lord, you have deceived me, and I was deceived; you are stronger than I, and you have prevailed. I have become a laughingstock all the day; everyone mocks me. For whenever I speak, I cry out, I shout, 'Violence and destruction!' For the word of the Lord has become for me a reproach and derision all day long. If I say, 'I will not mention him, or speak any more in his name,' there is in my heart as it were a burning fire shut up in my bones, and **I am weary with holding it in, and I cannot.**"

If you're called, you're called! You can avoid living it out, but you can't avoid feeling it. If God has spoken and called you to be a pastor, or to do anything for that matter, you know it. You feel it. You are weary with holding it in.

Jeremiah was. I have been there too. You pastor long enough, you will too.

Jeremiah speaks:

Jeremiah 25:3-5,7, "For twenty-three years, from the thirteenth year of Josiah the son of Amon, king of Judah, to this day, the word of the Lord has come to me, and I have spoken persistently to you, but you have not listened. You have neither listened nor inclined your ears to hear, although the Lord persistently sent to you all his servants the prophets, saying, 'Turn now, every one of you, from his evil way and evil deeds, and dwell upon the land that the Lord has given to you and your fathers from of old and forever. Yet you have not listened to me, declares the Lord, that you might provoke me to anger with the work of your hands to your harm.'"

Sometimes our message is difficult for others to hear and sometimes it is difficult for us to give. And sometimes it is both.

And if you are anything like Jeremiah or me, you will wonder out loud to yourself whether it is worth it or not. Do yourself a favor. Stop speaking. Let go. Tell yourself you're gonna quit. Tell God you're gonna quit. See what happens inside of you.

Feel it?

That's your calling. Whether it feels like it is worth it or not, it is WHO God has made you to be. The best way to overcome feelings of futility is to stop and see how much more futile you feel if you don't do what He tells you to do.

Just because people don't do what you tell them to do doesn't mean God can't bless you. Your blessing is not dependent upon the people you lead, but the obedience you choose to demonstrate in the face of the futility you feel from serving God's people day in and day out.

The second-best remedy to this hardship is silence. The best remedy is obedience.

Jeremiah employed both. If you go at this long enough, I have a sneaky suspicion, you will too.

In the midst of wanting to quit, Jeremiah faced harsh criticism and even lies.

HARDSHIP #4: PEOPLE WILL TRY TO DISCREDIT YOU WITH LIES.

James Wells, the hyper-Calvinist, wrote about Charles Spurgeon, "I have most solemnly had my doubts as to the Divine reality of his (Spurgeon's) conversion". Can you imagine as a pastor someone even doubting if you are even a Christian and declaring it publicly to all others?

Spurgeon's response:

> "Men cannot say anything worse of me than they have said."

This hardship is real, and like smelling someone's bad breath in the morning, it recoils you.

It is easy to shrink back. Especially when the Enemy uses God's people that you serve to go on the attack and say things about you that just aren't true.

I don't know how to break it to you, but people will lie and make up stuff about you in the ministry to hurt you.

The Psalmist addressed this. Everyone in the pastorate experiences it:

> **Psalm 120:1,2,6,7,** "In my distress I called to the Lord, and he answered me. Deliver me, O Lord, from lying lips, from a deceitful tongue. Too long have I had my dwelling among those who hate peace. I am for peace, but when I speak, they are for war."

The pastorate will feel like this at times. People will lie about you. They will say things about you that just aren't true. And here is the most painful part of that equation: for a time, people will believe them. And there is nothing you can do to change their minds.

Only God, over time, can change it. In the meantime, it will drive you crazy. I had a situation like this that went on for five-plus years. It was very difficult. Things were said about me by another believer, a leader, that just were not true. It seems like everyone I have ever compared notes with has had someone during their life have it out for them for whatever reason. They will say all manner of things against you and cause your blood to boil. The injustice will mark you, impact you, and, if you not careful, consume you.

At times it consumed me. I am not the only one.

Jeremiah suffered the same thing.

Jeremiah told Israel enough was enough. God was going to judge them and they would be carried off to Babylon into slavery. It was the moment of truth for Israel. While Jeremiah was trying to help Israel repent with these truths, Hananiah spoke to Jeremiah and told him the opposite of what he had just told Israel.

> **Jeremiah 28:1a,2,3,** "Hananiah the son of Azzur, the prophet from Gibeon, **spoke to me in the house of the Lord, in the presence of the priests and all the people,** saying, '**Thus says the Lord of hosts**, the God of Israel: I have broken the yoke of the king of Babylon. Within two years I will bring

back to this place all the vessels of the Lord's house.'"

In front of EVERYBODY, Hananiah bullies Jeremiah, and simply says, "You're wrong. You're an idiot. Here's the truth."

In the midst of feeling the futility of ministry, the Enemy will raise up people against you in the pastorate to try and finish you off. You MUST have the courage to stand your ground. You MUST have the courage to lead not in the flesh, but through the empowerment of the voice of the Lord Jesus.

A.W. Tozer understood this. He said in *The Pursuit of God*:

"Whoever will listen will hear the speaking Heaven. This is definitely not the hour when men take kindly to an exhortation to listen, for listening is not today a part of popular religion. We are at the opposite end of the pole from there. Religion has accepted the monstrous heresy that noise, size, activity, and bluster make a man dear to God. But we may take heart. To a people caught in the tempest of the last great conflict God says, "Be still, and know that I am God" (Psalm 46:10) , and still He says it, as if He means to tell us that our strength and safety lie not in noise but in silence.

It is important that we get still to wait on God. And it is best that we get alone, preferably with our Bible outspread before us. Then if we will, we may draw near to God and begin to hear Him speak to us in our hearts."

All the odds were against Jeremiah. Even Jeremiah was against Jeremiah. He was fed up. But he was faithful nonetheless. He spoke the words God asked him to speak, regardless of what it cost him. You can only measure your words for so long until God asks you to speak contrary to what you feel comfortable with. This was true for Jeremiah.

> **Jeremiah 28:15-17,** "And Jeremiah the prophet said to the prophet Hananiah, 'Listen, Hananiah, the Lord has **not sent you,** and you have made this people trust in a lie. Therefore, thus says the Lord: 'Behold, I will remove you from the face of the earth. This year you shall die, because you have uttered rebellion against the Lord." In that same year, in the seventh month, **the prophet Hananiah died."**

That's dramatic, and sometimes this will be the case, but most of the time these situations just linger on without resolution. What do we do if God doesn't allow us to hit it head-on like Jeremiah?

You must determine to live for Jesus and not turn and waste your efforts on silencing your critics. Instead, let them have at it. The Bible says eventually they will get what is coming to them.

> **Proverbs 7:13a,** "Behold, a wicked man conceives evil and is pregnant with mischief and gives birth to lies. **He makes a pit, digging it out, and falls into the hole that he has made**. His mischief returns upon his own head, and on his own skull his violence descends."

So, what do we do until they fall into the holes they dug for us? Fortunately, unjust criticism has been around for a while. David experienced his fair share of unjust criticism even as the King of Israel.

One time during King David's reign, He was falsely accused and attacked.

> **2 Samuel 16:5-7,9,** "When King David came to Bahurim, there came out a man of the family of the house of Saul, whose name was Shimei, the son of Gera, and as he came, he cursed continually. **And he threw stones at David and at the all the servants of King David,** and all the people and all the mighty men were on his right hand and on his left. And Shimei said as he cursed, 'Get out, get out, you man of blood, you worthless man!' Then Abishai the son of Zeruiah said to the king, 'Why should this dead dog curse my lord the king? **Let me go over and take off his head.'"**

Look at how he responds:

> **2 Samuel 16:10,11a,12,** "But the king said, 'What have I to do with you ... Leave him alone, and let him curse, for the Lord has told him to do so. **It may be that the Lord will look on the wrong done to me, and that the Lord will repay me with good for his cursing today.'"**

Ask God to bless you through the people who attempt to curse you. A long time ago, God made a promise to Abraham:

Genesis 12:3, "I (God) will bless those who bless you, and him who dishonors you I will curse, and in you all the families of the earth shall be blessed."

You might say, "That's great for Abraham." But you may be overlooking a promised blessing God has for you in the 21st century because of His promise to Abraham. It may just change the way you view the hardship of people telling lies and cursing you for the life you are trying to live for God as a pastor.

Galatians 3:29, "And if you are Christ's, then **you are Abraham's offspring, heirs according to promise."**

If you believe in Jesus, you are now a part of the promise God gave Abraham some five thousand years ago. The cursing and lies that people direct towards you are directly affected by the promise God gave Abraham. Just like David, who was certainly a part of the promise, it is important to ask God to bless you for the curses and lies people are saying against you. Don't wait for them to fall in the hole they dug for you, ask God to bless you for the curses they have leveled against you unjustly in your lifetime.

I have.

And He has.

Leave the revenge to Him, but allow this to increase your prayer requests exponentially. It's biblical.

Ask Abraham.

Ask David.

Ask me.

Ask others.

In God's time, truth always wins out. I have never seen it not.

Your attitude matters during this season. As a good pastor, your effectiveness depends on it. Paul exhorts us:

> **Philippians 2:14,16,17,21,** "Do ALL things without grumbling or disputing, holding fast to the word of life, so that in the day of Christ I may be proud that I did not run in vain or labor in vain. Even if I am to be poured out as a drink offering upon the sacrificial offering of your faith. I am glad and rejoice with you all. For they all seek their own interests, not those of Jesus Christ."

This was Paul's response to the Philippians when false teachers were lying about him to them.

Wait in silence for the Lord to rescue you. It will be dramatic and you won't ever forget it.

God sees the hardship of criticism you are in right now. In time, He will deliver.

Trust me.

Trust Jeremiah.

Ask Hananiah.

God's truth always wins, good pastor.

HARDSHIP #5: OVERCOMING PAST GRIEF TO LEAD IN THE PRESENT.

How many times have I said to myself, "Here we go again. Same song, different stanza."

After twenty years of pastoring, I was given a sabbatical for sixty-three days. It is the longest I have been away from the pastorate in twenty years. One of the things the Lord said to me during that time was this, "Kelly, if you are going to do this for twenty more years, you are going to have let go of the hurt of the past twenty and trust me with it."

Easier said than done, right?

No leader escapes disappointment in those they lead. No leader escapes the hurt that comes at the hands of those who disappoint us.

Samuel was no different.

Saul had failed as the King of Israel. Samuel had anointed him. Believed in him. Stood with him. But God said to Samuel, "No more."

Samuel said to Saul:

> **1 Samuel 15:28,** "The Lord has torn the kingdom of Israel from you this day and has given it to a neighbor of yours, who is **better than you.**"

That was not easy for Samuel to say. He loved Saul and believed in him.

> **1 Samuel 15:35,** "And Samuel did not see Saul again until the day of his death, **but Samuel grieved over Saul.**"

No big deal, right?

God anointed David through Samuel at seventeen years of age, but David didn't become King until he was thirty years old. He spent thirteen years running from King Saul. Guess who got to be prophet of Israel for those thirteen years?

Samuel.

He grieved Saul's death long before his death came. Thirteen years is a LONG time.

Grief is human. Grief is essential to moving on to the future. But grief tends to tarry, linger, and multiply on us if we are not careful. It becomes paralyzing to our future. It is prolonged, perpetual, persistent, and eventually pervasive if we are not careful. Not only can it steal our joy, but it can steal our future and land us in our past.

God said to Samuel:

> **1 Samuel 16:1,** "The Lord said to Samuel, 'How long will you grieve over Saul, since I have rejected him from being king over Israel?'"

How do you move past grieving the loss of people in your pastorate and lead again? Well, first, let's ask, how do you know if you have grieved too long? How do you know if it has moved into a pervasive mindset that is becoming damaging? How do you know if past grief is killing present pastoral productivity?

Here are some signs past grief has become more important to you than present pastoral productivity:

1) You think about the past more than the present.

2) You assume everyone in your present is like those in your past.

3) You have determined your future success based off your past.

4) You hear a pervasive voice telling you that you should quit.

5) You are starting to lash out at others over pain and grief from your past.

6) You are becoming divisive and won't listen to others.

7) You are becoming more and more defensive and refuse to trust those in your present.

8) You can't dream anymore for fear of more grief.

Henry Cloud, in his book, *Necessary Endings*, taught me how to get out of the pervasive mindset of grief and loss so that I could move on to the present pastoral opportunities God had given me.

God doesn't want you to live in past grief forever. Grieve it, but at His appointed time, move on. He tells Samuel this:

1 Samuel 16:1, "Fill your horn with oil, and **go,** I will send you to Jesse the Bethlehemite, for I have provided for myself a king among his sons."

God has a future for your pastorate. He has people in your future He wants you to anoint to do what He has called them to do. Just like David needed Samuel, there are people who still need you to be their pastor.

I am not saying this is easy. I have found this to be extremely painful to get through. Letting go of grieving the loss of people who used to be a part of my ministry is one of the most difficult things I have had to survive. I think this is why pastors leave the church they pastor, the city they are from, and move on. However, it certainly is easier to move on geographically than it is psychologically. Personally, I can't walk into a restaurant, a grocery store, a coffee shop, or a department store without running into people "who used to go to the church I pastor."

At some point, you must make peace with this. And the way you make peace with it, is by filling your horn full of oil, and asking God to send you to those He wants you to pastor and anoint for His service in the church He has called you to pastor.

There will come a time when He invites you to call some of those people back to join you and they will join you. Some won't, but some will, and you will learn and they will learn. This is not about assigning blame or even doing it perfectly the second time around. It is about continuing to move forward in the pastorate and anointing those God has called you to anoint and lead. It is about you doing what God has asked you to do. It is about taking responsibility for your part in the equation, and then letting go of them and their part. It is about recognizing God has a future for you.

Israel found herself in Babylon. When she arrived, she could have grieved for seventy years, but God had other plans.

> **Jeremiah 29:4-14,** "'Thus says the Lord of hosts, the God of Israel, to all the exiles whom I have sent into exile from Jerusalem to Babylon: **Build houses** and live in them; **plant gardens** and eat their produce. **Take wives** and have sons and daughters; take wives for your sons, and give your daughters in marriage, that they may bear sons and daughters; multiply there, and do not decrease. But **seek the welfare of the city where I have sent you into exile**, and pray to the Lord on its behalf, for in its welfare you will find your welfare. For thus says the Lord of hosts, the God of Israel: Do not let your prophets and your diviners who are among you deceive you, and do not listen to the dreams that they dream, for it is a lie that they are prophesying to you in my name; I did not send them, declares the Lord. For thus says the Lord: When seventy years are completed for Babylon, I will visit you, and I will fulfill to you my promise and bring you back to this place. For I know the plans I have for you, declares the Lord, plans for welfare and not for evil, to give you a future and a hope. Then you will call upon me and come and pray to me, and I will hear

you. You will seek me and find me, when you seek me with all your heart. I will be found by you, declares the Lord, and I will restore your fortunes and gather you from all the nations and all the places where I have driven you, declares the Lord, and I will bring you back to the place from which I sent you into exile."

God will eventually redeem all your grief from the past, but it may take seventy years. Until then, live. Live where you are like it is where God intended for you to be all along. He doesn't want you to live backwards. He doesn't want you to live preoccupied by the images in your rearview mirror, regardless of how they got there. He wants you to build houses, plant gardens, take wives, and pray for the welfare of the city you are exiled in. Everything in you might say, "It wasn't supposed to be this way." Don't worry about it.

LIVE.

Don't quit!

Don't fornicate!

Pastor.

It is not "worth it" right now, but it will be.

Spurgeon carried on pastoring thirty-eight years. George Muller pastored sixty years. How about you?

Live, Good Pastor, where you have been planted and let God sort out the grief of the past at His appointed time.

If you do, like Israel, you will discover a whole new life of anointing He has for you and those you pastor.

Hardships will come and stay longer than we like. We have to choose to sail into the seas of tomorrow, today, if we plan on letting go of the grief of yesterday.

Good pastor be determined to pastor through disappointments and hardships. The people in your future pastorate are dependent upon your ability to let go of those in your past.

CHAPTER 11

DETERMINED TO PASTOR THROUGH LEADERSHIP FAILURES

If at first you don't succeed, then quit.

No!

"If you don't pass the test today, don't worry, God will give it to you again tomorrow."

My good friend Richie Fike said this to me many years ago.

Do you know what it feels like to see the world you have spent your entire life building, crumbling all around you, and even some on the edges of your life taking pleasure in your impending failure?

This is what the pastorate can feel like at times.

You can't lead and never fail.

You can't fail and decide never to lead again.

You can't lead again, if you can't fail.

Failure is an essential ingredient to finding the grace God planned for you long ago.

The Apostle Peter knew this.

Jesus told Peter, "You will deny me three times."

Peter told Jesus, "Never."

Jesus was right, again.

The Bible records Peter's response:

> **Matthew 26:75, "**And Peter remembered the saying of Jesus, 'Before the rooster crows, you will deny me three times.' And he went out and **wept bitterly.**"

What is the difference between weeping and weeping bitterly?

Jesus wept, in John 11:35, at the death of Lazarus.

How was Peter's tears different than Jesus's tears?

If I were to say to you, "Fight to the bitter end." How would you interpret that?

The definition of a bitter end is one that you have done EVERYTHING you can and the outcome has not changed, but you gave it everything you could.

Peter had given it his best, but his best was NOT good enough.

He failed.

He denied Jesus in the darkest hour of Jesus's life.

Jesus had told him he would.

Peter didn't believe Him, and neither would I.

Peter failed.

I did too.

Vanguard had just experienced its BEST year of growth both financially and numerically in 2009. The church was twelve years old and headed up, up, and away like Superman. In 2010, the crash of our church hit, we had to cut $500k out of the annual budget, lay off staff that had been with us for years, cut ministries, renegotiate lease agreements for building space, and in one fell swoop 23% of our church left and never came back.

I fought to the bitter end, but I couldn't keep it from happening.

I gave it my best and my best wasn't good enough.

I failed on so many levels.

Like Peter, I saw my failure as permanent.

I wept bitterly.

I was walking through the valley of pastoral suck and I feared every evil.

How did I get there?

What did Peter feel like after he betrayed Jesus and failed Him? What were those next three days like? How did he go on?

His Savior needed him most and he denied three times in the darkest hour of Jesus's life that he ever knew Him.

The story says, "Your accent betrays you."

Peter was a fisherman, an uneducated fisherman from Galilee who talked like a hick from Kentucky.

Everywhere he went his accent betrayed him.

I wonder if he stopped talking. I wonder if he thought about taking speech classes. I wonder what went through his mind those three days after betraying his Savior?

Failure is real. And it hurts for a LONG time.

How many sermons have I given while feeling like a failure as a pastor? Let's see…

I think it was five years before I didn't feel like a failure. I gave over 500 sermons during that time.

I want to talk to you about the common failures we face as pastors.

COMMON FAILURE #1: WASTED RESOURCES.

I pride myself on being a good steward of the Lord's resources. I hate wasting anything.

2 Chronicles records the story of a man who hated wasting resources too.

> **2 Chronicles 25:1,2,** "Amaziah was **twenty-five years old** when he began to reign, and he reigned twenty-nine years in Jerusalem. His mother's name was Jehoaddan of Jerusalem. And he did what was right in the eyes of the Lord, yet **not** with a **whole** heart."

The passage caught my attention for many reasons, but one, I started Vanguard when I was twenty-five years old. Great responsibility at an early age will result in some failures, guaranteed. He didn't do it perfectly.

I can relate.

However, he did seek to follow God's Word and obey the commands given to him as the King of Judah. The Scriptures tell us:

> **2 Chronicles 25:3,5,** "And as soon as the royal power was firmly his, he killed his servants who had struck down the king his father. But he did not

put their children to death, **according to what is written in the Law, in the Book of Moses**, where the Lord commanded, 'Fathers shall not die because of their children, nor children die because of their fathers, but each one shall die for his own sin.'"

Amaziah's dad was King Joash, he committed a repulsive crime and was assassinated. King Amaziah's first act as King was to punish by death those who had killed his father, but from the text you can see his heart was to follow God's Word as he led, and he did. During this time, a border war broke out with Edom.

> **2 Chronicles 25:5,** "Then Amaziah assembled the men of Judah and set them by fathers' houses under commanders of thousands and of hundreds for all Judah and Benjamin. He mustered those twenty years old and upward, and found that they were 300,000 choice men, fit for war, able to handle spear and shield."

The text doesn't yet tell us this but he was fearful that his army was not strong enough. We will learn this in a bit. So, he goes and hires 100,000 mercenaries.

> **2 Chronicles 25:6,** "He hired also 100,000 mighty men of valor from Israel for 100 talents of silver."

This is roughly four tons of silver. After the large sum was paid and the army was on hand, a prophet of God comes to King Amaziah.

> **2 Chronicles 25:7,** "But a man of God came to him and said, 'O king, do not let the army of

Israel go with you, for the Lord is not with Israel, with all these Ephraimites. But go, act, and be strong for the battle. Why should you suppose that God will cast you down before the enemy? For God has power to help or to cast down.'"

King Amaziah was king of Judah. Israel was far more disobedient than Judah. But Amaziah was fearful and wanted help, so he hired an extra 100,000 Israelites to help him. The man of God, his name left out of the story, warned him against this. He listened, but look at his question. It is the question all frugal stewards of the Lord ask.

> **2 Chronicles 25:9,** "And Amaziah said to the man of God, 'But what shall we do about the hundred talents that I have given to the army of Israel?'"

The man of God was suggesting King Amaziah NOT follow through with his plan, but the King was concerned about the "resources he would be wasting" if he did not follow through with his plan.

Don't get me wrong, stewardship is important. Wasting resources is NOT good, but following through with a plan because you "have already spent the money" is not a good enough reason.

King Amaziah was faced with an issue all pastors are faced with at some time. Do I obey God's directive and take a turn even if it means "wasting resources" that I have spent out of fear of whatever? Or do I fall headlong into this regardless of what the Lord says because I want to be "a good steward?"

This is a tough dilemma. Because the money was spent because he was fearful. Now he is fearful the money will be wasted.

The man of God responds to King Amaziah:

> **2 Chronicles 25:9a,10,** "The man of God answered, 'The Lord is able to give you much more than this.' Then Amaziah discharged the army that had come to him from Ephraim to go home again. And they became **very angry** with Judah and returned home in **fierce anger.**"

Doing what's right is never easy especially when it means going against what you have already decided.

I hate wasting resources, but look at what occurs because obedience mattered more to King Amaziah than stewardship.

> **2 Chronicles 25:11,** "But Amaziah took courage and led out his people and went to the Valley of Salt and struck down 10,000 men of Seir."

He won! God gave him the victory in spite of his wasting resources due to his fear he couldn't win. He realized God is SOVEREIGN, even over His failure.

That gives me great hope as a pastor to lead. My good success as a pastor is not primarily determined by my ability to lead or make good decisions but by my obedience to do what God says regardless of what I have decided to do at that point.

The consequences of failure have no bearing on the outcome God has for your pastorate if you choose to obey at the point at which you realize you can't do this without God's directive.

King Amaziah realized this. He had a choice. Do I follow my plan and try and salvage the resources I have wasted or do I abandon my plan and trust the sovereign God to do what the man of God said?

I remember, in 2010, when we had to cut $500k from the budget, renegotiate contracts, and figure out how to survive. In the midst of this confusing season, I was told more than once, abandon the loan you have on the church building, abandon the unsecured loan you have with the former landlord and move on.

I wanted to.

Everything in me wanted to. I wanted to walk away from the mistakes I had made. I wanted to be done with the pressure that lay before us. I was in the opposite predicament of King Amaziah. If I walked away, we could start over in a building elsewhere and those who were committed to funding would stay with me.

I had a Christian finance company telling me not to pay the unsecured loan to our former landlord. I had some of my church leadership telling me not to pay the mortgages to the Christian finance company.

Here is what I know, "wasted resources" is not a good enough reason to walk away. "Wasted resources" is not a good reason to ignore what God is saying.

Be determined to pastor through leadership failure.

I take full responsibility for the mess we were in at the time.

I learned in that season from 2010 to 2017, "God is able to give you much more than this."

I was told we had a building we can't afford to pay for. We had a roof and HVAC that needed replaced, with no money. Our church had dwindled by 23%. We had laid off staff that mattered more than a building. The accusations were thick. And many of them were true.

I remember taking a stand. I looked the President of our Christian finance company in the face and said, "The same integrity that pays you pays our former landlord's unsecured loan."

I looked my leadership in the face and said,

"I led us into this, by God's grace I will lead us out."

People may not want you to lead them when you have failed them, but God does.

He wants you to get to the end of yourself.

It takes great humility to have the courage to trust God when you have royally screwed it up.

You don't stop swinging the sword because your aim is off.

You take better aim.

Seven years later, here is what I know.

By God's grace, I did.

And so can you.

In that seven-year period we NEVER missed a payment on anything, we received four $100k gifts, an insurance settlement of $700k, we launched a church planting center, helped partner to plant seventy three churches and counting, have seen 3300 people, in twenty-four years, follow Christ in believer's baptism, launched two new locations for Vanguard in addition to our original location, and our church's finances have NEVER been better.

I am a better leader now, but not because I have more confidence in myself because I led us out of this, but because I have a greater awareness of my need of Him.

COMMON FAILURE #2: WORSHIPPING YOUR SUCCESS.

I remember when our worship pastor, Richie Fike, co-wrote, "We Believe." Yes, the song Newsboys made famous. Part of it was crafted in the hallowed halls of Vanguard after our crash as a church. Pretty cool! Didn't see that coming.

Fike said he remembered how the Enemy would attack him before he wrote this song. The Enemy would say, "You don't have what it takes." But once he had a song "make it" the voice changed from "You don't have what it takes" to "Aren't you something?"

The Enemy will never relent. If he can't destroy you by reminding you of your failures then he will use your success to tempt you to bow down and worship him over your Holy God.

This is called Idolatry. It is failure to worship God for your success.

King Amaziah had this problem. He started out good but his success led to his sinful demise.

> **2 Chronicles 25:14-17,** "After Amaziah came from striking down the Edomites, he brought the gods of the men of Seir and set them up as his gods and worshiped them, making offerings to them. Therefore the Lord was angry with Amaziah and sent to him a prophet, who said to him, 'Why have you sought the gods of a people who did not deliver their own people from your hand?' But as he was speaking, the king said to him, 'Have we made you a royal counselor? Stop! Why should you be struck down?' So, the prophet stopped, but said, 'I know that God has **determined** to **destroy you**, because you have done this and have not listened to my counsel.'"

God won't throw you away because of your failures, or destroy you. However, He will NOT tolerate you taking credit for His work in you and not giving Him the glory. If you bow down and worship your success over Him, He will strike you down like He did King Amaziah.

> **2 Chronicles 25:17-20,23,** "Then Amaziah king of Judah took counsel and sent to Joash the son of

Jehoahaz, son of Jehu, king of Israel, saying, 'Come, let us look one another in the face.' And Joash the king of Israel sent word to Amaziah king of Judah ... You say, 'See, I have struck down Edom,' and your heart has lifted you up in boastfulness. But now stay at home. Why should you provoke trouble so that you fall, you and Judah with you?

"But Amaziah would not listen, for it was of God, in order that he might give them into the hand of their enemies, because they had sought the gods of Edom. **And Joash King of Israel captured Amaziah.**"

Eventually, Amaziah was assassinated, not because of his failure, but because of his "success."

Failure doesn't keep you from "good success" with God but "success" idolatry does.

I have "failed" much in my pastorate and I am sure there are other failures that await me.

My humility to take better aim and trust God to lead me is however not my greatest challenge. It is remembering where my strength comes from when the success comes.

God told Israel:

Deuteronomy 8:7.9-11,17-19, "For the Lord your God is bringing you into a **good land**, a land in which you will eat bread without scarcity, in which you will lack nothing, a land whose stones are iron ... And you shall eat and be full, and you shall bless the Lord your God for the **good land**

he has given you. Take care **lest you forget the lord** ... Beware lest you say in your heart, '**My power and the might of my hand have gotten me this wealth.**' you shall remember the Lord your God, for it is he who gives you power to get wealth ... if you forget the Lord your God and go after other gods ... I solemnly warn you today that you shall surely perish."

Your greatest failure could be your success.

Repent of pride, daily, and ask the Lord to do whatever He has to do to keep you dependent upon Him.

Paul understood this:

> **2 Corinthians 12:8,9,** "Three times I pleaded with the Lord about this, that it should leave me. But he said to me, 'My grace is sufficient for you, for my power is made perfect in weakness.' Therefore, I will **boast** all the more gladly of my **weaknesses**, insults, hardships, persecutions, and calamities. For when I am weak, then I am strong."

Don't ask for success or failure. Ask for dependence.

It will enable you not to hide your failures or worship your successes.

COMMON FAILURE #3: MISUSE OF ANGER.

Most great leaders are passionate leaders. Most passionate leaders can be angry leaders.

James 4:19,20, "Know this, my beloved brothers: let every person be quick to hear, slow to speak, slow to anger; for the **anger of man does not produce the righteousness of God.**"

The anger of man does not accomplish the righteousness of God. Then I won't be angry as a pastor.

Easier said than done. One of the humblest men to ever live was Moses.

Numbers 12:3, "Now the man Moses was very meek (humble), more than all people who were on the face of the earth."

Moses was charged with leading God's people. They eventually wore him down as they have me and will you.

Psalm 106:32,33, "They angered him (Moses) at the waters of Meribah, and it went ill with Moses on their account, for they made his spirit bitter, and he spoke rashly with his lips."

Previously, Moses's staff had been used as a representation of God's presence. He held it up and the waters parted. Earlier he touched the rock and water came out. But at Meribah, he lost it and hit the rock. Water came out. His leadership was effective, but not God-honoring. You can get the result you are looking for the wrong way.

God is NOT after results.

He is after obedience to His voice.

He does not want us to use our unrighteous anger to motivate people to do what He wants them to do.

He doesn't want us to use our "force" alone to get His people what they want or to accomplish what we want. My friend Richie Fike once said to me, "I think you can make anything happen even if it isn't God's will." I am not sure that is true, but it has caused me to pause often over the years and ask myself if my accomplishments are born out of the root of my strength and sheer determination or by the prompting and leading of the spirit of God?

How you accomplish something is just as important to God as what you accomplish.

> **Numbers 20:2,3,6-9,** "Now there was no water for the congregation. And the people quarreled with Moses and said, 'Would that we had perished when our brothers perished before the Lord!' Then Moses and Aaron went from the presence of the assembly to the entrance of the tent of meeting and fell on their faces. And the glory of the Lord appeared to them, and the Lord spoke to Moses, saying, 'Take the staff, and assemble the congregation, you and Aaron your brother, and **tell** the rock before their eyes to yield its water. So you shall bring water out of the rock for them and give drink to the congregation and their cattle.' And Moses took the staff from before the Lord, as he commanded him."

> **Numbers 20:10-12,** "Then Moses and Aaron gathered the assembly together before the rock, and he said to them, 'Hear now, you rebels: shall

we bring water for you out of this rock?' And Moses lifted up his hand and **struck** the rock with his staff **twice**, and water came out **abundantly** ... And the Lord said to Moses and Aaron, 'Because you **did not believe in me**, to uphold me as **holy** in the eyes of the people of Israel, therefore you shall not bring this assembly into the land that I have given them.'"

You know why you are so angry as a pastor. Same reason I am at times. You are doing what God called you to do in your strength and you think it is your job to provide for God's people instead of realizing you are the conduit not the source. You are the glove not the hand.

He is the potter. You are the clay.

He wants to mold you as a pastor into a shape the people you lead can see and experience His holiness through, but you feel the pressure to be Him. He doesn't want you to be Him. He wants you to be you.

You don't have to take up a reproach for God against His people or for His people against Him. You can't solve everyone's problems like they want you to but neither does He expect you to. God is not looking for pastors who can be expert hands.

The glove doesn't get to tell the hand how to hand. It just gets to be the glove. But like me, like you, like Moses, the glove sometimes gets tired of getting the unholiness of God's people all over their lives while being expected to live holy on the inside due to the hand of God, the holy hand of God.

God is not looking at the success of the glove to determine His worth or its. He is looking at the glove to see if it cares more for the hand than how it is being treated by the exterior forces against it like ministry.

Moses was angry and anger clouds our judgment and causes us to function in roles that are effective at times but not honoring to God.

I remember the first time we fired someone at our church. At the time, the elder board had to rule on this from my recommendation. I recommended they fire a staff member after a series of attempts to restore him. I met with them, they agreed we should fire him. Then we brought him in and fired him. He slowly started picking apart the board and they caved (in my opinion) and said they didn't want to fire him they were just going along with me.

I dismissed the staff member and when I walked back into the room, I was irate. I closed the door and I slammed my fist on the table and said, "I will be damned if I am going to submit to a board that doesn't have my back." When I hit the table, the elder's coffee cup nearest me jumped off the table and went all over the table and all over him and others. I was right in being hurt. I was wrong in being angry and taking it out on them in that way.

I lost elders that day and others who eventually left the church and never came back. I regret it, but I can't reverse it and neither could Moses. He lost his opportunity to lead Israel into the promised land because of his anger. I lost the opportunity to lead them because of this.

God is more concerned about your holiness, "how you go about something for Him," more than "what you accomplish for Him." The world and even the church you pastor will often be the opposite. And you may even get fired for making holiness more important to you than effectiveness, if so, so be it. Don't use it as an excuse to not be effective, but equally don't make it more important than it is.

Moses learned the hard way and so have I over the years. The result is loss of blessing over the long haul and eventually ineffectiveness in the pastorate because of lack of holiness. The anger of man NEVER accomplishes the righteousness of God. Sheer determination of will is not enough to please God because eventually our calling outruns our will and failure and anger become our partner and motivational means.

You won't last long in the pastorate at that burn rate.

Peter learned this the hard way. He burned out at Jesus's darkest hour and ran.

I don't know what Peter felt and thought those three days after his failures. Maybe a lot of anger toward himself, others, and maybe even God. I don't know.

But I do know what went through Jesus's mind. The Bible records it.

> **Mark 16:1,2,5-7,** "When the Sabbath was past, Mary Magdalene, Mary the mother of James, and Salome bought spices, so that they might go and anoint him (Jesus). And very early on the first day of the week, when the sun had risen, they went

> to the tomb. And entering the tomb, they saw
> a young man sitting on the right side, dressed in
> a white robe, and they were alarmed. And he said
> to them, 'Do not be alarmed. You seek Jesus of
> Nazareth, who was crucified. He has **risen**; he is
> not here. But go, tell his disciples and **Peter** that
> he is going before you to **Galilee.**'"

Jesus made a point of telling the angel to tell the women, he would meet the disciples and Peter in Galilee.

Galilee, the place Peter was from. The place that gave him his accent. The accent that betrayed him to the young servant girl and led to his triple denial of Jesus in the darkest hour of his Savior's life.

He could still hear the words he spoke to Jesus, "Never Lord, I will go to death with you."

Jesus wasn't trying to pour salt in Peter's wounded heart. He was trying to bandage a heart that believed his failure was permanent and God's grace was limited.

Jesus was headed back to where it all began for Peter because he had EVERY intention of showing Peter his failure was not permanent but His calling was.

Jesus knew Peter would fail. He even told Peter He would fail. Peter didn't believe Him.

Failure is inevitable.

How you handle that inevitability will shape the rest of your life and pastorate.

"Never let success go to your head and never let failure go to your heart." Author Unknown.

Easier said than done. Right?

Winston Churchill said,

"Success is not final, failure is not fatal: it is the courage to continue that counts."

And it does take courage and lots of it because the voices are never louder than when your failure is the talk of those who once followed you.

This can destroy your heart as a pastor to the point that you start condemning yourself like those you once led are condemning you. Even the strongest heart in the pastorate faints, eventually.

I know what it feels like to have your heart condemn you.

What do you do? At this point, the voices don't care as long as it doesn't involve continuing on the journey you were once on.

The legendary basketball coach of UCLA, John Wooden, said:

"Failure isn't fatal, but failure to change may be."

The grace of God doesn't excuse your failure, it redeems it.

John tells us:

> **1 John 3:20,** "For whenever our heart condemns us, God is greater than your heart and he knows everything."

This is why the discipline of meditation is so important because the voices inside of us get loud, especially loud during failure. The voices become feelings that are pervasive and can quickly become permanent. To me this is the hardest thing about staying somewhere you have "failed." But if you weather it, they might just name a fish after you. ☺

The voice of God speaks again to Peter:

"Go tell the disciples and Peter, 'See you in Galilee.'"

"See you in the town where it all began."

I have been to Galilee. I have eaten the white fish that is fished out of the Sea of Galilee, known as the "Fish of Saint Peter."

I have sat on the edge of the Sea of Tiberias, incredible town, and wondered out loud, "Why does Peter have a fish named after him in a region where he failed so miserably?"

Thousands of years ago, Peter heard a group of women repeat the words of the angel who spoke on behalf of Jesus. He heard them say, "Jesus said, go tell the disciples and Peter, I will meet them in Galilee."

His failure didn't keep him from hearing the voice of God. Matter of fact, it made his ability to hear God's voice sharper still.

He wanted to believe, again. It was his choice. Just as it is your choice.

Just as it takes courage, it also takes faith. It takes faith to believe that failure can be redeemed and God's grace can swallow our greatest mistakes.

It takes hope to believe that the future doesn't have to be defined by the past, but can be used to shape a more effective present.

It takes patience to wait for Jesus to come get you after you have royally screwed up the pastorate.

But none of this is out of our reach. And the story of Peter proves this to us.

Look at how Peter responded to the voice of the angel through the women.

Luke 24:12, "Peter arose and **ran** to the tomb."

Hope restored requires action.

Failure drives us away from God and closer to our prideful center. Hope drives us back to the empty tomb.

And just as Jesus was no longer in the tomb, Peter was soon to learn his failure was no longer a part of his future.

> **John 21:1,4,7,12,15,** "After this Jesus revealed himself again to the disciples by the Sea of Tiberias, and he revealed himself in this way. Just as the day was breaking Jesus stood on the shore;

That disciple whom Jesus loved therefore said to Peter, 'It is the Lord!' When Simon Peter heard that it was the Lord, he put on his outer garment, for he was stripped for work, and threw himself into the sea. Jesus said to them, 'Come and have breakfast.' When they had finished breakfast, Jesus said to Simon Peter, 'Simon, son of John, do you love me **more** than these?'"

Peter responds:

John 21:15a, "'Yes, Lord; you **know** that I love you.' He said to him, 'Feed my lambs.'"

Meaning, pastor my people.

We know Jesus asked him two more times. But the second and third time He didn't ask him if he loved Him **more** than the other disciples.

Peter had learned his lesson. He didn't need to be the "greatest" pastor. He needed to just be great for God. And all he had to do to do that was to love Jesus. The greatest gift a pastor can give his church is to love Jesus with all his heart, soul, mind, and strength. If you and I as pastors love Jesus, love of Christ will be permeated throughout the body of Christ.

But what about our failures?

What about them?

Do they define us?

Maybe, for a time.

But ultimately, Jesus defines us by our love for His sheep, His people.

He wants us to get up out of our failures and love His people well.

The most important call to the pastorate is certainly the initial call, but after that don't forget the recall. Before you quit because of your failure, ask God to recall you.

In 2014, I stood on the edge of the Sea of Galilee by the Papyrus of Peter asking God to recall me.

Paul said:

> **Philippians 3:12-14,** "Not that I have already obtained this or am **already perfect**, but I press on to make it my own, because Christ Jesus made me his own … But one thing I do, **forgetting what lies behind** and **straining forward** to what lies ahead, I press on toward the goal for the prize of the upward **call** of God in Christ Jesus."

As a pastor, my dad used to say, "You know what a rut is, don't you?" "It is a grave with both ends kicked out of it."

It will require effort on your part to get out of the rutted season you find yourself in, maybe right now.

I re-read the story of Peter. I remember the deep pain I felt from my failures as a pastor in 2010 and beyond. I was paralyzed by those failures and defined by my past.

I was finished. I had come to that sea's edge to see what limitation and failure looked like and as I looked out over those waters, I remembered on these waters where Peter walked and then almost drowned, he was later met by His Savior, whom he failed, thrice, and was reminded that Jesus was not yet done with him. For his calling was permanent, but his failure was temporary.

Failure was not his death sentence but his tutor to prepare him for the rest of the calling Jesus had on his life. His failure was behind him, but his calling was ahead of him.

> **John 21:18,19,** (Peter) "Truly, truly, I say to you, when you were young, you used to dress yourself and walk wherever you wanted, but when you are old, you will stretch out your hands, and another will dress you and carry you where you do not want to go. (This he said to show by what kind of death he was to glorify God.) And after saying this he said to him, '**Follow me.**'"

You know why they named a fish after Peter?

Because he didn't let his failure dictate his calling.

He kept going.

He asked for a recall.

You know what a recall is, don't you? It is when a manufacturer "recalls" a product because it has a defect. Peter detected a defect and knew he needed a recall to his manufacturer.

People admire failures who don't give up.

They even name fish after them.

Johnny Cash said:

> "You build on failure. You use it as a stepping stone. Close the door on the past. You don't try to forget the mistakes, but you don't dwell on it. You don't let it have any of your energy, or any of your time, or any of your space."

Let me say it another way:

Your failure doesn't dictate your calling, Jesus does.

He is asking you to follow Him into your future. He is asking you to learn what you need to learn from the failures of your pastorate. But He is also asking you to lead, again, in the pastorate. He is asking you to let Him be Lord and you be servant. He is asking you to trust Him to redeem your failure and to have faith to believe in His sovereign grace over your life. Just like Peter, He **knew** before He called you, you would fail. He is asking you to let go of that failure. Turn your back on it like I did that day on the edge of the Sea of Galilee.

As I look back on that season, I learned these things contributed to my failure:
1) I made assumptions about growth off of what people told me, others' experiences, and what I thought God was telling me.
2) I signed agreements too early off of future assumptions of success.

3) I let one elder have too much influence. I must be accountable to a board of elders not one elder.

4) I told people what God was saying instead of discovering with them through a process of God's direction.

5) Like David, I made numbers too important.

6) I tried to force people into things instead of leading them into them.

7) I let my woundedness cause me to become defensive and shortsighted in my decisions.

8) I realized people don't do what you expect they do what you inspect.

9) I mistook selfish ambition for zeal to do God's work. I needed a certain measure of success to feel important and it tempted me to risk too much too quickly.

10) I allow my envy of others' success to dictate decisions.

From these self-discoveries,

1) I learned to better listen to teams not individuals.

2) I probed new opportunities slower.

3) I remembered why I started in the first place.

4) I ask for new vision.

5) I realized to err is human.

6) I continue to assess what can be learned without feeling like a failure today.

7) I realized you need to grow too as a pastor, but many aren't mature enough to see this about you to stay with you, but Jesus is.

My pastor friend, Jon Elsberry, taught me a lot about number seven.

8) I learned some will stay with you because they believe in the calling God has on your life more than they believe in your ability to do it perfectly. (This is a good thing)

9) I realized the hardest thing about the pastorate is forgiving yourself when others won't.

10) I realized, if at first you don't succeed, ask for a recall! ☺

Jesus will meet you on the shore's edge of your failure as He met Peter and as He met me.

With tears streaming down my face, I learned that day the difference between tears and bitter tears. Bitter tears don't believe they can ever be redeemed. Tears believe redemption is just beyond our failure mixed into the future calling God has on our lives.

I am reminded of the good words of the Psalmist:

> **Psalm 73:26,** "My flesh and my heart may **fail,** but God is the strength of my heart and my portion forever."

Good Pastor, let go of the bitter tears of your past failure. They don't define your future pastorate. Your best doesn't have to be good enough because His grace is.

He doesn't expect your best to be "good enough."

He never did.

He wants your love.

The only failure that matters is whether or not you will stop loving Jesus as a pastor.

Go tell the disciples and Pastor Peter.

He is waiting for you at the empty tomb of past pastoral failure.

Run.

Your future pastorate is dependent upon it, **be determined to pastor through failure, Good Pastor!**

CHAPTER 12

DETERMINED TO PASTOR THROUGH TEMPTATION

Do you remember the first time you heard the voice of the Devil?

I do.

He said to me as clear as day, "Why don't you call her? I bet she's home and her husband isn't. Better yet, why don't you just drive by her house and see if she is home?"

I was a young church planter in my twenties working on a sermon. I was fasting and attempting to hear from God.

All I could hear was the Devil's voice that day.

And my flesh wanting to agree with the words I was hearing.

I won't ever forget that day.

Franklin P. Jones says:

"What makes resisting temptation difficult for many people is they don't want to discourage it completely."

I could unfortunately relate that day.

When I was eighteen years old, I made a commitment to God to walk in purity in my mind and in my actions in all areas of my life.

I have walked in this battle for over three decades now and I have learned a few things along the way.

C.S. Lewis understood the battle when he said:

"No man knows how bad he is till he has tried very hard to be good."

ALL of us have temptations in our lives that we think at times will inevitably get the best of us, if we are honest.

Sometimes we can be so discouraged by our struggles and temptations that we begin to believe the lie that the only way to get rid of a temptation is to yield to it.

Jesus told Peter:

> **Luke 22:31,32,** "Simon, Simon, behold, Satan demanded to have you that he might sift you like wheat, **but I have prayed for you that your faith may NOT FAIL**. And when you have turned again, strengthen your brothers."

Jesus is praying for you right now that your faith may not fail. Your purity, pastorate, integrity, family, and other brothers and sisters are dependent upon you recognizing and acknowledging that Jesus is praying for your purity in the battle of temptation you are in right now.

You and I have an Enemy who seeks to destroy us. He wants to "sift us as wheat." Meaning, he wants to tear our faith apart. He will say things to you like:

> "Your ministry doesn't matter anyway. You can't do this. No one cares. It won't make a difference if you do or you don't. You have earned this. You deserve this. God doesn't care. You have done enough good to earn the right to do some things you want to do."

The Enemy wants to isolate you. He wants to overwhelm you. He wants you to feel the darkness and assume there is no one in the darkness with you because you can't see them or feel them at times. He wants you to quit, give up, give in, indulge, and then, he will destroy you.

Jesus told Peter, "Satan has DEMANDED to have you that he might *sift* you like wheat." What does that mean?

Sifting wheat means to "tear apart." He wants to tear apart your faith.

Peter tells us later:

> **1 Peter 5:8,** "Be sober-minded; be watchful. **Your adversary** the devil prowls around like a roaring lion, **seeking someone to devour.**"

Peter has learned from first-hand experience what Jesus previously warned him about. He had a powerful adversary seeking to devour him.

You have an adversary who hates you and your faith in Jesus. He HATES you, your faith, and your pastorate. He wants to consume you.

If you and I are going to pastor through temptation we must first:

1. ACKNOWLEDGE YOUR POWERFUL ENEMY, SATAN

He is REAL.

You want to know how arrogant the Devil is? He tempted Jesus with Scripture. He ain't afraid of you!

Satan is not intimidated by you, regardless of how well known of a pastor you are in Christ's Kingdom.

He seeks to unleash hell on ALL of us who claim the name of Jesus.

He speaks to your soul and you can hear him. Especially when your flesh wants to agree with him. This is why it is SO important to learn how to hear the voice of God. I guarantee you, the longer you are in the pastorate, the more the Enemy will speak to you to discourage you, tempt you, and seek to defeat you.

He is powerful. God tells us this. Jesus calls him "the ruler of this world" in John 16:11. Paul refers to him as "the god of this world" in 2 Corinthians 4:4 and "the prince of the power of the air" in Ephesians 2:2. The story of Job best shows the role Satan plays and the power God has allowed him to have for now.

> **Job 1:6,7,** "Now there was a day when the sons of God came to present themselves before the Lord, and Satan also came among them. The Lord said to Satan, 'From where have you come?'"

Do you see and get the implication here?

God talks to the Devil and the Devil talks to God. We see this in Job. We see this when Jesus told Peter, "Satan has demanded to sift you as wheat."

Here is HOW it works. God is sovereign. Satan has to ask to do anything to God's children. God has to say yes for anything of Satan to touch us. I know, "Why does God do this?" Stay with me. We will get to that way later, but it is important for you to realize that God KNOWS you have an Enemy. He talks to him. Satan can't talk to us UNLESS Jesus lets him. We see this in the story of Job.

> **Job 1:7a,8,** "Satan answered the Lord and said, 'From going to and fro on the earth, and from walking up and down on it.' And the Lord said to Satan, '**Have you considered my servant Job, that there is none like him on the earth, a blameless and upright man, who fears God and turns away from evil?**'"

Good Pastor, could Almighty God say this of you to the Devil?

Job was the richest man in the world, but God didn't mention this in His description of Job to the Devil.

God is not impressed with our wealth or success. The size of our bank account or the size of *our* (aka HIS) church. He is not impressed with our talent or treasure. He gave it to us.

But here is what God is impressed with from Job: "None like him on the earth." Why? Because he is: 1) A blameless man, 2) an upright man, 3) he fears God, 4) he turns away from evil and not towards it.

How about you pastor? Are you blameless, upright, fearing God, and turning away from evil?

In your pastorate, are you turning *away* from evil or *to* it?

> **Job 1:9-12,** "Then Satan answered the Lord and said, 'Does Job fear God for no reason? Have you not put a hedge around him and his house and all that he has, on every side? You have blessed his work of his hands, and his possessions have increased in the land. But stretch out your hand and touch all that he has, and he will curse you to your face.' And the Lord said to Satan, 'Behold, **all** that **he has is in your hand.**' So Satan went out from the presence of the Lord."

In Job 1:13-19, Satan took everything Job had and killed all of his children. We have a powerful Enemy.

Job responds:

> **Job 1:20-22,** "Then Job arose and worshiped. And he said, 'Naked I came from my mother's womb, and naked shall I return. The Lord gave, and the Lord has taken away; blessed be the name of the Lord.' In all this Job did not sin or charge God with wrong."

Job proved God's point. A man stood up to the most powerful angel in the universe.

Satan had lost to Almighty God, Yahweh.

Satan had now lost to Job, a man.

Satan is the god of this world. He took ALL of Job's worldly possessions and his children.

Job REFUSED to bow down.

Satan was bent.

> **Job 2:1,3,** "Again there was a day when the sons of God came to present themselves before the Lord, and Satan also came among them to present himself before the Lord. And the Lord said, to Satan, 'Have you considered my servant Job, that there is none like him on the earth, a blameless and upright man, who fears God and turns away from evil? He still holds fast his integrity, **although you incited me against him to destroy him without reason.**'"

I have heard MANY people over the years say, "Well, Job, must have done something to deserve what happened to him." So many people don't want to accept the way the world really is. Good people suffer bad, a lot. And for a time, God allows it. We see this in the text.

Satan keeps pressing Job through the Lord:

> **Job 2:4-6,** "Then Satan answered the Lord and said, 'Skin for skin! All that a man has he will give for his life. But stretch out your hand and touch his bone and his flesh, and he will curse you to your face.' And the Lord said to Satan, 'Behold, he is in your hand; only spare his life.'"

God gave Satan complete access to Job, except for the taking of his life. He would NOT allow that.

> **Job 2:7,9,10,** "So Satan went out from the presence of the Lord and struck Job with loathsome sores form the sole of his foot to the crown of his head. Then his wife said to him, 'Do you still hold fast your integrity? Curse God and die.' But he said to her, 'You speak as one of the foolish women would speak. Shall we receive good from God, and shall we not receive evil?' **In all this Job did not sin with his lips.**"

Job was a righteous stud! But he was also human.

> **Job 3:1,** "After this Job opened his mouth and cursed the day of his birth."

Every human being has their limitations. The Psalmist says:

> **Psalm 103:13,14,** "As a father shows compassion to his children, so the Lord shows compassion

to those who fear him. For he (God) knows our frame; he remembers that we are dust."

Job knew he was up against a powerful Enemy. But he knew God to be MORE powerful.

We should not curse God in our temptations. We may curse the day of our birth like Job, but we don't curse God. He is our ONLY source of HOPE. Job knew this and told his wife so.

He spends thirty-five chapters pleading his case to God in front of his friends who, unfortunately after seven days, open their mouths and remove all doubt that they didn't know the same God that Job knew.

Job addressed his concerns, pain, anguish, hurt, and frustration to God. This is what we are supposed to do. When we do this, we are acknowledging that God is SOVEREIGN over Satan.

We have a powerful Enemy. We have a more powerful Savior.

The Enemy can't touch anything God doesn't allow.

However, when you are tempted, I am not suggesting you blame God. James, Jesus's brother, addresses this:

> **James 1:13,** "Let no one say when he is tempted, 'I am being tempted by God,' for God cannot be tempted with evil, and he himself tempts no one."

Satan is called the Tempter for a reason. But Job's life is not an exception to the redemptive story of God. Peter's interaction with Jesus proves this. Satan has to ask permission from God to come after us.

I am glad.

He doesn't just wreak havoc on us whenever he wants to. Otherwise, he would never let up.

God has to give him the green light.

Why?

This is a tough reality no believer wants to embrace.

> **Romans 8:17,** "And if children, then heirs—heirs of God and fellow heirs with Christ, provided we suffer with him in order that we may also be glorified with him."

We can't be glorified with Jesus if we are not willing to suffer with Him.

Suffering is our ticket to glorification with Jesus. You can't get on the bus to Christ's redemption for your life without it. Suffering is the Devil's means to beating us down and then temptation is His way of destroying us. It is his swift one-two punch that God allows him to unleash on each of us, including Jesus.

Jesus modeled this for us when He walked this earth.

> **Hebrews 5:7-9,** "In the days of his flesh, Jesus offered up prayers and supplications, with loud

cries and tears, to him who was able to save him from death, and he was heard **because of his reverence.** Although he was a son, **he learned obedience through what he suffered.** And being made perfect, he became the source of eternal salvation to all who obey him,"

That's beautiful. He got on the bus of suffering and passed EVERY test of temptation. He cried out to God the Father in reverence. He knew God the Father was His ONLY hope. He took every one-two punch Satan could throw at Him and came out sinless at the end of the train ride on the other side of the cross.

He learned obedience through suffering, and because He passed every test, He was made perfect in His flesh. This is the path God expects us to take too.

> **1 Peter 4:19,** "Therefore let those **who suffer according to God's will** entrust their souls to a faithful Creator while doing good."

Peter got it. Jesus perfected it.

This enabled Jesus to become the source of eternal salvation to all who obey Him.

> **Hebrews 4:14,15,** "Since then we have a great high priest who has passed through the heavens, Jesus, the Son of God, let us hold fast our confession. For we do not have a high priest who is unable to sympathize with our weaknesses, but **one who in every respect has been tempted as we are, yet without sin.**"

And by the way, temptation is not a mark of sinfulness. It is simply a mark of humanness. Jesus was tempted too. To be tempted is to be human. Pastor, you are not evil because you are tempted. You only become evil if you give into that sin.

How do we remain determined to pastor through temptation?

2. FOLLOW CHRIST'S MOST POWERFUL EXAMPLE.

Job set it up. Christ perfected it.

> **Hebrews 4:16,** "Let us then **with confidence draw near to the throne of grace,** that we may receive mercy and find grace to help in time of need."

Because Christ overcame every temptation that is common to you and me, He got off the bus to hell, and so can we.

There is no temptation you can face that Christ has not already faced and defeated its power.

We have to remember the example we have been given to follow and the power that comes with that example. I could dedicate this chapter to talking about the different temptations that pastors face. But I want to give the bulk of this chapter to teaching you how to resist and overcome temptation, and even thrive in God's presence, as you serve Him faithfully as a pastor, like Jesus did. And I want you to know something else before we go on this journey of discovering the steps to overcoming temptation as a pastor.

You have the MOST POWERFUL God of the universe living inside of you. He believes in you. He believes in you so much, He died for you. He believes in you so much, He called you. He believes in you so much. He stands with you *right now* swinging the sword and fighting off the enemies that seek to devour you.

Say this out loud:

> **1 John 4:4a,** "For he who is in you (me) is greater than he who is in the world."

Jesus lives inside of you. The force of Christ is greater than the force of Satan. He is not only within you. He is actively talking to God on your behalf when you find yourself facing the devastating ambushes the Enemy has set up against you. Remember this promise:

> **Romans 8:34a,** "Christ Jesus is the one who died—more than that, who was raised—who is at the right hand of God, who indeed is interceding for us."

What does it mean to intercede? It means Jesus is talking to the Father right now about you and me.

He loves us that much! And He assures us in that same passage:

> **Romans 8:39a,** "(Nothing) will be able to separate us from the love of God in Christ Jesus our Lord."

NOTHING!

James 4:7,10, "Submit yourselves therefore to God. Resist the devil, and he will flee from you. Humble yourselves before the Lord, and he will exalt you."

What does it mean to submit yourself to God? It means to voluntarily place yourself under the authority of Jesus. You are making yourself subject to His rules, His ways, and His law for you. It means you are abiding by the commands He has given you. You are humbling yourself before Him.

I remember when I was nineteen years old and working as an intern at a church in the Clearwater/Tampa area. I was housesitting for a family and I turned on the television where there was a less than appropriate scene on the television and sadly, I watched it longer than I should have. I finally turned it off and went into the bathroom to engage in behavior that every day since I was twelve years old and exposed to a pornographic movie had taught me how.

However, about six months prior I had gone through an accountability group and had learned how to overcome in this area of my life and take every thought captive in obedience to Christ. All the work I had done to get to this place of freedom was zapped during those few moments of engaging in that movie I shouldn't have been watching.

I was alone. I was vulnerable. I was exposed again and I was headed back down the path of addiction and stronghold. As I sat on the throne, the demons surrounded me, consumed me, and welcomed me back to the failure prison I had lived the last seven years of my life in. It didn't feel to me like I had a choice. It had me and I was once again a victim of its overwhelming power.

But here is what I learned that day.

I have a choice. As a follower of Jesus, I do not have to ever choose sin, but given the stronghold of the past, I would not overcome this through sheer will power. Some sins, maybe, but not this one.

As I went down the dark path of bondage again, I cried out to God and said, "God this is too overwhelming. I can't do this. I can't overcome this. I can't do this without you."

It was a powerful moment that was super vulnerable and embarrassing for me to share, but I share it in hopes that pastors will be saved from the dark grip of addictive behavior that leads to the destruction of their pastorate and sadly their families, marriages, and walk with the Lord.

In that moment, I heard the Lord say distinctly to me, "Drop to your knees and cry out to me."

Embarrassed and ashamed, but desperate, I fell off the toilet on to the floor sobbing and crawling across the floor out of the bathroom to the edge of the bed. Begging God to purify me from my bondage. I wept. I wept bitter tears like Peter after He had betrayed Jesus because I was so tired of sinning and giving into my fleshly desires to appease my flesh in the quiet and solitude of my life and betraying Jesus for my sin.

And on that day, I wrote this journal entry:

July 7, 1990: "It seems as if I cannot win, no matter how I try, my problem overwhelms me. God, I place my problem totally in your control and if I ever do something like I did tonight I pray that you take me on to glory. God, I want to serve you and you alone. And I am begging you to please deliver me from this mind game with Satan. Give me strength over the problem of being alone by myself and being tempted. Help me to realize that you are the one I am accountable to. Dear God, I love you and all I want to do is please you. So, I pray, God, give me strength and victory in this area. Thank you! My attitude is: broken and sorrowful."

I humbled myself that day, alone, in that house where no one but God could see me. But I knew I was naked before my Lord and victoriously pure in His presence. Hebrews tells us:

> **Hebrews 4:13,** "And no creature is hidden from his sight, but all are naked and exposed to the eyes of him to whom we must give account."

3. LIVE NAKED BEFORE HIM IN HUMILITY.

It could be the difference in the outcome of your pastorate many years later. It could be the difference in saying yes or no to a temptation to fantasize about someone other than your spouse. It could be the difference in you continuing to focus on the message you have to write or getting in your car and driving by their house to see if they are home alone. The Devil will find you. That is a guarantee. But will you find God's voice in that moment to guide you to humble yourself under His mighty hand so He can lift you up in His time for His glory?

That night, after weeping uncontrollably for longer than
I can remember and feeling God's presence in a way
I never had, I got up from the side of that bed victorious.
I felt more "saved" than I had ever felt in my life. I felt
free. Not free from the battle. Not free from the temptation.
But yes, free from the bondage. I knew I had a choice and
His strength was greater than the temptation of the Devil
that lured my flesh then and many times since to return.

Will you have a July 7 in your life? Will you come to the place,
alone, that you want God more than you want the pleasure
that comes from fulfilling the indulgence of your flesh?

It won't happen if you don't humble yourself under the
mighty hand of God. I can assure you of that. Resistance to
temptation is futile if God is not leading. The Lion will find
you and he will devour you.

When the disciples asked Jesus to teach them how to pray.
He said to them at one point in the prayer to pray like this:

> **Matthew 6:13,** "And lead us not into temptation,
> but deliver us from evil."

You won't overcome sin apart from Christ's strength. It is
not possible. But with His strength, nothing is impossible.

A few years ago, I got to go to Africa with Compassion
International. Toward the end of the trip, we made our
way to the savannah to see the wild life. It was amazing.
We got to drive up and sit right next to lions just a few feet
away. I asked the driver, "Why don't they try to attack us
in the open-air jeep? I will never forget his response. With
his British-African accent, he said:

"They can't distinguish between you and the jeep when you are in this jeep. Therefore, they don't realize they can get you. But the moment you step out of this jeep, they would crush your body and kill you instantly."

As I sat there staring at these man-eating lions, and observing this overwhelming power just a few feet away, it dawned on me that Jesus has been my "jeep" for a long time. Apart from Him, the Lion would have already devoured me alive a long time ago.

My strength comes from the "Jesus Jeep" that surrounds my heart and soul. I learned that for the first time on July 7, 1990, but I saw the picture of what it looked like when I sat in that jeep on the savannah a few years go. Thank you, Lord, for protecting me from the Lion and from myself as well.

I invite you to live naked before Him. It will give you the courage to do the next thing.

Peter says:

1 Peter 5:9, "Resist him, firm in your faith,"

4. STAND FIRM IN YOUR FAITH AGAINST SATAN.

Why is standing firm in your faith so important?

Isaiah 7:9a, "If you are not firm in faith, you will not be firm at all."

King David was not firm in his faith and it cost him, greatly.

> **1 Samuel 11:1-5,27a,** "In the spring of the year, the time when kings go out to battle, David sent Joab... It happened, late one afternoon, when David arose from his couch and was walking on the roof of the king's house, that he saw from the roof a woman bathing; and the woman was very beautiful. And David sent and inquired about the woman. And one said, 'Is not this Bathsheba ... the wife of Uriah the Hittite?' So David sent messengers and took her, and she came to him, and he lay with her. And the woman conceived, and she sent and told David, 'I am pregnant.' But the thing that David had done displeased the Lord."

I bet if you went up to David and said, "You are going to go on the balcony, see a beautiful woman, find out she is married, sleep with her, impregnate her, have her husband killed, and marry her."

He would have said to you, "You're crazy!"

But that is exactly what he did.

He never planned on falling, no one ever does. But if you are not standing firm in your faith as a pastor, you will NOT stand at all.

You have to choose purity and faithfulness *today*. No one will choose it for you or foster an environment where you don't need it. The Enemy will bombard you continually if you are not standing firm in your faith. He will destroy you.

Many years ago, I struggled with an attraction to another woman. I have since written about it in the marriage book my wife, Tosha, and I wrote together called *Real Marriage: Where Fantasy Meets Reality.*

Thankfully it never left the confines of my heart, but it was nonetheless lodged in my heart and I had to weed it out. During that season, someone gave me a book by Tom L. Eisenman called *Temptations Men Face: Straightforward Talk on Power, Money, Affairs, Perfectionism, and Insensitivity.*

I read it.

I have never read a book that explained the process a person goes through to reach the point of having an affair. I had no idea I even had an emotional attraction for someone besides my wife, but this book dug it out of me.

Tosha and I moved to Colorado Springs to start a church. Three years in we needed a break, bad. It was on that trip, my first trip away from the church, that I was convinced I was so burned out I could never come back. Over the days to follow, I started to come alive again and during this time of journaling, reflecting, and confessing I realized my heart had drifted and I went to work to do something about it.

I am so grateful for the help I got during that season of my life to learn myself. I had drifted in my heart and I didn't even know it. I wonder about David. Had he drifted and didn't even know it? God tells us David was a man after

His own heart. I want to be that kind of man, but even that kind of man drifts.

How do you stand firm in your faith against Satan?

Step #1: Know Thy Self.

Without going into great detail, I want to share the twelve steps Tom outlined in his book and then encourage you to explore it more in his book. These steps helped me to learn internal me and understand how I tick. I hope it does the same for you.

1) **Readiness.** The condition of emotional readiness that is causing you to lean away from your responsibilities. (I would both at home and at church)

Tom writes this:

> "If we look closely at the story of David and Bathsheba in 2 Samuel 11, it appears that this kind of emotional readiness was present in David. Several things indicate that his situation was abnormal. It was spring, 'The time that kings go off to war,' but David did not go. He stays at home (v.1). David was in bed, but could not sleep. He got out of bed to walk around the roof of the palace (v.2). Why did he not accompany his troops into battle?"

When we disengage our calling, we lose sight of ourselves and fill that void with something that will cost us greatly if we don't realize it quickly.

2) **Alertness.** You have a growing awareness of a particular person in your web of relationships.

3) **Innocent Meeting.** You have a "chance" meeting, but would deny any interest in each other.

4) **Intentional Meeting.** You have frequent meetings which look coincidental, but you have acted in an intentional way to increase the potential of crossing paths.

5) **Public Lingering.** You spend time together while in group settings.

6) **Private Lingering.** You find you are still together long after everyone else has left.

7) **Purposeful Isolating.** You start to plan times to be together, alone.

8) **Pleasurable Isolating.** You start planning times to be together for the sheer fun of it.

9) **Affectionate Embracing.** You start having secret longings for each other and you start embracing without letting go.

10) **Passionate Embracing.** You start touching and embrace for the purpose of passionate interchanges.

11) **Capitulation.** You give into sexual intercourse.

12) **Acceptance.** You admit, "We are having an affair."

How fast can you move through these stages? King David went through all twelve in one day. I found these stages to be very helpful in identifying my thoughts and the people in my life that I needed to limit their access to me if I wanted to go the distance in the pastorate and avoid moral failure.

Attraction is inevitable. You can't get married and turn off your attraction button. You have to protect your heart because no one else will. You have to know thy self. You have to know what makes you susceptible to temptation. You have to know what lures you in. You have to know the kind of people you can be attracted to and you have to build safeguards and talk freely and honestly with those in your life. You also have to make sure you don't lie to yourself. But most importantly you have to stay engaged in the battle.

Why did King David disengage the battle? We don't know. Was success becoming boring to him? Was he tired of winning? Was he tired and fatigued? Was he arrogant and felt he was above going to war? We don't know. But here is what we do know: He didn't go. And because he didn't go, it put him within proximity to Bathsheba on that day.

Remember July 7, 1990? I turned on the television and there was Bathsheba, so to speak. I had a choice to make. It would have been better had I never turned the television on by myself in a strange location. It would have been better had King David gone to war, but he didn't. And you and I will find ourselves in situations we shouldn't be in, but we are, and then we have to decide, where do we go from here?

King David got up and walked out on his balcony and saw her. He liked her. He wanted her. He got her. He had her. He killed her husband. He married her. God was not pleased.

How do stand firm in your faith against Satan?

2. Stay engaged in your calling.

I have had my fair share of opportunities to choose the wrong thing along the road of life. What has helped me more than anything is to remember the calling God has on my life. The text says, "At the time when Kings go off to war, David stayed home." You can't avoid sin if you refuse to engage your calling. It is the engagement of your calling that increases your protection against the attacks of the Enemy. (I know you also need breaks, accountability, rest, and reminders of God's promises to keep you dependent upon the Lord. We will talk about that in the final section of this book.)

But right now, you need to stay engaged. You need to remember your calling and you need to do what pastors do. So many guys I know over the years stop going into the office. They stop leading the parts of the church they just don't enjoy leading. They stop building into others because they have been hurt by people in their past. I beg you, good pastor, stay engaged in your calling. So, you are not as successful as you hoped you would be at this point. If you pull back like King David, you will be less.

The final thing David needed to do to stand firm in his faith against Satan was to:

3. Ask God to Make Sin Exceedingly Sinful.

My long-time prayer partner, Jon Elsberry, told me his dad, a Wesleyan pastor, who has since gone to heaven, used to pray, "Lord, make sin exceedingly sinful."

He got this idea from Romans 7:13 in the King James Version.

Romans 7:13a, "Sin ... might become exceedingly sinful."

As best as I can tell, when Paul wanted to overemphasize sin and how bad it was, He didn't use another adjective because there isn't one to describe sin worse than it is. When Paul says, "Sin ... might become exceedingly sinful." He was saying, "It is my prayer we realize just how bad it is."

Sin is against God. God represents EVERYTHING AND EVERYONE that is good. When we sin, we represent the opposite. He wants us to realize that is how bad sin is.

King David understood sin well. Matter of fact, when Nathan confronted him, he responded like this:

Psalm 51:3,4, "For I know my transgressions, and my sin is **ever before me**. Against you, you only (Lord), have I sinned and done what is evil in your sight."

Why was King David able to say with such confidence, "I have sinned and done what is evil in your sight, Lord"?

Is it because he got caught? No. I have known people who got caught and they refused to accept what they had done.

King David could say with confidence what he had done was sin because he humbled himself and was honest and God had made his sin exceedingly sinful to him. How?

Nathan the prophet came to King David after he confessed and told him what his punishment would be:

> **2 Samuel 12:13,14,** "David said to Nathan, 'I have sinned against the Lord.' And Nathan said to David, 'The Lord also has put away your sin; you shall not die. \Nevertheless, because by this deed you have utterly scorned the Lord, the child who is born to you shall **die.**'"

The child died soon after. Confession and consequence make sin real. And making it real makes it what it is, evil. When we feel the evil of our sin, sin becomes exceedingly sinful to us.

Is there a way to confess the temptation of sin before you have to confess the result of the temptation and live with the consequences? Trust me, anyone who has sinned as David has sinned would tell you, "Don't do it! Don't go there. It isn't worth it. The pleasure is never worth the pain."

Sin will always take you further than you want to go. Keep you longer than you want to stay. Cost you more than you want to pay.

For me, here is how I get sin to feel like sin before I have to experience the consequences to remember. When I am struggling with a sin, I will either write out that sin or say out loud to God these words, "God, I want to sin." And I will fill in the blank how I want to sin. Whatever it is. And it is embarrassing. I remember when I was struggling with having emotions for someone other than my wife. I said out loud,

"Lord, right now I want to commit adultery with someone who isn't my wife. Would you please take this out of my heart? Would you please allow me to feel what it would feel like to commit this sin, so I can know what it would cost me if I went there? Lord, I want to want you more than this sin, but I can't overcome this without you."

This prayer has taught me how to feel the exceeding sinfulness of sin without having to go there and learn the most difficult way.

Let these two verses sober you in the temptations of your life:

> **Numbers 32:23,** "Be sure and know your sins will find you out."

> **Hebrews 4:13,** "No creature is hidden from his sight, but ALL are naked and exposed to the eyes of him to whom we must give account."

The next time you hear the Devil's voice, take a page out of Jesus's playbook.

> **Matthew 4:8-10,** "The devil took (Jesus) to a very high mountain and showed him all the kingdoms of the world and their glory. And he said to him, 'All these I will give you, if you will fall down and worship me.' Then Jesus said to him, 'Be gone, Satan! For it is written "You shall worship the Lord your God and him only shall you serve."'"

I can't follow Jesus as a pastor and at the same time be chasing someone else's wife or amassing the kingdoms of popularity and success to gratify my flesh. I have to make a choice regarding what I want to worship, my flesh or Jesus, but I can't chase both and neither can you. But if you choose Jesus, the Devil must flee.

> **Matthew 4:11,** "Then the devil left him (Jesus), and behold, angels came and were ministering to him."

Good Pastor, you are no match for the Devil, but when we choose Jesus, the angel, Satan, must flee. Then the angels of God will minister to us as they did for Jesus and as they did for Job thousands of years ago.

They are pretty good at it.

Good Pastor, don't wait, like King David, until she's "pregnant," so to speak, to be intentional about a game plan to get yourself out of a temptation. It will be too late then.

You have two options: sin or submit?

There are no other options.

Stay submitted and engaged in the calling Jesus has on your life and His voice will take care of the rest. Or fall.

The choice is yours. I invite you to:

Remain determined to live out your calling as a pastor through temptation.

It won't kill you.

Hebrews 12:4, "In your struggle against sin you have not yet resisted to the point of shedding your blood."

Jesus did though.

And He overcame for you and for me.

And with Him, we good pastors can too.

SECTION #4:

DEPENDENCE ON GOD

CHAPTER 13

DEPENDENCE ON GOD THROUGH ACCOUNTABILITY

Vision always comes through an individual, but the accomplishment of that vision is always best served and lived out through a team.

The Bible tells us:

> **Proverbs 15:22,** "Without counsel plans fail, but with **many** advisers they succeed."

My good friend Vance said to me once, "You won't pull this off by yourself. No one is smart enough, strong enough, or talented enough to go it alone for a lifetime."

In twenty-plus years of pastoring, I have learned this valuable lesson over and over and over again.

You have heard the African Proverb: "If you want to go fast, go alone. If you want to go far, slow down and go **together."**

Everyone needs someone else to help fulfill God's purpose for their existence.

If no one in your life knows the real you, the fake you will eventually implode.

But it doesn't have to be that way.

Paul told the Ephesian elders:

> **Acts 20:28, "Pay careful attention to yourselves, and to all the flock,** in which the Holy Spirit has made you overseers, to care for the church of God, which he obtained with his blood."

You can go the distance and finish this race of pastoring, but you can't just lead others and be successful. You can't be a good pastor and not pay careful attention to yourself while tending to the flock entrusted to you.

Just as the best gift you can give your children is a healthy marriage, the best gift you can give your flock is a healthy you.

Your sermons eventually won't mean anything if you stop living them out yourself.

Are you paying as close attention to yourself as you are to your flock?

Who have you asked to help you pay close attention to you?

As we age, we have to learn how to be more dependent upon the Lord. And this strangely enough requires you to depend upon others. God didn't make you to live in a vacuum. He didn't make you to live isolated. Matter of fact, the Bible tells us the opposite.

> **Proverbs 18:1,** "Whoever isolates himself seeks his own desire; (not God's) he breaks out against **all** sound judgment."

My worst decisions have been made alone.

Isolation heightens selfishness. And selfishness kills sound judgment.

It doesn't matter how godly you become, you will always need others. Without others, your pride will get the best of you. With others, your humility will set you free to soar to the honor God has determined for your existence. Proverbs tells us:

> **Proverbs 18:12,** "Before destruction a man's heart is haughty, but humility comes before honor."

Do you know how to be dependent upon God through accountability with others? It is not just a good idea; it is the only idea that will sustain you for a lifetime to be a good pastor.

You can't check yourself enough not to wreck yourself. Someone has to help you.

Galatians 6:2, "Bear one another's burdens, and so **fulfill** the law of Christ."

You know what the law of Christ is? Love God and love others. If you bear each other's burdens, you will fulfill this. It is possible. I can love God and love others for a lifetime if I choose to live in dependence with others through accountability.

In 1989, during my first semester of college I had a guy ask me, "Do you want to be a part of an accountability group?"

My response, "What's that?"

He said, "It's where a group of guys get together and share their real lives and what is really going on, the good and the bad, and we pray for each other to become who God created us to be."

I said, "Sure, why not."

I had no idea this would change my life and pastorate forever.

It is in that group, and others since, that I have learned these truths that have sustained me thus far. I pray these do the same for you, good pastor.

There are a few keys to holding yourself accountable.

KEYS TO ACCOUNTABILITY:

Key #1: Right Attitude

It is important to have a right understanding of yourself in order to experience God's grace and favor for our lives.

I think Paul gives us the best view of self as a spiritual leader of others.

> **1 Timothy 1:15,16,** "The saying is trustworthy and deserving of full acceptance, that Christ Jesus came into the world to save sinners, **of whom I am the foremost. But I received mercy for this** reason, **that in** me, as the foremost, Jesus Christ might display his perfect patience as an example to those who were to believe in him for eternal life."

Let me say it in my vernacular.

No one is worse than me, but God is using my life to make Jesus wildly famous.

Some of us think too highly of ourselves and some of us think too lowly of ourselves. Neither is God's will. He wants us to have a right understanding of ourselves.

As pastors, we are not celebrities, we are servants. In the pastorate, some will treat you like a celebrity and some will treat you worse than dirt. Remember, you are neither.

I think the writer of Ecclesiastes captured this attitude best:

Ecclesiastes 7:16-19, "Be not **overly** righteous, and do not make yourself too wise. (in your own mind) Why should you destroy yourself? Be not **overly** wicked, neither be a fool. (in your life) Why should you die before your time? It is good that you should take of this, and from that withhold not your hand, for the one who fears God shall come out from both of them. **Wisdom gives strength to the wise man...**"

I have watched pastors be overly righteous and destroy themselves through legalism. I have watched pastors make fun of holiness and strict boundaries and live loose and fast with their lives and flame out way too soon.

Here is the bottom line, if you want a good view of yourself, fear God and apply His wisdom. How can you best fear God and get wisdom? The Bible has already told us through a multitude of counselors. If you are going to fear God and be dependent upon Him, you have to see yourself as **in need of others input** into your life. This is how God imparts wisdom to the areas of your life you can't hear Him on your own.

We ALL need this.

Key #2: Proximity

Accountability with others is best lived out with people who live near your real life.

I know pastors who have elder boards that hold them accountable that are made up of other pastors of other churches. This is the totality of their accountability. It is a flawed model and seldom works. Humanity needs proximity for holy sand paper to produce righteousness.

> **Proverbs 27:17,** "Iron sharpens iron, and one man sharpens another."

I am best served to be accountable to people who see my real life. Now you might say, "But I will be honest and tell them." You are assuming you have within yourself the ability to see and say everything that needs to be said. You have blind spots in your character. Do you know why they call them blind spots? Because you don't see them, but others will. Accountability from a distance is better than none, but proximity is the best form of accountability.

This is why church attendance is so important for believers. It puts them in proximity to other believers who, over time, can see things about their life they can't see on their own.

The best form of accountability is with people who are in proximity to your real life and pastorate.

Key #3: Honesty

You have to believe you truly need this.

You can't be helped if you can't be real. Accountability is a waste of your time and everyone else's if you are not going to discuss the difficult, embarrassing, and gut-wrenching truths about your life. You don't have to wallow in the details, but you can't just pretend they don't exist.

On churchleaders.com I found an article entitled, "10 Reasons Pastors Quit Too Soon."

These reasons are the areas where we as pastors need to have someone in our lives to whom we are honest about all of them with. They are as follows:

1) Discouragement.

2) Failure.

3) Loneliness

4) Moral Struggles.

5) Financial Pressures.

6) Anger due to comparison.

7) Burnout due to insecurity.

8) Physical Health.

9) Marriage/Family Challenges.

10) Busyness/Drivenness Challenges.

These are the areas that will trip you up the most as a pastor.

Are you intentional about addressing the issues of your life while helping your congregation with theirs? This is one of the hardest things about being a pastor.

Do you have someone (or some ones) in your life that you are discussing these ten areas of your life with? You don't have to discuss all ten with the same person, but do you have different people in your life holding you accountable in these areas?

Tosha and I have a very good marriage, but the pastorate puts so much pressure on our lives that we need a release valve. Jon and Sandi Elsberry have pastored us over the years and Shari Edgell Walker has counseled us. We have needed both, often. I have a sneaky suspicion, you do too.

It is sad how few pastors are known by anyone while carrying the burdens of so many. The pastorate is lonely and always will be. But lonely and alone are not the same thing.

People can't hold you accountable if you can't be real about what is really going on in your life.

I recently read an article about a pastor who fell morally. He lost his wife and family. Seems like a really nice guy. He had a couple hundred thousand followers on social media and the article was describing how destructive social media had been to his marriage, family, and ministry and how now that he was no longer in the pastorate, he was going to stop using social media because it had been, in his mind, a contributing factor to his demise. He was consumed with others liking his life more than liking it himself.

You can't fall in love with the ideal life you have created on social media for your followers, Pastor. It is not real. Reality requires honesty. Honesty creates a life you can love even when it is not ideal for social media.

I find it interesting that one of the first things pastors who have fallen morally do is stop using social media, at least for a time. It shows how it is not the core of your life and who you are. And it never will be.

Like your life whether anyone else on social media ever does and, Lord willing, you won't ever have to make that decision.

Use social media to share your life with others, not as a tool to prop up its "importance."

As they say, "Honesty is the best policy."

KEY #4: CONSISTENCY

Vince Lombardi once said, "Perfect practice makes perfect."

Accountability must be a discipline you practice consistently if you want it to yield good results.

> **Hebrews 3:12-14,** "Take care, brothers, lest there be in any of you an evil, unbelieving heart, leading you to fall away from the living God. But **exhort one another every day**, as long as it is called 'today' that none of you may be hardened by **the deceitfulness of sin.** For we have come to share in Christ, if indeed we hold our original confidence firm to the end. As it is said, 'Today, **if you hear his voice, do not harden your hearts as in the rebellion.'"**

The writer of Hebrews says the deceitfulness of sin hardens our hearts. Sin is deceitful, it lies to us continually. God's voice heard through others softens our hearts to the lies we are prone to believe about ourselves and gives us a better chance of hearing His truth.

It is important to have routines and rhythms of accountability. I will talk later about the levels of accountability you need in your life, but now I just want to emphasize the need for regular and consistent accountability. The text says, "Exhort one another every day." It needs to be a part of your day, week, month, year, and life if you want it to help sustain you through the good times and the bad times.

You have times in your life when you can't hear God, and others will need to hear on your behalf. I have been there, and I bet you have too. You may be there right now.

So many think accountability is needed just to deal with your struggles, and yes that is true. But you may need accountability the most to deal with the successes of your life and ministry. We all need someone to remind us:

> "God may have said your feet are beautiful, but they are still clay and they can crumble easily if you forget the source of your success."

I have more than one in my life that does that for me.

It has been a life saver MANY times.

Key #5: Application

My dad used to tell a story about a farmer who said to the other farmer, "You need to feed your cows, they are really skinny." The other farmer would reply, "Corn right by them." One day the farmer went to look at the "corn right by them." He discovered it was in the bin next to the lot they were in. They had no access.

If you don't apply what you learn in accountability, it won't make any difference in the final outcome of your real life.

You will starve to death spiritually if your life is full of accountability with no application.

You have to be accountable. You have to listen. You have to be honest, but if you don't apply it, it can't help you. If I go to the doctor and get meds for a sickness, but never take the prescription, I wasted his time and mine.

It is not enough to share your problems or successes with others, you have to figure out how to apply what they are suggesting to you if you want it to make a difference in your life.

Good ideas won't change your life, but good ideas *applied* will.

I have learned something over the years when I meet with people more than once and they talk to me about the same thing twice. I ask, "Did you try to apply what I suggested last time?" Sadly, the answer is "no", more than I care to remember. I stop them and say:

> "Talking about the same struggles and never applying what you already know is the definition of accountability insanity. I can't help you, sorry. Don't waste my time if my suggestions aren't worth your time."

Respect the time of the people you are accountable to, apply what they say, at least try. Or else don't patronize them, tell them:

> "I wish I had the courage to apply what you said, but I don't." Or, "I tried it and it just didn't work. I need help figuring out what went wrong."

This leads to the final key of accountability:

Key #6: Reboot

You will need to modify your accountability over time. You may realize, as painful as it may be, that the people you are accountable to can't help you. They don't know how. You may need to add others to your accountability, explore some books that can help on the topic, or seek out some professional counseling to dig into some areas you just can't seem to unlock and understand. You may need to see a doctor about some of the challenges you are facing and you may need to consider alternative medicines or traditional medicines to deal with some chronic mental or physical challenges.

The key is to explore. The key is to modify as you go. In sports, we call it the halftime adjustments. You have to be committed to rebooting your accountability strategy and plan for greater effectiveness over time. If at first you don't succeed, modify and reboot, but whatever you do, don't give up. You can and will find the necessary help to carry you through this season and time. Keep asking the Lord to guide your steps to the necessary people and resources to get you the help you need.

However, you may see no hope and be so depressed that you want to end your life or at least your pastorate. That doesn't make you "unholy." Paul dealt with the same thing and he understood it clearly. Listen to his words to the Corinthians:

> **2 Corinthians 1:8-11,** "For we do not want you to be unaware, brothers, of the affliction we experienced

in Asia. For we were so utterly burdened beyond our strength that we **despaired of life itself.** Indeed we felt that we had received the sentence of death. But that was to make us rely not on ourselves but on God who raises the dead. He delivered us from such a deadly peril, and **he will deliver us.** On him we have set our hope that he will **deliver us again.** You also must **help us by prayer,** so that many will give thanks on our behalf **for the blessing granted us through the prayers of many.**"

The best reboot in accountability is to ask those you are accountable to "keep praying for you."

Sometimes, the breakthrough has nothing to do with a "golden solution", but simply a willingness to stay engaged and ask for prayer from others. This is the best modification, medicine, and reboot.

Keep asking your accountability partner to pray for God's blessing on whatever area of your life or pastorate that seems to be leading you, like Paul, to despair of even life itself.

Reboot, my friend, through the prayers of others. I can't tell you how many times Jon Elsberry has rebooted my life through his prayers. Thank you, Jon!

LAYERS OF ACCOUNTABILITY:

Ask God to help you, through others. Some of the godliest people in biblical history have. They knew they needed the help of others to do what God had called them to do.

The favor of God often comes through others we know.

I love how Elisha asked Elijah for a double portion of his spirit:

> **2 Kings 2:9-10,** "When they had crossed, Elijah said to Elisha, 'Ask what I shall do for you, before I am taken from you.' And Elisha said, 'Please let there be a double portion of **your spirit on me**.' And he said, 'You have asked a **hard thing; yet**, if you see me as I am being taken from you, it shall be so for you, but if you don't see me, it shall not be so.'"

I bet Elisha never left his side. 😊

That's the mindset we have to have when it comes to accountability. It has to be consistent, constant, and essential to existence.

Elisha understood this.

But he also understood this, people won't provide you accountability unless you ask them to.

People will assume you have it unless you ask.

The first move is yours.

Now accountability is not one-size-fits-all. It says, "Within a multitude of counselors there is wisdom." What is a multitude? Well, it is at least two. You should have at least two others speaking into your life. I suggest more, but this is a minimum.

Here are the levels of accountability in my life and how they function:

LAYER #1: Family/Marriage

This is a long term and everyday accountability from my wife and five children. I have given my five children and my wife permission to say anything they want to say to me as long as it is in a protective or private environment or setting. They don't have to hold back or worry about hurting my feelings.

I go on five to six dates a year with my children and one of the questions I ask them is, "What do you not like about me?" They get better at answering this with age. ☺

Without them knowing it, they all pretty much tell me the same two or three things. I find it extremely helpful.

I also ask them what they like about me, that's important too.

When Tosha and I were dating, we went through a book by Bill and Lynne Hybels called *Fit To Be Tied*. Through it, we found it extremely helpful to establish our ability to say to each other whatever needs to be said and we have lived by this philosophy our entire marriage.

My wife has full authority to read my journals at any time. This is where I confess the truth of who I am.

I also made a commitment to my children to give them my journal starting at nineteen when they reach the corresponding year of their life. This is sobering, but builds immediate accountability into my life for the long haul and for the long term. I find this helpful, though embarrassing at times, but humility never hurt anyone. Jesus said:

> "You shall know the truth and the truth shall set you **free**."

Live true, it's the quickest path to freedom. Begin with your kids and spouse.

LAYER #2: Long-Term Friends

This is a long term and big life decision accountability.

Longevity and loyalty trump everything else in my mind when it comes to friendship and accountability.

People must earn the right to know the truth about your life. Trust is essential to healthy and long-term accountability. Don't give it until people deserve it. I have a few friends in my life that date back to the late 1980s and early 1990s. I have other friends that I have met since then who play a significant role in my life as well. But time and consistency determine my willingness to go there with them. My sister, Ellen Goad, has known me all my life. She has been a friend and a partner in ministry most of my life. My roommate from college, Joel Willitts, knows me. We have now journeyed through thirty plus years of life. There is no substitute for longevity.

You don't need a lot of long-term friends, but you need a few. You need people who can get on the phone with you and, in seconds, say, "What's wrong?" They know you better than you know yourself. You can't lie to them.

Have you ever tried to define what a true friend is to you?

Oprah Winfrey said once, "A friend is someone who loves you, respects you, but doesn't want your life."

Wow! That is an incredible definition of friendship. Find that and make yourself accountable to them.

LAYER #3: Other Ministry Leaders and Pastors

It is VERY important to have other people in your life who lead organizations or churches at the same level as you do. They don't need you to explain it to them. They get it. This kind of accountability is more ... I smell what you are stepping in ... Here is how I got out of it or survived it. This is very important.

I have a couple of pastors in my life. One from a distance and one up close that I stay in close contact with. We probably average a couple of communications or connections by phone, lunch, or text a couple of times a month. The pastor that is local, we have lunch together once a month, every month. We eat, share our lives, ask each other for advice, and pray for one another. The pastor from a distance, we text, share over the phone at times, and have lunch together a couple of times a year.

I am extremely thankful for John Pauls and Armin Sommer. They have been tremendous pastor friends to me over the years. I am very grateful for their accountability and encouragement in my life. Two true men of God who love their families and their churches well.

LAYER #4: Life Group Men

I have five men in my life who have been in my life for the past six years. We meet once a month and share our lives and pray for one another. Each of them run their own business, so I get good insights from them on how to handle situations that are of the entrepreneurial nature. These guys are an encouragement to both my personal and professional life. I am grateful for their input into my life. I am able to bounce ideas for my life and pastorate off of them. I find the accountability of this group to be more of "an encouragement to me that helps me feel like a normal guy," even though I just so happen to be their pastor as well. They do a great job of checking their church agenda for me at the door and treating me like one of the guys. I appreciate that.

LAYER #5: Prayer Partner

Jon Elsberry and I have been meeting since 2002 and praying together for a couple of hours every Tuesday when I write my sermons. We usually meet in the afternoon, after I have spent the morning sermon writing. It started out as a mentorship of Jon to me. He is about twenty years my senior. He pastored for twenty-seven years in the Wesleyan denomination. And though our theology may be different at times, like David and Jonathan, God has knit our hearts together for ministry. He intercedes for many pastors and I am grateful I am one of them. We share a friendship and a professional relationship as well. He is in my men's life group and he leads the prayer ministry of our church.

This is where I experience consistent counsel and prayer. I see this accountability as heart accountability first and partnership accountability. Because Jon has been a pastor, and he attends the church I pastor, he is able to see and respond to things from a multi-faceted perspective.

Jon got asked to be an elder at our church a few years ago. He asked me what I thought. I told him he would make a great elder, but it would limit what I could discuss with him because I couldn't give him biased treatment at the expense of all the other elders. He decided he could have a greater influence in my life by being a sounding board on church issues before I go into elder meetings. I am grateful for this partnership in the ministry and the counsel he freely gives to me. It has been invaluable.

Over the years, he hasn't always agreed with my leadership and he has told me so in our times of communion, prayer, and sharing. However, he is quick to support me and pray for me to follow Christ. I mean this with the greatest of sincerity. He can cry at the drop of a hat and he doesn't need a hat. Jon has the unique ability that my mother had and that is to disagree and yet love you even more. That's a great gift.

A long time ago, someone who knows him and me asked me, "What do you get out of meeting with Jon Elsberry? He is nothing like you."

I said, "Exactly."

I get everything I am not. He keeps my heart soft to the Lord. I am gritty, determined, and unfortunately at times ready to fight at the drop of a hat (and I don't need a hat). He keeps me even-keeled and focused on the heart of the Lord in a way that I can't do without him in my life. I have grown to greatly appreciate the investment he and his wife, Sandi, have made in Tosha and me over the years. We are very grateful for their help in our marriage as well. They intercede for our kids and we are very grateful for this. The Elsberry family has loved our family well including, as Jon would say, the moms, Velma (Sandi's mom), and Elaine (Jon's mom), who both were pastor's wives. We feel so blessed to have these godly people in our lives. They have made ministry and life so much richer because of it.

There are a lot people who have impacted my life, but few who have had the impact Jon has had on my life. Thank you, Jon!

I call this accountability, "holistic accountability." It runs the aggregate of our entire lives and we are so thankful.

LAYER #6: Church Pastoral Leadership Team

Presently, this is made up of four other pastors on staff at the church I am called to lead as Senior Pastor. I rarely make any decision without first consulting them. We meet every other week and then I meet every other week with each one of them individually. This has been huge for the health of our church, our team, and each other. They have made me a MUCH better Senior Pastor. Thank you, pastoral leadership team, for building into my professional decision making and leadership. I am extremely grateful for Danel Smith, Aaron McClain, Richie Fike, and Jenni Ehrlin.

This Vanguard Pastoral Team provides me "wisdom" accountability for the direction of the church.

LAYER #7: Church Elders

Our church's elder board is comprised of six volunteers who meet once a month with me and once a month with the entire Pastoral Leadership Team. We have crafted a document called, "The Leadership Matrix" to guide our decision making process.

I am accountable to this board for every decision I lead the church to make. The Leadership Matrix outlines our lanes and how we function as a team. They are also responsible for reviewing my salary, benefits, and job performance annually, and keeping a close eye on my walk with the Lord, what I am teaching, and how I treat my staff.

Our elders serve three years and then rotate off for a year. They are then eligible to come back, if invited by the board to do so, for another three-year term. This cycle can continue into perpetuity.

I feel HUGELY supported by this team. I call this accountability "protective accountability." It is their job to keep an eye on me in proximity to the church and to ensure my life does not get out of balance at home. We meet twice a month and go away for an annual retreat every year to review the past, dream the future, and address the present. I meet once a month with the Chair Elder for greater and more effective communication and professional oversight for the church.

The board has created so many good boundaries for me. My risk-taking spirit needs them. I became a MUCH better leader and pastor the day we crafted the Leadership Matrix. I don't have a problem living in boundaries as long as they are established. But, if I don't have any, well, I don't live a very balanced life and I don't lead the church in a very balanced way. This I know of myself.

I am extremely grateful for this "protective accountability." I couldn't have gotten this far without it. Thank you, Vanguard Elders, who have invested your "free time" in my life and the life of the vision of Vanguard Church. I am extremely grateful.

They help me run in my professional lane well.

These seven layers of accountability have protected me from myself and enabled me to pastor for twenty-plus years at the same church my wife and I founded. This doesn't happen often, I know, and I give credit to the scores of people who have invested in my life and honestly my willingness to listen and let go of control over everything and everyone. It is a must if you want to go the distance as a good pastor.

And I do want to go the distance. I hope you do too.

BENEFITS OF ACCOUNTABILITY:

1) You make WISER decisions.
2) You are happier and more emotionally healthy because you don't carry it all.

3) You are more effective and supported. A cord of three is not easily broken.

4) You may feel lonely, but you know that you are not alone.

5) You have people who care about you. You get to take breaks.

6) You have others to fight for you when you can't fight for yourself.

7) You can feel somewhat "normal" as a human being because they care for *you* and not just what they can get from you as their pastor.

8) You get a chance to be served the way you serve so many.

9) Your family gets to feel the love that comes from those who look after you.

10) You are protected from yourself.

I would have made a lot of dumb decisions without these seven layers. I am just not myself when I don't have accountability. And I bet, neither are you.

PITFALLS OF ACCOUNTABILITY:

I wish I could tell you that being accountable always produces positive things, but it doesn't. It has some pitfalls you have to choose to avoid.

PITFALL #1: LETTING ONE PERSON'S OPINION CONTROL YOUR ACCOUNTABILITY.

I believe this may be the most frequent pitfall of accountability. You decide to be accountable to one person. I have made this mistake more than once in my life with the elder board. It took me a long time to learn that there is "wisdom in a multitude of counselors."

You can't let one person dictate and influence you to the point that no one else gets to. And there is a certain type of personality that loves for you to be accountable to them and no one else. A number of years ago, I had to repent to my board and ask them to forgive me because I had allowed myself, more than once, to be accountable to just one elder on the board. I had chosen not to weigh into what the totality of the board thought.

I don't make this mistake anymore and I don't worry about that type of personality falling out with me. It took me a while, but I am there. I don't EVER listen to just one person's opinion and then make a major decision for myself or the church. It requires a multitude and that means at least "more than one."

Is there an individual in your life that has too much influence over your accountability? You better do something about it. And the best way is to start listening to others and taking back some of the authority and influence you have given that one person over your life. More than likely, they won't stay in your life long after that. But you will be healthier and so will your family and the organization you lead.

PITFALL #2: YOU MAY LOSE THE COURAGE TO MAKE DECISIONS WHEN PEOPLE DISAGREE WITH YOU.

I go from being a maverick in my decision-making ability to being fearful that not everyone whom I am accountable to will agree with my decision. This can cause you to second guess your leadership and paralyze your ability to lead because you so want unity, consensus, and harmony with those you are accountable to.

But the misnomer is, accountability doesn't mean you agree, it means you submitted yourself to a process and consider it from other people's perspectives before you made a wise, informed decision. But I find my personality either wants to make the decision upfront or figure out a way to get everybody to like the decision before I make it. Neither are healthy or necessary to make a wise decision.

PITFALL #3: OVERSHARING WITH PEOPLE YOU SHOULDN'T.

Because you want to be accountable and live with full-disclosure, you may lack discernment at times as to who you should share what with. This is no easy task to figure out. As pastors, we live complicated lives. Our social life, personal life, and professional life collide over and over again. I have had to learn how to compartmentalize my accountability and ask myself these three questions: 1) Why am I telling this to this person? 2) Do they have any authority to affect the decision at a formal level? 3) What do I hope to accomplish by sharing this with them?

For example, I don't share everything that happens in the elder room with my wife. I don't share everything that happens with my wife in the elder room. Accountability is not a substitute for discernment and propriety. If I come home and share certain things with my wife and kids, I get over it in a day, they may linger on it for days, weeks, months, years, and some things they struggle to release, ever.

Accountability doesn't mean I share everything with every layer I just talked about. It means I have these seven layers in my life to first off protect me from me. Second of all, to discern who it is God wants me to share certain things with so I can be the best possible person, pastor, and follower of Jesus Christ. I have found those three questions to be invaluable in this process.

PITFALL #4: ASSUMING YOUR ACCOUNTABILITY PARTNER IS RESPONSIBLE

If I share this with them, then I am no longer responsible. Accountability doesn't mean you abdicated your authority. It means you allow others to influence it. But you are forever responsible for what you are responsible for. If your accountability partner gives you bad advice. Guess what? It is still your responsibility and even your fault.

When you are the point leader of an organization, you have to accept the burden that comes with it. You include others in the process, so you can be a better leader. But when it goes wrong, you are responsible. You don't get to say, "Well, I was just doing what my accountability partner suggested I do."

Accountability doesn't give you a get out of jail free card for your decisions that you are responsible for making nor does it erase the consequences of your sin once you have confessed it to them.

Accountability helps you lead better and make wiser decisions, but it does not abdicate your responsibility.

Point leaders are always responsible, regardless.

CONSEQUENCES OF NOT BEING ACCOUNTABLE:

A few years ago, I had the privilege of going to Africa with Compassion International and my second-born daughter, Christianna. At the end of the trip, we got to go out on the savannah where all the wildlife lives and sleeps on this compound in the middle of the savannah. There are two visible images I will never forget and one haunting sound that filled a cacophony of animal sounds.

The first day we went out and saw all the amazing wild animals just grazing in their herds on the savannah. That night, we could hear the different sounds, lurks, and screams of the animals from the hippos, the lions, to the monkeys, and everything in between. My heart rate was a little higher than it is normally at night.

The next morning, we went out to get in our jeep to go observe the animals again, and when we walked toward our jeep, a hyena came out of the bush and stood before us just a few feet away. He was a brave soul and it got my attention. The guide who had a gun and stick ran him off thankfully. But it got my heart rate up again.

And then when we were out on the savannah, watching predators like hyenas and lions chase their prey. We got to see a group of lions single out a water buffalo. I am sure you have seen this on television even if you haven't seen it in person. The lions run out on the savannah and single out their prey from a large herd running by. They isolate the prey, and before long, it falls victim to their appetite.

I sat in a jeep with others and listened to hyenas just a few feet away crush the bones of their deceased victims and eat them whole.

Satan is the hyena of your soul. He is the lion seeking to kill you. He will devour you, if he can.

Peter said, "Satan is like that roaring lion seeking whom he may devour."

Satan wants you not to be accountable. You are easier to isolate, and eventually destroy, if you are alone in the real issues, struggles, and successes of your life.

He will tell you that you are not worth God's blessing. And then when you get it, he will tell you that you deserved it.

He won't relent.

If you go it alone, he will isolate you, devour you, and destroy you.

There are many consequences to no accountability:

1) Poor decisions.

2) Anxiety disorders due to trying to carry too much on your own.

3) Dark secrets that are eating you alive.

4) Selfishness that is running rampant.

5) The body of Christ not functioning the way God intended (as a body not an individual).

6) Believing the deception of sin.

7) Arrogance unchecked.

8) Success not shared but horded.

9) Making success the focus, not service to each other.

But I think number 10 is the most devastating one.

Show me someone who has had a moral failure and I will show you someone who did not exercise their accountability correctly or maybe they had none at all.

10) Moral Failure and Public Humiliation.

I know without a doubt that if I had not had accountability in my life, I would have had multiple moral failures as a pastor.

You have heard people say, "But for the grace of God go I," when a pastor falls.

Listen, it is grace, but not just grace. It takes hard work and humility to let others see the real you.

But it is worth it.

Trust me.

The Bible says it best:

> **Ecclesiastes 4:8,10-12,** "Two are better than one, because they have a good reward for their toil. For if they fall, one will lift up his fellow. But woe to him who is alone when he falls and has not another to lift him up! Again, if two lie together, they keep warm, but how can one keep warm alone? And though a man might prevail against one who is alone, two will withstand him—a threefold cord (accountability) is not quickly broken."

Accountability does not guarantee you won't have a moral failure, but what it does do, is slow down the possibility because accountability makes your life not quickly or easily broken by the attack of the Evil One.

It is not full-proof, but it is your best option.

Dependence on God, Good Pastor, begins with accountability.

CHAPTER 14

DEPENDENCE ON GOD THROUGH BOUNDARIES

Only one out of ten pastors will retire as a pastor.

The most difficult person you will ever lead in your life or pastorship is yourself.

My dad has a story he has told for years that makes the point. One morning, while the man was shaving, he said to his wife, "I don't think I am going to church today."

To which she replied, "How come?"

He said, "I will give you two reasons. I don't like them and they don't like me."

To which she replied, "I will give you two better reasons. You are the pastor and today is Sunday." ☺

All of us as pastors fall into this mindset from time to time.

You have to learn to lead yourself because, at the end of the day, no one else will.

But to do so, you need boundaries, strong boundaries for yourself that you commit to live by regardless of the circumstances, relationships, geography, temptations, struggles, or fatigue. You name whatever it is, it can NOT trump your boundary.

Boundaries in sports tell you when you are out of bounds. In basketball, you can make the greatest shot in the history of the game, but if you are out of bounds, it doesn't count.

When God created the nation of Israel under Joshua's leadership, he established **boundaries** in Joshua 15. The word is used no less than nineteen times. Boundary is key to possessing and maintaining the inheritance and blessings God has for your life. This is what enables you to steward well what God gives you.

In the pastorate, you can have some of the greatest accomplishments in the world, pastor the largest church in the world, have the most followers on social media in the world, write the best books in the world, and be a NY Times Bestselling author, but if you don't have boundaries for your life, you will shipwreck your pastorate and destroy the "success" of your life and be left in shambles confused by the divorce and departure of those you meant to love the best.

Paul said it best:

1 Corinthians 9:24-27, "Do you know that in a race all the runners run, but only one receives the prize? So run that you may obtain it. Every athlete exercises self-control in all things. They do it to receive a perishable wreath, but we an imperishable. So I do not run aimlessly; I do not box as one beating the air. **But I discipline my body and keep it under control, lest after preaching to others I myself should be disqualified.**"

There it is, "I discipline my body (boundary) and keep it under control (boundary) so that after I preach, I don't disqualify myself (boundary).

There are three boundaries in this passage:

1) I live a disciplined life.

2) I am intentional at keeping me under control.

3) I want to keep doing this for a lifetime.

Do you?

I do.

If you and I are going to go the distance and finish strong in the pastorate, then we have to be intentional about how we structure our lives and how we keep ourselves "in bounds" so that our performance is legit for the Kingdom for a lifetime.

In the Bible, King Asa was considered one of the godlier kings of Judah.

2 Chronicles 14:2. "And Asa did what was **good** and **right** in the **eyes of the Lord** his God."

If he were a pastor, we would call him, "a good pastor."

Asa served as king for forty-one years. That's a long reign by anyone's standard. That would be a very long pastorate. Remember the characteristics we are going for in the passage Paul shared with us ... keep yourself disciplined, self-controlled, for how long? For a lifetime. I saw a statistic that said, "Only one out of ten pastors will retire as a pastor."

Asa was told when he started:

> **2 Chronicles 15:1,2,** "The Spirit of God came upon Azariah the son of Oded, and he went out to meet Asa and said to him, 'Hear me, Asa, and all Judah and Benjamin: The Lord is with you while you are with him. If you seek him, he will be found by you, but if you forsake him, he will forsake you.'"

Asa served the Lord faithfully for thirty-five years. That is pretty impressive, but here is the problem, he was king for forty-one years.

What happened?

In the thirty-sixth year of the reign of Asa, he decided to take matters into his own hands. It is a temptation we all face regardless of our age or experience in the pastorate. Matter of fact, I think this temptation grows with age.

The longer we live the more pragmatic we are tempted to become and less dependent on the Lord. It makes sense to our human minds and so it must be what we should do.

> **2 Chronicles 16:1-3,** "In the thirty-sixth year of the reign of Asa ... Asa took silver and gold from the treasuries of the house of the Lord and the king's house and sent them to Ben-hadad king of Syria, who lived in Damascus, saying, 'There is a *covenant* between me and you, as there was between my father and your father.'"

Here is the problem. Asa's dad, Abijah, was not a good man for his entire lifetime. He only reigned for three years before he died.

> **1 Kings 15:3,4,** "And he (Abijah) walked in all the sins that his father did before him, and his heart was not wholly true to the Lord his God, as the heart of David his father. Nevertheless, for David's sake the Lord his God gave him a lamp in Jerusalem, setting up his son (Asa) after him, and establishing Jerusalem."

Abijah started out good, but ended very poorly. This is true for a lot of pastors. It is not how you start that matters, but how you finish the race. Yet, Abijah had hope because of God's promise to David and Asa was that hope. Long after Abijah had died, Asa walked with the Lord faithfully for a long time, but in the thirty-sixth year, for whatever reason we don't know, he changed his mind. He took matters into his own hands and chose to follow his earthly father's example over his heavenly Father.

2 Chronicles 16:7,9,10, "At that time Hanani the seer came to Asa king of Judah and said to him, 'Because you relied on the king of Syria, and did not rely on the Lord your God, the army of the king of Syria has escaped you. For the eyes of the Lord run to and fro throughout the whole earth, to give strong support to those whose heart is blameless toward him. You have done foolishly in this, for from now on you will have wars.' **Then Asa was angry with the seer and put him in the stocks in prison, for he was in rage with him** because of this. And Asa inflicted cruelties upon some of the people at the same time."

We don't know what happened in the thirty-sixth year of Asa's reign to cause him to go rogue on his walk with God. The Bible doesn't tell us, but it is a good reminder to all of us, our dependence on God is for a lifetime not just when we are young and unsuccessful. It must also be when we are older and more successful in our "careers."

Living in Colorado Springs, I have had the privilege of crossing paths with well-known Christian leaders and pastors. Some are just as impressive up close as they are from a distance and some, well, they must have eaten what Asa was eating in his thirty-sixth year.

Here is what we do know, arrogance and self-reliance lead to poor choices, when confronted as leaders, if we don't repent, poor choices lead to anger, rage, and mistreating those who oppose you.

Don't ever get "so important" in your life that God can't discipline you otherwise He will have to humiliate you to get you to listen.

Asa wouldn't listen. This godlier-than-most king would not listen to the seer God sent to confront him. Look at what happens to him in just three short years of arrogance and unrepentance.

> **2 Chronicles 16:12, "In the thirty-ninth year** of his reign Asa was diseased in his feet, and his disease became severe. Yet even in his disease he did not seek the Lord, but sought help from physicians."

He had become so prideful and self-reliant that he wouldn't even call on God in his misery and disease. He relied on his own physicians. God gives us many chances to repent as pastors, but if we don't take them, we can be guaranteed the worst is still yet to come.

Asa started off great. He took EVERYTHING to God in prayer, but as his success came and his experience grew, he acted as if he could do it all himself.

Sad.

Boundaries and disciplines are not just good things to do when you are young and unsuccessful, they are equally important when you are older, more experienced, and may have some resources you didn't have when you were younger.

Dependence doesn't get easier with age and success, it gets harder, this is why boundaries are so important. They have to govern our every move.

Two years later, look at what happened to Asa:

2 Chronicles 16:13, "And Asa slept with his fathers, dying in the forty-first year of his reign."

It didn't have to be that way. In just five short years, his thirty-six years were overshadowed by his self-reliance, arrogance, rage, and unwillingness to repent.

All of us need boundaries in our lives more than anything to keep us humble and dependent on God. It doesn't matter how successful you become or don't become, your age, or your knowledge or financial resources. Boundaries are important to sober us to who we are apart from Christ as pastors.

The boundaries of your life are the rules you self impose upon yourself to enable you to never disqualify yourself in the pastorate like Asa did as King.

It is not about legalism it is about wisdom and protecting yourself.

Accountability is about letting others protect you from you.

Boundaries are about protecting you from you. And providing you the ability to care for your spouse and children well.

It is God's grace that ultimately keeps you from self-destruction, but it is your boundaries that keep you away from stupid places you don't need to be and develop bad habits that keep you from your optimum effectiveness.

BOUNDARIES FOR 7 AREAS OF A PASTOR'S LIFE:

BOUNDARY AREA #1: WORK WEEK

Psalm 122:1, "I was glad when they said to me, 'Let us **go** to the house of the Lord.'"

You have to learn how to find joy in going to "work" as a pastor. God wants us to enter His house day in and day out with joy and gladness. It takes some time to learn how to do this. Here are some suggested boundaries that might help.

1) I have found that I can work 48-52 hours every week and still be a good husband, father, friend, and pastor. How's your work-week hours?

2) I have found I can prepare about 35-40 messages a year and speak about 130 times (multiple services a week) a year and stay balanced, but realized my fatigue grows as the ministry year wears on. How often do you get a break from sermon writing and preaching? We now have a teaching team that we have developed over the past five-plus years that does just about all the teaching when I am not teaching.

3) I try to work five days a week realizing my work week may bleed into a sixth day often. If our staff work more than four hours on a day off, we give them a flex day for them to use later.

4) I do not counsel people on an ongoing basis. I will meet with anyone from our church and help but,

if ongoing counseling is needed, we either refer to a professional or connect them to an older mentor in our church through huddles.

5) Many years ago, I made a difficult decision not to meet with females one on one by myself, ever. And especially not to counsel them by myself.

This has caused a lot of hurt feelings over the years in the pastorate. Females say this makes them feel like they are second-class citizens to the pastor and feel as though it leaves them limited in their spiritual counsel.

Over the years I have had females tell me the following things:

"I just want to know your heart."

My response, "Only one woman will ever know my heart, my wife."

"Pastor, you understand me in a way no one else does."

My response, "We have some great women in our church who would love to get to know you and help journey with you in your walk with the Lord."

"Pastor, can I have your phone number, I have something I want to discuss with you."

My response, "My assistant would be more than glad to set up a time for the three of us to meet and discuss what is going on in your life."

6) I don't meet with the opposite sex alone and I don't text or talk with them over the phone alone about their personal matters.

I made a decision a long time ago not to meet with the opposite sex one-on-one. I will however meet with them with my assistant or another female leader or another pastor present when we meet.

Why is this? I have learned that people have more control over what they share with you when a third party is present. I have found that people tend to share things one-on-one that they later feel embarrassed about having shared. When there is a third person in the room, especially a female it creates a much less intimate experience not only for them but you as well.

People like to share their secrets and when they can share them with someone of the opposite sex in private the enemy then will use this to destroy you and them. Don't go there, it is not worth it. I know so many pastors who counsel the opposite sex one-on-one and inevitably it leads to a huge statistic of people who are no longer in pastorate.

Why is this so dangerous? Like it or not, most men are not emotional with their spouses. There are a lot of lonely godly people who go to the church you pastor. They listen to you week in week out share your heart, your emotions, they see what they wish their spouse was like. Innocently, they feel drawn to you like a friend of the same gender, but this is dangerous for them and you.

When two people of the opposite sex share anything in isolation of your spouse being present it inevitably leads to bad places. However, when a third party is present it helps keep your emotions and theirs at a different level, a more professional level. It makes it more objective and you have a third party there to observe and give wise feedback about the person and about you if need be.

You can ignore this boundary, but it could be the undoing of your pastorate. When a someone says to you, "Pastor, you understand me better than my spouse." they have already attached themselves to you emotionally in a way that is unhealthy. They may not have meant to, but it has happened nonetheless.

I find it very important to share with my wife anything I believe creates an emotional connection for me or the other person to me. Secrets are sweet. Sharing them with your spouse makes them bitter, quick. 😊

I will never forget, I asked my pastor, John Yeats, how do you handle potential attractions to the females in your congregation? And by the way, it will happen. It is not an if, but a when, the question is, how will you handle it?

He said, "I don't have long conversations with the opposite sex by myself."

Limit the time you spend in one-on-one conversations with the opposite sex.

I have adopted this boundary in my life as well.

You may see this as extreme. I see it as wise.

For a moment, I want to put my toe in the water on an issue that I doubt a pastoral book has ever addressed. What if you are a pastor and you have same-sex attraction impulses, what do you do?

First of all, let me say, I believe the Bible teaches that homosexuality is a sin, it is not THE sin, but it is a sin. I talk a lot about this in the book *Friend of Sinners: Taking Risks To Reach The Lost.*

I believe there are pastors out there both male and female who are married or single who battle same-sex impulses for a myriad of reasons. They do NOT give into them, but they are prone to these impulses. I know that you fear being able to tell anyone in your ministry for fear of losing your job. If you feel you can't share it with your leadership, do your spouse and your children a favor and identify a professional mentor or counselor who can know this about you and help craft a game plan of boundaries that enable you to go the distance in the pastorate.

No impulse is sin until you act on it, remember that. Temptation is not sin. You don't get to choose your temptations, but you do get to choose your boundaries. Choose them wisely.

If this is you, you need to let your accountability partner know this and you need to let them help you build a model of boundaries in this area that protects you from you.

It is inevitable that we will find ourselves attracted to people in our ministries that are not our spouses. Attraction is a normal desire created by God. Do you have a game plan for dealing with it?

If people leave your church over you having boundaries, as sad as that might be, let them. It is better for you to make it to the finish line with purity and healthy God-honoring boundaries than to allow the kryptonite of your soul to destroy you, your family, and others.

My final thought on work week is management of conflict.

7) It is important to slow down the process of conflict by having a process by which you deal with all conflict.

Rarely should you deal with it on the spot if you can at all avoid it. My staff know we have weekly meetings, write it down and bring it up in our meeting. Most immediate conflict is unhealthy and usually is not real. It is important to stay focused on your work week. I have learned over the years with a five-day work week to compartmentalize my tasks and block my work week. We have services Saturday and Sunday and I am preparing to speak. We have individual staff meetings on Mondays. I prepare messages on Tuesdays. Wednesday, we have group meetings and I meet with people one-on-one from the church and community as well.

I try and end my work week every week by writing thank you notes.

8) It is important to me to reflect on the work week and end it recalling the highlights.

I attempt to write at least two thank you notes a week to leaders and I write thank you notes to new givers, large givers, and three regular givers a week. I also try and reflect on the week and think of those in our community that need words of encouragement and I try to drop them a line or two letting them know how much I appreciate them and their ministry to our church, community, or to their family and friends.

I find ending my work week being an encouragement to others equally lifts my spirits as well and it also enables me to cross paths with them over the weekend in services and have conversations with them. We try and get the cards out on Thursday and by the weekend they have received them in the mail.

I am still a big believer in sending hand-written notes to people. I send a personal thank you note throughout the year to anyone who gives to the church at least once in the calendar year. I cannot tell you how many people have said to me, "You know I have been giving to the church for thirty, forty, fifty years and I have never gotten a hand-written note from a pastor thanking me for giving to the church."

That's sad.

I know, everyone is worried about the Senior Pastor being this far into the finances, but I believe it is important that we honor those who enable everyone else to have jobs and do ministry through the church. I encourage you to become a letter and card writing pastor who seeks to honor as many people as possible in the work week through the hand written note. And you can thank my wife for this. She taught me well.

I save this last one for last for a reason. It is that important to your work week.

> **Psalm 150:1,** "Praise the Lord! Praise God **in his sanctuary.**"

9) Worship God **in front** of the people you pastor.

I think it is extremely important that the people you lead SEE you worship God. If you are not careful you can get the "celebrity" mindset where everyone is there to hear you. Or you can fall into the "this is my time to do my job and fulfill my service." It is called the "Martha syndrome."

> **Luke 10:40a,** "But Martha was **distracted** with **much serving.**"

That is what the pastorate feels like often, no doubt.

One of the greatest challenges in the pastorate is to worship God authentically week in and week out and then get up and give the people of God the message of God and fulfill your service to God and to them.

I believe it is important that you are the lead worshipper as the pastor, especially as the Senior or Lead pastor of a church. Let people see you worship God in His sanctuary. It will give them tremendous encouragement to do the same and it will help keep your feet squarely placed where they need to be.

BOUNDARY AREA #2: MARRIAGE

> **1 Chronicles 16:43,** "Then all the people departed each to this house, and **David went home to bless his household.**"

Hebrews 13:4, "Let marriage be held in honor among all" (including pastors and their spouses).

You are NOT married to the church, so don't live like it.

The church is God's bride.

Most pastors, especially male pastors, need to be reminded of this important fact.

So many women have suffered slightly under the reality that their husbands loved the church they pastored more than they loved them. I remember as a kid, my dad saying to me, "The church comes before family."

He wasn't neglectful of us, but he did put the church above us, he genuinely thought that is what he was supposed to do as a pastor.

When A. W. Tozer died, his widow, Ada, eventually remarried. Several people who were close to Ada lovingly inquired about her happiness. Her responses were consistent. She was quick to honor A.W., but she also was honest. She said:

> "I have never been happier in my life. Aiden (A.W.) loved Jesus Christ, but Leonard Odam (2nd husband) loves me."

The Apostle Paul tells us,

> **Ephesians 5:25,** "Husbands love your wives as Christ loves the church and gave himself up for her."

Pastor, does your spouse know she/he is more important to you than the church?

Pastor, would your spouse utter these words:

> **Song of Solomon 7:10,** "I am my beloved's, and his desire is **for** me."

That is a beautiful statement to describe the marriages God wants us to have as pastors. He wants our spouses to know they are ours like no other and our desire is for them.

Paul tells us married people need to live like they are married, even pastors.

> **1 Corinthians 7:33-35,** "But the married man is anxious about worldly things, how to please his wife, and **his interests are divided**. And the unmarried or betrothed woman is anxious about the things of the Lord, how to be holy in body and spirit. But the married woman is anxious about worldly things, **how to please her husband**. I say this for your own benefit, not to lay any restraint upon you, but **to promote good order** and to secure your undivided devotion to the Lord."

Paul is telling us, if you are married and a pastor, you can't act and live like you are not.

Here are some boundaries I have in regards to my marriage to help me remain dependent on God as a pastor instead of making the church too much of my focus.

This is how I make sure I am married to my wife and not the church:

1) I take her on at least three dates a month. We share the real us on these dates.

2) We are committed to intimacy at least twice a week and usually three times a week. This is a great rhythm for us. This is really important for all married couples in the pastorate. If you don't keep your connection with each other, you will find it with someone else, it is inevitable.

3) We have her take a week away from the family in the summer.

4) It is my goal to always be growing in my sensitivity to my wife and sharing more of my spectrum of emotions with her not just my desire for intimacy or my occasional moments of frustration or anger.

5) I help her keep the house clean and carpool the kids when I can.

6) I cook at least one meal a week.

7) We seek to get away on trips at least twice a year.

8) We celebrate our anniversary away every year.

9) I encourage her to pursue the things that matter to her.

10) I work to create space for her to live out the calling God has on her life.

11) I never share a story about her that she doesn't approve first.

12) I look for ways for us to do ministry together as often as possible.

I want my spouse to know she is more important to me than the church I pastor.

Pastor, the best gift you can give the church you pastor is a good marriage. Like it or not, if your marriage goes so goes your pastorate. This is not true of most vocations, but it is true of this one.

Sadly, many pastors and their spouses don't enjoy each other. They use all their social time to be with church-related activities and people and then the rest goes to their children. At the end of this draining process, their marriage always gets the leftovers. Our kids have activities, the church has activities, our marriage date night is more important than all of this. Yes, there are exceptions, but this isn't the norm.

Date your spouse, Pastor, the church you pastor will benefit whether they ever realize it or not.

If you lose your marriage, the church can get another pastor, but you will have lost the most important relationship of your life. You will then spend who knows how many years trying to figure out how to navigate the pain this causes your children. Avoid it all, remember you're married to your spouse not the church.

If you do these things, you will find: happy wife, happy life. ☺

> **Psalm 128:3a,** "Your wife will be like a fruitful vine within your house."

THE GOOD PASTOR | *Kelly M. Williams*

BOUNDARY AREA #3: FAMILY TIME

> **2 Chronicles 8:1,** "At the end of twenty years, in which Solomon had built the house of the Lord and **his own house."**

As a pastor you have responsibility to build both.

1) I take each of my children on one-on-one dates five times a year.

On these dates, I take them out to eat and I have a list of twenty-four questions I ask them. I ask the questions and listen. Sometimes the answers are painful. I ask them what they don't like about me and what they do. The same about themselves. I ask them about all the major categories of their life. They can choose not to be honest with me. That is their choice, but I ask and engage them. I want to know my children. I want them to know their father pursues them and cares about the details of their life. I understand that their view of me as dad will shape their view of God the Father more than any other relationship in their life.

No pressure! ☺

Many years ago, I read a book comparing Sigmund Freud to C.S. Lewis.

The book said, "In October 1896, Sigmund Freud's father died. Freud wrote a letter to Fliess (his friend) that this death 'has affected me profoundly ... has reawakened all my early feelings ... I feel quite uprooted.' He noted that the death of one's father is 'the most important event, the most poignant loss, in a man's life.' However, Freud was not close to his father. He considered his father a failure."

Regardless of how good or bad your relationship is, it shapes your view profoundly.

2) I don't share anything about my children in my messages without their permission.

3) We eat together at least three times a week around the table.

> **Psalm 128:3b,** "Your children will be like olive shoots **around your table.**"

A few years ago, we had Leonard Sweet speaking at our annual Multiply Conference. He referred to a study that talked about the one trait that all families had in common that gave families the greatest amount of potential for success as a family. Ironically enough, it was whether or not families sat down together and ate three meals together in the course of a week. We have done this for years in our home. You would hope you could get more than three in, but in the crazy fast-paced world we live that is the magical number for connectedness for your family.

We have a "no-phone policy" at our table. No electronic devices are allowed at the table.

We are there to connect with each other.

4) Read through the Bible as a family.

We have been working on this boundary/goal for thirteen-plus years now. We should have the entire Bible read at the end of fourteen years.

5) Be emotionally engaged with my family on my days off by abstaining from social media, work emails, and phone calls.

6) Take an annual vacation together and go camping or take a road trip.

7) Have five family days a year where we spend a whole day together.

It is very important your family also gets times where they can be together unencumbered by the work of the pastorate.

BOUNDARY AREA #4: SOCIAL MEDIA/ TELEVISION/COMPUTER/SMART PHONE:

> **Psalm 101:2a,3,** "I will walk with integrity of heart within my house; **I will not set before my eyes anything that is worthless.** I hate the work of those who fall away; it shall not cling to me."

What you allow yourself to watch on television or the internet could be the downfall of your pastorate.

It is important to walk with integrity especially in your own home where you may be the most susceptible to viewing things and participating in things you should not and would not normally. The Psalmist knew a little something about observing things he shouldn't observe in his own home. This is where he saw Bathsheba naked and bathing. He learned: 1) Don't watch things you shouldn't in your home. 2) Hate the work that causes you to fall away. 3) Don't let rebellion cling to you.

Here are some boundaries to help practice these principles:

1)   Follow Television/Social Media/Internet boundary.

Here is my commitment. If I see something on social media or television and I do not immediately turn it off, then I have to write about it in my journal for my wife and, eventually, children to read too at their corresponding age I was at the time of writing it.

These are built-in boundaries that help me keep a short account on temptation to lust sexually.

2)   Abstain from social media when I am on summer break.

I have made a commitment to stay off of social media completely because I cannot get on social media and not think about work. It is impossible for me. So, I take pictures of my family vacations and break and, a few days before I re-enter work, I start posting chronologically what our family did for the summer. This helps me to be in the moment with my family and it enables me to share with a large group of people at once what we did all summer. This helps people feel connected with me and my family as I re-enter. It also makes my re-entry much easier and simpler as I am an introvert and struggle to be extroverted with a lot of people at once especially when I have been on break for a long time.

3) Abstain from work emails, text, and social media on day off.

I find this to be the most difficult boundary to maintain in the week-in-week-out ministry season. I don't find it difficult to abstain from social media during my summer break. Matter of fact, I find it hard to re-engage social media after a long break from it.

4) Use social media primarily to disciple the people you lead and secondarily to share your life with them.

Social media is not a place a pastor needs to go to get validation of their life. Reserve that for your levels of accountability and relationships. Use social media primarily as a means to help your congregation to know what a healthy life lived out with Christ can look like and then, secondarily, to share your life. See it as a means of leadership and secondarily as connection.

BOUNDARY AREA #5: DIET AND EXERCISE

1 Timothy 4:8, "For while bodily training is of some value."

1) Annual Family Sugar Fast

Every year our family fasts from sugar for the month of August. This resets our sugar intake and binds us together as a family. It resets my disciplines of cravings and helps me to better manage my desires. It helps my children be honest and purifies their ability to be dependent upon something other than sugar. We have great conversations through this shared family experience. And yes four-year-olds can do this as well as forty-year-olds.

2)   Fast every Tuesday when I write a message

I have already touched on this one earlier in the book. I want God's voice to scream louder than my physical desires. This trains me in that direction.

3)   Have some form of physical activity two to three times a week

I usually play basketball twice a week for two-plus hours. This is huge for my mental health. I read a statistic that says men who have at least two hours of physical activity are many times less likely to be aggressive physically with their wife or kids.

I have no desire to be ripped like some pastors are today, but I do have a desire to be fit.

4)   Take juice-plus supplement daily

This is huge for energy and digestive consistency for me. I usually take it in the afternoon during the week to give me an extra measure of energy to focus and get work done during the time of day when I am prone to exhaustion. I also take it just a couple of hours before I preach, I find it helps sustain me through the grind of speaking. It gives me energy without the heaviness that can come from eating something with high amounts of sugar in it.

Since I have been taking this, it has lowered the number of times I get sick during the year.

5)   Try not to eat more than two meals a day on average.

I do this for health reasons and because the pastorate is a very sedentary job. It is important to do what is necessary to take good care of your physical body. It is the only one you will get. How you take care of it could determine your ability to stay in the pastorate longer.

6)   Get a stand-up desk for work.

Obesity and sedentariness could be the next big killer for pastors and other vocations where you are seated a lot. I have a desk that can go up and down and enable me to use my desk in an upright or seated position. I find this helpful for studying and for responding to an excessive number of emails. I find as the day wears on it gives me more energy and focus to get work done.

BOUNDARY AREA #6: FINANCES

> **1 Timothy 5:17,18,** "Let the elders who rule well be considered worthy of double honor especially those who labor in preaching and teaching. For the Scripture says, 'You shall not muzzle an ox when it treads out the grain.' And, 'The laborer deserves his wages.'"

1)   Don't be afraid to ask for a raise from your elder board.

It is important your elder board review you annually as the senior pastor, or, if you are associate, then your boss review you. It is important they review your benefits and salaries. Most senior pastors feel on an island with this part of their job.

2)   Tithe

It is amazing to me how many pastors don't tithe. When I was eight years old, I got my first pay check from my dad on the dairy farm. He paid me $10.00. He told me, "Now you need to tithe to God what you made." I said, "What is a tithe?" He said, "A tithe is 10 percent of what you make." I looked at my $10 bill and said, "But that means I will only have nine after that." He said, "That's right. But son, you need to know this, the more you make and the longer you wait to tithe the harder it will be. You will never make enough to feel comfortable tithing." God asked us in the Old Testament and the New Testament to tithe.

>   **Hebrews 13:5,** "Keep your life free from love of money and be content with what you have."

Tithing is your best chance of keeping your life free from the love of money, being thankful for what you make and content with what you have.

3)   Save 10% for retirement and kids college

I have had a retirement account since I was twenty-five years old. It wasn't much when I first started, but it has grown over the years. I also made a commitment to save $100 a month per child in a SMART529 for my kids' education. We have been able to save roughly $25,000 for each of our five kids. We give this amount and tell them, "This is yours and you are responsible for figuring out how to pay for the rest." I want my kids to be self-sustaining.

I also want each of my kids to be able to lead whatever organization they work for. We have sought to raise our four daughters the same way we have raised our son, to be entrepreneurs.

We want to be able to retire at sixty-six from making a salary from the church and we would like to have a large enough retirement and have no debt including mortgage so, if the Lord permits, we could continue to minister in some capacity without needing any income for it.

4)   Live off of a budget

Keep up with your expenses and income. Know what you make and what you spend your money on each month. It is important for stewardship.

BOUNDARY AREA #7: DAYS OFF

> **Genesis 2:2,** "And on the seventh day God finished his work that he had done, and he rested on the seventh day from all his work he had done.

It is extremely important to have days off for your family, your marriage, and for your mental and physical health. You need a rhythm that frees you each week from the grind of the work week. You need to keep fighting the temptation to fall into the trap of just working for the ministry.

On your days off you need to rest and you need to recreate. In the next chapter, we will address these two all important issues that enable you to be dependent upon God as you serve Him as a pastor.

Time off and recreation cannot be an option any more than your spiritual disciplines. It is also very important that you keep pressing into your time with the Lord during your days off. This is where you regroup each week. For me, I have found that working five days in a row and then having two off give me the best chance to stay replenished and fresh throughout the year, but as the year wears on my days off become less restful for me and I find work creeping in more than I care to admit.

I think it is important to have two days a week off. I don't think you can sustain a six-day work week over the long haul in the pastorate, especially if you have a family. Without margin you find yourself either always sleepy when you are at home or frustrated and angry. Your family learns to stay away from you.

I think it has taken me twenty years to find a good rhythm with this.

In the next chapter, we will discuss rhythms of rest and recreation. This plays a huge factor in our willingness to follow boundaries in our lives.

Boundaries in your life, Good Pastor, may be boring, but they are the self-imposed bumpers you have placed in your life to protect you from you. And remember King Asa, he had thirty-six years of faithful kingship to God, but he crossed one of the boundaries of his life and sought out help from the King of Syria instead of depending on God. In just five short years, Asa undid what he had spent thirty-six years being faithful to God in as the King of God's people. Unrepentant sin causes very good men and women of God to fall away, and the longer they wait to repent or turn to God, the more boundaries they cross, both of God and of their own.

Your past faithfulness does not dictate future success for God in the pastorate, but your boundaries followed NOW do.

If you want to go the distance and not burn out in the thirty-sixth year of a forty-one-year pastorate like Asa, Good Pastor, **then live dependent on God through boundaries in all areas of your life for a lifetime.**

CHAPTER 15

DEPENDENCE ON GOD THROUGH REST AND RECREATION

Fatigue makes cowards of us all.

When you feel like quitting the pastorate, realize this is a sign you need a break.

The hardest work of the pastorate is resting.

Spurgeon said to his students:

> It is wisdom to take occasional furlough. In the long run, we shall do more by sometimes doing less. On, on, on forever, without recreation may suit spirits emancipated from this "heavy clay," but while we are in this tabernacle, we must every now and then cry halt, and serve the Lord by holy inaction and consecrated leisure. Let no tender conscience doubt the lawfulness of going out of harness for a while.

EXCERPT FROM MY JOURNAL 7/17/2017:

Today marks the 36th day of my sabbatical break. We have twenty-seven days left until all the madness of ministry kicks back in. At times now I find myself wondering how Vanguard is doing. I pray for it but glad, honestly, not to know how it is doing. I am glad to rest, relax, recover, and refresh. The human body is not made to always be in charge. Leadership takes its toll on us and only rest and reflection restore the weary soul.

Fatigue creates the greatest threat to ministerial disaster.

Question I felt like the Lord asked me this morning:

"Do you crave to praise me more than you crave praise for yourself?" He told Israel, "I will share my glory with no other."

If you don't learn to rest and recreate, the probability decreases with time.

I think Augustine said it best:

"Thou hast formed us for Thyself, and our hearts are restless till they find rest in Thee."

If you have ever seen the movie, "Schindler's List" you know it personifies what the pastorate feels like 24/7. At the end of this movie, after the heroics of Oskar Schindler, he had saved 1200 Jews lives, he was full of angst because "he should have saved more."

Pastors can relate. We always do a lot, but we never do enough!

Any pastor, who truly cares, wishes he or she could have done more.

But it is, "the more" without rest, that eventually leads to burn-out and even worse, moral failure. Oftentimes, this burn-out eventually results in leaving the pastorate all together.

I'm convinced a lot of good pastors failed in ministry, fornicated, and quit because they refused to do one simple thing:

Rest.

Remember what my professor said to me?

"You want to be great for God? Don't quit, don't fornicate, you will be the only one left and you will be great."

Few consider rest as a means of avoiding this, but as the statement goes, "Fatigue makes cowards of us all." We are just not ourselves when we are fatigued. Sin looks far more appealing to us when we are fatigued as pastors.

I can't tell you how many pastors over the years have said to me, "What do you do to rest and to recreate?"

Lady Gaga once said:

"I will rest when I die."

Sadly, this is a lot of pastors' mottos as well. It seems admirable, but it is not human or sustainable.

John Piper said about rest in the pastorate:

In my pastoral experience, I can testify that time off is crucial for breathing a different spiritual air. When we take time away from the press of duty, Spurgeon recommends that we breathe country air and let the beauty of nature do its appointed work. He confesses that "sedentary habits have tendency to create despondency . . . especially in the months of fog." He then counsels, "A mouthful of sea air, or a stiff walk in the wind's face would not give grace to the soul, but it would yield oxygen to the body, which is next best.

At this point, let me add a personal word to you who are younger. In my years of pastoral ministry, I noticed significant changes in my body and soul. They were partly owing to changing circumstances, but much was owing to a changing constitution. First, I had to reduce my calorie intake to keep from gaining unhelpful weight. During the course of my ministry and aging, my metabolism stopped functioning the way it once did.

*Second, I grew to become emotionally less resilient when I didn't get adequate sleep. There were early days when I would work without regard to sleep, and afterward I would feel energized and motivated. However, **as I entered my forties, adequate sleep was no longer a matter of staying healthy, but a matter of staying in the ministry.***

Spurgeon was right when he said...

The condition of your body must be attended to . . . A little more . . . common sense would be a great gain to some who are ultra-spiritual, and attribute all their moods of feeling to some supernatural cause when the real reason lies far nearer to hand. Has it not often happened that dyspepsia has been mistaken for backsliding, and bad digestion has been set down as hard heart? Rest as you can see, is critical to going the distance in the pastorate.

The word "rest" means:

To cease work or movement in order *to relax*, refresh oneself, or recover strength.

The word recreation means:

Activity done *for enjoyment* when one is *not working.*

So, we rest by ceasing from work (so we can relax), and we recreate by doing something we enjoy (when we are not working).

Sounds simple enough.

Actually, sounds like something we would all enjoy doing.

But the pastorate and the demands of the 21st century place high pressure on us. Along with the increased pressure we place on ourselves, due to access to social media and the prevailing opinions of our society bombarding us, we get caught in the rat race of work … work …work …and more work.

Rest and recreation become the last priority on our list.

How do we depend on God in rest and recreation?

1. REALIZE REST TAKES WORK AT FIRST.

The writer of Hebrews understood this:

> **Hebrews 4:7a,9-11,** "Today, if you hear his voice, do not harden your hearts. So then there *remains* a Sabbath rest for the people of God (including pastors), for whoever has entered God's rest has also rested from his works as God did from his. Let us therefore *strive* to enter that rest, so that no one may *fall* by the same sort of disobedience."

Rest, naturally, gives you time to listen to God. Rest gives you time to hear God speak to you as a person, not you as a pastor. This is very important as time goes on. It is easy to hear God for others, but God wants to speak to us for us. I am not just a pastor. I am a person. I am a personal follower of Jesus and much of it has NOTHING to do with being a pastor. But, because we give so much of our time and energy to hearing God on behalf of *others* through His Word, we stop resting to hear from Him for *us*.

He tells us, "There remains a Sabbath rest for God's people." The New Testament still calls us to rest like He called His people to rest in the Old Testament. Granted, it can't be Sunday because that is the hardest day of our week, but we need a Sabbath.

We need a time to hear God through rest. He sounds different. He feels a lot more compassionate and relatable.

When we enter this rest, we are resting from the work of God. He DOESN'T want us to work for Him all the time. This is a lie that the Enemy uses to try to destroy our walk with the Lord by making us feel guilty. He wants us to feel "important" to the equation. He wants us to "fear" something good will happen without us. He wants us to feel like, if we stop, the church will realize it doesn't need us anymore. You can't be happy as a pastor if you only pastor because they need you. You must learn they don't just need you they want you and they will *wait* for you.

But this rest requires "striving." Rest will not naturally happen in the pastorate. You have to *strive* for it.

In my experience, all rest (especially at first) requires some "striving." But the writer of Hebrews makes it clear, rest is what keeps us from *falling.*

You can't memorize enough Scripture to avoid a moral failure. If you refuse to never rest and find some recreation for your life, fatigue will dull your ability to hear God's voice. And eventually, you will make a poor choice. But with the proper rest, you learn to depend upon God in a new and powerful way. And believe it or not, rest may very well be the discipline that saves your ministry and allows you to go the distance for Christ as a pastor.

But you need to know, NO ONE will fight for rest for you if you don't fight for it for yourself.

This has to be a priority to you.

Now, I have noticed that younger pastors are starting to work out more, eat better, and seemingly take better care of their physical bodies.

But if I am honest, it seems like this is a reaction born out of social peer pressure from our society, rather than being something pastors are doing to take better care of themselves by resting and recreating.

It seems that the most "appealing" kind of pastor is one who is "buff" in his or her physique, but a mess emotionally.

People today seem to want pastors who are emotional wrecks, but physically cut.

I am not sure if this trend is creating "rest" and "recreation" or just adding one more burden to the already burdened pastor.

Please know I am not anti-exercise. I play a couple of hours a week every week of basketball and I live on a small farm where I am able to keep myself in decent shape.

When I refer to rest and recreation in this chapter, I am referring to the things that **replenish you** physically, mentally, and spiritually **while also finding enjoyment in them**.

If you enjoy working out two hours a day with weights and so forth and so on, good for you. But if you do this to make yourself look a way that makes more people enjoy looking at you through livestream or in person when you speak or preach, then you have missed the point. But see how hard it is to "rest" and "recreate?"

How do you get away from the job of being a pastor? And then how do you get away from your thoughts about "how I can be a better pastor?"

See, I find, my "rest time" can be consumed with "how I can work better as a pastor" time.

My "recreation time" can be consumed with "I wonder how this might help me 'look' better, 'feel' better, 'connect' more with people I want to influence as pastor".

Even as simple as putting a picture of your family on social media when you are on vacation can lead to you thinking about work depending on who responds to your social media page. It can go something like this.

You post the picture.

You wait a few moments . . . no one likes it . . . oh no . . . what's wrong? . . . what are people not telling me? . . . do they think I shouldn't be on vacation? . . . is something wrong at church and no one wants to respond to my vacation?"

Then a flood of "likes" come in . . . oh, that's cool . . . (momentary peace) . . . then you say to yourself, "It is really cool being a pastor."

Then someone responds with a comment . . . "Looks like you are having fun with your family pastor, we miss you at church..."

That comment gives you a momentary high that they need you and miss you, then a few seconds later you start saying to yourself.

"I shouldn't have taken such a long time off."

Guilt runs rampant in your heart.

You are restless inside.

Your kid or grandkid runs up to you on the beach and asks you to play with them. You immediately feel the pressure of being a pastor and being a father or mother or grandparent. You have a choice to make.

You momentarily say to the child, "Not now."

You sit on the beach and stew in the guilt, regret, and begin to wonder what is really going on at church. You hope everything is okay.

The curse has bit you and the rest is:

OVER!

You are fried emotionally as if you had been at work all day and all you did was post a picture of your "fun time" with the family to social media.

Most pastors are control freaks. Sadly, it is what makes us good at what we do. However, it kills our souls over time.

Learning to rest requires discipline just like preparing sermons.

How do we depend on God through rest and recreation?

2. DISCONNECT FROM ALL KNOWABLE SOURCES OF PASTORAL FEEDBACK.

It is impossible to have a "staycation" in your own city of pastoral employment and never run into anyone from your church.

I am not talking about "controlling" what you can't control on your rest and recreation time. I am talking about stewarding well what you can.

Set an auto-reply for your email with the date you will return to the office and a way to connect with someone else.

But what if people think I have too long of a time off? What if people complain? What if...

Did your authority give you approved time off?

Then let them deal with it.

What if the person I refer them to ends up being someone they like and want more than me and while I am gone their hearts grow more toward them and away from me?

People are fickle and this will happen to a degree. It is human nature.

Be confident in your calling and trust that God called you there and He will sustain you. And if He doesn't, then He must want you somewhere else, but don't let this insecurity rob you of rest.

I am convinced the inability to rest from God's work as a pastor is fundamentally an inability to trust God with the work.

How do we depend on God through rest and recreation?

3. TRUST GOD AND YOUR TEAM WITH THE WORK.

You will not be around forever to lead the church, so you might as well start trusting God and your team now because eventually they are going to have to lead without you. And believe it or not, when you retire the work still won't be fully done.

Look at the life of Joshua:

> **Joshua 13:1,** "Now Joshua was old and advanced in years, and the Lord said to him, 'You are old and advanced in years, and **there remains yet very much land to possess.**'"

Regardless of how hard you work, the work of the Lord at your church will NEVER be complete. When you retire from it or die, it still won't be done, so rest and learn to live in the tension of God's Kingdom. He doesn't expect you to complete it, so rest when it is your time to rest.

This helps me to realize I need to trust it to the source that was in charge before I got there and will be in charge after I am gone.

Say to the Lord:

> "God, I commit my calling to you. I trust that you have called me here and when I return, I trust you will restore me to my call and continue to use me for as long as you desire as the pastor of this church."

Over twenty-plus years of being at the same church does not guarantee you job security. Matter of fact, I have had a few years where I wondered if my church would want me when I came back. I also have had a few years where I wondered, during my time off, if I wanted to come back.

Both processes are good to go through because they either strengthen your calling or open your eyes (and theirs) to the reality that maybe this season has come to an end.

It is hard to know if God has called you to stay somewhere if you never take a break from it.

He can't speak to you afresh and anew like He did when He called you there.

When I go on break, I don't assume anything, except, it is time for a break to rest.

You have to force yourself to let go of the results of what is going to take place while you are gone and you will face when you return. That fear is real and hard to let go of.

But rest shows me that much of what I do is striving to get approval from myself, God, or others. My "striving" with fatigue, mixed with fear, kills my ability to feel loved by God.

> **1 John 4:18-20** says, "There is no fear in love, **but perfect love casts out fear**. For fear has to do with punishment, and whoever fears has not been perfected in love. We love because **He first loved us."**

Fatigue as a pastor, makes fearful cowards of us all in the ministry.

Rest restores my ability to feel loved by God.

Whatever you do for God as a pastor, you do not do it to be loved, but *because you are loved.*

So much of what we do, we do to get people to love us and that is the quickest way to destroy yourself in the pastorate. It is like a mom saying to herself, "I want to have a child so I can feel better about me."

Good luck!

Don't go into the pastorate or parenting if you want the church or the child to meet an unmet need in your life. You go into both to serve and meet *their* unmet needs.

You bring to them what you experienced through the "rest" of your life . . . in rest I bring the excess presence of God that spills over out of my life and soul into others' lives, not unlike Moses, when he went to meet with God on the mountain.

How do I depend on God through rest and recreation?

4. SEEK HIS PRESENCE THROUGH REST.

Look at what God said to Moses:

> **Exodus 33:14-17** says, "And he (God) said, (to Moses), 'My presence will go with you, and I will give you **rest.**'"

See, it is His presence that ultimately gives us **rest.**

I am convinced rest is the opposite of fear. When I am "resting" in God's presence I am casting off fear and feeling the love God has for me regardless of the outcome or "success" of my ministry. When you seek God's presence *through rest* you find God's favor for your life and the distinction of what makes you who you are.

Moses says it:

> **Exodus 33:15-17,** "And he (Moses) said to him, (God) 'If your presence will not go with me, do not bring us up from here. For how shall it be known that I have found favor in your sight, I and your people? Is it not in your going with us so that we are **distinct**, I and your people, from every other people on the face of the earth?' And the Lord said to Moses, 'This very thing that you have spoken I will do, for you have found favor in my sight, and I know you by name.'"

> **Exodus 33:19-23,** "And he (God) said, 'I will make all my goodness (presence and favor) pass before you and will proclaim before you my name "The Lord." And I will be gracious to whom I will be gracious, and will show mercy on whom I will show mercy.' But, he said, 'You cannot see my face, for man shall not see me and live.' And the Lord said, 'Behold, there is a place by me where you shall stand on the rock, and while my glory passes by **I will put you in the cleft of the rock, and I will cover you with my hand until I have passed by.** Then I will take away my hand, and you shall see my back, but my face shall not be seen.'"

Do you know what God was telling Moses?

During your rest time, in the cleft of the rock, I will cover you with my hand until I have passed by. Then, I will remove my hand and allow you to see my back, but my face shall not be seen.

God gives us a greater glimpse of His presence through rest. When you and I are in a posture of rest, after a season of battling on His behalf like Moses, we are in the best position to receive the most impact from the presence of God. This gave Moses greater confidence to lead God's people and be a better prophet for God.

However, it is important to remember, I don't take a break to ultimately be a better pastor when I return, though that happens.

Rather, I take a break, so I can seek His presence through rest and not just through a posture of work.

I get to know God differently in rest than I do in work.

He wants me to accomplish things in His name. He wants me to bring glory to Him through my work. But He also wants me to bring glory to Him by just resting and spending time with Him.

When I rest and spend time with the Lord four things are able to naturally occur over time without trying to force or rush the process.

1) Time to think: organize your experiences

2) Time to feel: allow yourself to go there, wherever, there is

3) Time to process: put your thinking and your feeling together on paper

4) Time to heal: ask God to take it and use it as He desires in your life

Every human being needs this and especially pastors. You need time to heal from the brokenness ministry has caused you and your family. Even more importantly, you need time to heal from the bumps and bruises that life itself has caused you.

I have learned over the years that ministry is difficult, but if you never rest you start assuming that "all" the difficulties of your life are due to ministry, and that is just not true.

Ministry is difficult. Being a pastor is difficult. But never forget, just being human is difficult. We all live in a fallen world that wants to tempt us at every turn to quit on the good of our lives and give into the bad. The Psalmist reminds us that even our best days are full of trouble.

> **Psalm 90:10a (NLT)** "But even the best years are filled with pain and trouble; soon they disappear, and we fly away."

But it is also important to remember, we need to rest and recreate **in God's presence.** You can't find rest outside of His presence. You can't find recreation outside of His presence and expect it to restore you. Your rest and recreation have to be in rhythm with who and where God has called you to be and do.

Even God worked six days and then **rested** from His work. He trusted the completed work of His creation. I wonder if Adam and Eve fell on Sunday? 😊

Your rest has to be in rhythm with the work God has called you to do for it to be effective.

I would be a rich man if I had a quarter for every time someone asked me the question, "Pastor is it okay to work on Sunday?"

Uh, yes.

The title Pastor by definition **requires** you to work on Sunday.

Spurgeon said:

> *"Our Sabbath is our day of toil, he said, "and if we do not rest upon some other day we shall break down."*

When I was a kid my dad would say, "If the ox is in the ditch, Jesus says to get him out." And then he would add, "Just make sure you don't put him there," meaning, don't work on Sundays because you want too, work on Sunday because you have too. Just make sure the "have to" is real.

When you and I work and do what God has asked us to do and then rest, our rest is more meaningful. As we learned in the life of Moses, God goes with us and gives us rest through His presence. But sometimes, we don't rest properly because we don't have proper rhythms of rest and recreation. Sometimes we sabotage the process of work and rest by trying to manufacture rest and recreation where God never intended it to be.

I have seen this occur in scores of pastors' lives because they go so long without rest, they begin to break down and try to manufacture rest and recreation in seasons where they were supposed to be about the Father's business.

King David gives us a prime example of what rest looks like in a season when he was supposed to be working.

> **2 Samuel 11:1,** "In the spring of the year, **the time when kings go out to battle, David sent Joab, and his servants with him, and all Israel.** And they raved the Ammonites and besieged Rabbah."

None of them were kings.

Senior pastors are meant to lead their churches into the most important battles.

It is ALWAYS dangerous to be resting and recreating in a season where you are supposed to be working and leading God's people into battle.

Rhythms of rest are just as important as rest.

> **Ecclesiastes 3:1** says, "For everything there is a season, and a time for every matter under heaven."

King David chose to rest and send others to war when Kings normally go out to battle. Look at what happens when we seek rest and recreation when it is not in rhythm with who God has called us to be and do:

> **2 Samuel 11:1a,2,** "But David **remained** at Jerusalem. It happened, late one afternoon, when David arose from his couch and was walking on the roof of the king's house, that he saw from the roof a woman bathing; and the woman was very beautiful."

You know the story. On a day when he was supposed to be off in battle, he remained in Jerusalem.

Rest has to be in rhythm with what God has called you to be and do.

Rest has to be as intentional as work, otherwise you will remain in a place you are not supposed to be and end up doing something you are not supposed to be doing.

How do you depend upon God in rest and recreation?

5. MAKE SURE IT FITS THE RHYTHM OF YOUR WORK.

David was a King. Everyone knew the season kings went to war. He knew it. His troops knew it. His Enemy knew it.

The Enemy wants you to work when you should rest, and rest when you should work. You need the wisdom to discern the difference through accountability with those around you.

Your rest and recreation should fit into the rhythm of your work, be planned, and full of intention.

Here are the rhythms of my rest and recreation that I follow year end and year out:

1)   Take **TWO** days off a week from work.

Why two? Because if you take two you will consistently get one. If you take one, you will consistently get none. This is how pastoral ministry works. It bleeds into your days off whether you want it to or not.

2) Do something twice a week that you enjoy doing that brings recreation into your life.

I find my days off create space for me to do this.

3) Take a break from speaking every fifth weekend if possible (especially if you do multiple days and multiple services of speaking on the weekend).

Studies that I have read show that you exert the same amount of energy for a thirty-minute message as you do for an eight-hour work day. I speak three times a weekend most of the time. This means I am stressing my body and, more importantly, my mind as if I am working twenty-four hours each weekend.

4) Take a week off in the Spring and Fall of the year to give yourself time to rest during the week even if you end up speaking on the weekend.

It is better if you can plan your work schedule so you have the whole week and weekend off when you do this.

5) Take four to five weeks and weekends off every summer.

My experience is, it takes me fifteen long emotional days in a row to reach the point where I have a day of "rest" when I go on break. I start to feel rested around days 21-23. I could go back to work then, but I find I start to have fun at this time and enjoy my life, wife, and family. So, then around day twenty-eight I start to catch vision for the church and the future of the ministries of the church. My mind naturally drifts to what I am called to do and it reaffirms my confidence, but it takes time and I have to face my fears that maybe this is my last year and I need to move on, but without fail like a boomerang I come back to it.

I find days 28-35 are full of imagining how God can use us as a church team, staff, community, and I get excited about a dozen or so ideas. I don't assume this is ALL from God and mandated that we do it, I just initially see it as God's way of affirming in me that I am called to this and a little rest makes me energized and excited again about what I am created to do.

Now you may say, "That's great for you! But how in the world can I do this when I am the ONLY pastor who speaks at my church?"

Even when Vanguard was small, I decided to identify key volunteer leaders in the church who could give ONE message a year about what matters deeply to them that fits into the vision of the church.

Yes, the teaching may suffer a bit, but my experience is, you need a break from them and they need a break from you to regain a deeper appreciation for you and the gifts God has entrusted to you.

You are the primary communicator for a reason. It is more than likely because you are better at communicating than others or you are the most impactful to the church's vision, but that does not mean you can't take a break and let others share in that vision.

Recently, one of our teaching pastors spoke two weeks in a row, and afterwards, someone came up to them and said, "Great message, Pastor. I used to go here when Kelly was the pastor." The team member said, "How long have you been back?" The person said, "Two weeks." The team member said, "Kelly is still the senior pastor, he has just been gone for two weeks."

It is okay for others on your team to get the glory of teaching while you are gone. And yes, there will be people in your church who like the other speakers better than you. But see this as a win for everyone, including yourself.

Seven years ago, we developed a teaching team of volunteers and staff. We now have over fourteen teachers on a team that has enabled us to expand to three locations. This has been one of the greatest victories that has come out of the "rest" model we have at Vanguard.

Ironically enough, I am writing this chapter (as you noted from the beginning of the chapter) after being on "rest and recreation" time.

Good things happen when we rest in rhythm with our work. I have found over the years that when I rest in rhythm with my work others get a chance to succeed in seasons of the church when less is expected and this gives young and new leaders a chance to have success without the pressure that comes from the seasons of "when kings go off to war."

6) Every five years take a sabbatical and give yourself and your full-time staff an extra 20 days off in conjunction with their regular time off.

I have now done this twice and have found it to be extremely helpful to me, the church, and to my family. It rewards longevity and builds lasting trust between you and your staff.

What about recreation?

1) Do something every day you enjoy, regardless of how small and insignificant it is to others as long as it matters to you. (Drink coffee, go for a walk, watch or read sports highlights, read a short story, draw, sketch, find your daily recreation.) It will get you through some tough days. You will be amazed at how a simple little sinless pleasure can help you endure a long day of meetings that are beating the life out of you.

2) Do something every week that you look forward to like a date with your spouse, a nice meal, a drive in the woods, country, mountains, or a walk by the ocean or lake, join an adult sports team or pick-up sport at the local gym or fitness center.

3) Do something every month that requires you to get out of your regular rhythm and you look forward to it. Like going fishing, climbing a mountain, painting a picture, sketching, going to a sporting event, play, or musical.

4) Do something every year like go on a long road trip, buy something for yourself, go to an adult sports camp and have fun, sit by the ocean, camp by a camp fire in the mountains for multiple days.

Ministry is difficult, even in the best-case scenarios. It is exhausting and it requires an immense amount of personal energy and emotion to perform at a very high level over a long period of time. If you don't rest and recreate consistently, your body will eventually tell you to, as it breaks down emotionally, physically, medically, and psychologically. I have suffered from so many chronic issues because of my inability to properly handle stress and rest correctly. Your body and mind need rest and recreation to replenish itself. If you don't give it what it needs, eventually it will take it in a season like David when you are supposed to be off to war.

How about you? Are you finding yourself looking for "escape" routes while working? Are you remaining "at work" while "remaining in rest/recreation mode" so to speak? Are you caught in that middle place where you are no longer effective in your work or effective in resting? Have the lines blurred in your life to the point that you are thinking about taking someone else's spouse to find the relief you can't seem to find in your regular routine of life? Is the stress of ministry breaking your body down physically and emotionally? Are you going to send everyone else out to war while you stay home and try to figure out how to recover from your fatigue?

It is important that you find rhythms in your rest and recreation that compliment your work. Rest and recreation must be as intentional and purposeful as work. Otherwise, they will be swallowed by the tyranny and urgency of the work at hand, until your capacity to resist the temptations that so easily beset you breaks down completely. Be wise, be intentional and purposeful, today. Use what you have read here to plan your rhythm of rest and recreation, so that you can depend upon God in rest and recreation, and go the distance in the pastorate at a high level for a lifetime.

I give you permission as a fellow pastor to *enjoy* your life.

Don't wait until your dead to rest.

You won't make it.

You will quit or have a moral failure before then.

Realize rest and recreation is the hardest work that leads to your greatest accomplishment: being faithful to God for a lifetime through the pastorate.

Well done, thy rested and recreated servant!

Now get back to work, Good Pastor!

It is time for kings to go off to war, again!

CHAPTER 16

DEPENDENCE ON GOD THROUGH TRUSTING HIS PROMISES

Faithfulness is best measured over time, but it begins with where you are now.

My professor, Dr. John Hannah said, "You want to be great for God? Don't quit, don't fornicate, you will be the only one left and you will be great."

He said that to our class when I was twenty-one years old. The "don't fornicate part" resonated with me deeply then. At the time, I had no idea why anyone would want to quit on the pastorate. But now, as a fifty year old man who has been in the pastorate for twenty-five-plus years, I get it. The young need to remind the old not to quit, and the old need to remind the young not to fornicate.

When we are younger, our selfishness comes out in our ambition to succeed and feel successful at any cost. But as we age, our selfishness leaks out through our desire to quit because we are just not sure it is worth the sacrifice it has exacted on our selfish ambition.

The young see the hypocrisy of the old and the old see the naïveté of the young.

This is why we need each other in the pastorate, regardless of our ages.

I was once young and fornication was probably my greatest temptation, but I am now older and my desire to quit honestly exceeds my temptation to sin sexually.

I had a seasoned leader tell me when I was younger, "The great thing about getting older is youthful lust doesn't have as strong of a hold over you, but the bad thing about getting older is your ambition and your desire to 'stay at it' wanes as well." In every season, we have temptation, it just looks different depending on our age. Now don't get me wrong, I'm not dead. Both are still very real temptations, just one takes priority more often over the other depending on the season.

Throughout the past twenty-five plus years, I have learned a few things I sometimes forget. Such as, faithfulness is not dependent upon your ability, appearance, or success. It is strictly determined by your willingness to keep showing up regardless of the circumstances or the cost that is exacted upon your life.

I think every pastor, if he or she is honest, is discouraged by their professional ministry from time to time. Either they are discouraged that the success of their ministry was not as fulfilling to them as they hoped it would be or the success of their ministry never measured up to the dreams or aspirations that they once had when they entered the pastorate. But either way, we all fight the demon of:

"Was this really worth giving my life to...?"

I think the Apostle Paul addresses this and says it best:

> **Acts 20:23,** "But I do not account my life of any value nor as precious to myself, **if only I may finish my course and the ministry that I received from the Lord Jesus**, to testify to the gospel of the grace of God."

This would be Paul's "Don't quit, don't fornicate" mantra.

There comes a point in your life when you stop thinking about "success" and start thinking about finishing what God has asked you to start and do with your life.

It is not an easy moment or season, but it is a good moment and a good season, when you find out deep down why you signed up for this thing called the pastorate and what you are truly made of in the midst of the grind.

I can't think of anyone who modeled the grind of this challenge any better in the Bible than Joshua.

He began his "professional career" for God when he was forty. He records this in Joshua 14:7:

"I (Joshua) was forty years old when Moses the servant of the Lord sent me from Kadesh Barnea to explore the land."

Joshua's first ministerial assignment from his boss, Moses, was to go into the land and spy it out and come back with a report on how they could go about capturing the land for God.

Like Joshua, we all have high aspirations when we first set out on the journey.

How do you educate your naiveté without giving in to the temptation of going through the motions of the pastorate and becoming a hypocrite to the people you lead?

Easier said than done.

Jesus knew this wouldn't be easy when He walked the earth and He told us:

> **Luke 6:28,** "Bless those who curse you, pray for those who abuse you."

Wow! If I had a dollar for every time a person has cursed me or abused me as a pastor, I would be a rich man.

Do you remember what age you were when you began your "professional ministerial career" as a pastor? Do you remember who your first ministerial employer was?

I was twenty-two years old. South Park Baptist Church in Grand Prairie, Texas, hired me for my first official pastoral role as the youth pastor serving three-quarter time as

I went to seminary at Dallas Theological Seminary in the fall of 1993.

I was eager to live my life by the convictions of God's Word just like Joshua:

> **Joshua 14:7a,** "And I (Joshua) brought him (Moses, my first employer) back a report according to my convictions, [8] but my fellow Israelites who went up with me made the hearts of the people melt in fear."

Do you remember the day you were no longer sure that what God promised you as a pastor would come true? Or whether you could endure the people He had entrusted to you? And even more so, whether you cared any more or not?

For me it was about a year and half into my ministry. My senior pastor resigned and moved away, and they made me the interim-senior pastor. My first week on the job a guy came into my office and sat down and within a few minutes he had unloaded on me some of the worst comments and insults I had ever experienced in my life. He verbally ripped me to shreds. I sat there in complete disbelief as he told me every reason why I wasn't qualified to be the pastor of that church. And when he was done, he got up and walked out. I was left to process what he had said and make a decision to believe I knew I was called to be a pastor regardless of what he saw in me or didn't. And by the way, he never changed his mind.

Just like the ten spies caused the people of Israel's hearts to melt because of fear, that guy caused my twenty-three-year-old heart to melt in fear. What little did I know it would be the beginning of a long journey where I would have numerous opportunities to doubt my calling, who I was, and whether I had what it took to be a pastor.

I loved Joshua's response to the critics who said they couldn't do it:

> **Joshua 14:8a,** "I, however, followed the Lord my God wholeheartedly."

There is no substitute for following the Lord your God wholeheartedly.

You can't do what God has called you do while exhausting yourself with doubt as to whether He has called you to do it. At some point, you have to TRUST the promises of God and do what He has called you to do and be with your life.

Everybody will have that watershed faith moment (or moments!) in your pastorate where you will have to decide to trust God's promises more than relying on God's people. No offense to God's people, but they will hurt you, harm you, and disappoint you to the point that you might decide you would rather do something else with your life.

Just this morning, I doubted God's call on my life because of God's people. My daily devotions led me through Acts 12-22 and here is what the Spirit said to me through the life of Paul and his ministry:

> **Acts 18:9,10,** "And the Lord said to Paul one night in a vision, '**Do not be afraid, but go on speaking and do not be silent**, for I am with you, and no one will attack you to harm you, for I have many in this city who are my people.'»

I needed to hear those words this morning. It has been twenty-seven years since that guy laid into me and began my journey of doubt as a pastor, and yet, I still get tripped up by my own humanity and insecurities.

We as pastors need to be reminded of the promises of God just like Joshua, especially when we are caught in the crosshairs of discouragement and intense criticism that lead us to doubt. Joshua said:

> **Joshua 14:9,** "So on that day Moses (my boss) swore to me, 'The land on which your feet have walked will be your inheritance and that of your children forever, **because you have followed the Lord my God wholeheartedly.**'"

God has promises for you and me that are not tied to our abilities, appearances, or accomplishments, but simply our willingness to remain wholeheartedly faithful to His calling on our lives.

Recently, I was at a pastor's conference in Southern California and I struck up a conversation with a pastor. I asked him how long he had been pastoring. He said, "Thirty-plus years." He then said back to me, "How long for you?"

It was like we were exchanging terms of our prison sentences. 😊 (And sadly, sometimes that is what the pastorate can feel like, sometimes for long stretches.)

I said twenty-plus years. He immediately said to me, "You gonna stay after it?"

We both stood there in silence for what seemed like an eternity. I am not sure what ran through his mind, but it seemed like we didn't need to speak. We got it. We smiled at each other and then I said,

> "It certainly gets harder with time to pull the arrows out of your back and go on."

He looked at me, not needing to ask me what I meant by what I said. We both just stared at one another with relief, in agreement, and in some strange way our presence momentarily brought comfort to each of us. And then he said, "Yeah it is."

We exchanged a few more pleasantries and then walked away from one another. We both knew the cost to continue, but we also knew what it felt like to experience the faithful hand of God who gives us the grace to keep going despite the challenges that come against us.

I love Joshua's words:

> **Joshua 14:10,11,** "Now then, **just as the Lord promised,** he has kept me alive for forty-five years since the time he said this to Moses (his boss), while Israel moved about in the wilderness. So here I am today, eighty-five years old! I am still as strong today as the day Moses sent me out; **I'm just as vigorous to go out to battle now as I was then."**

Can you say that?

The Lord has kept His promise to me and kept me alive for these past twenty-five plus years. I can honestly say, I don't

continue on because of my strength, ability, or success.
I remain in the battle committed to the call because of the
faithfulness of the Lord to His promises to me.

I may not have as much energy or naiveté now that I had
twenty-five plus years ago, but I have something now,
I didn't have then. I have a faith that has been tried and
tested and I have chosen not to give in to the hypocrisy
of my soul and teach the people of God the promises of
God without believing them myself. I STILL believe God is
faithful, His Word is true, and He will reward those who
diligently seek Him. I still have dreams from God for God
and I am still eager to ask God to do through me for His
people what I can't do without Him. I love the tenacity and
the determination of Joshua even after forty-five years of
disappointment and waiting.

This morning I wrote in my journal:

"I trust you, Lord, with the weight in the wait."

And the best way to handle the weight in the wait is to
keep asking Him for what He has promised to give you.
Moses promised Joshua the Lord would give him and his
children the land. Joshua was faithful to keep asking God
for what He had promised him.

> **Joshua 14:12,** "Now give me this hill country
> that the Lord promised me that day. You
> yourself heard then that the Anakites were there
> and their cities were large and fortified, but,
> the Lord helping me, I will drive them out just as
> he said."

If you are going to depend upon God through trusting His promises, you are going to have to do three things:

1) Remember what God has promised you.
2) Trust Him that He will fulfill it through you.
3) Do your part and keep fighting the good fight.

The promise is from God, but it will be fulfilled through you.

You still matter to the equation, just as Joshua did.

He had a battle to fight at the age of eighty-five, forty-five years into his professional ministerial career, he still had a job to do. And so do you. You have to rise up above your disappointment, stop focusing on the amount of time it has taken you to get here, and look forward in anticipation as you continue to remain faithful to who God has created you to be and do. Some days you will be more successful than others, but you keep treading along regardless of the little progress you seem to be making at this time.

Don't give up! Keep trusting His promises. Keep applying them to your heart, your life, and to your pastorate.

You and I have been on a pastoral journey through the past fifteen chapters. I thought it would be fitting to end this book by reminding you of the promises God has given YOU as a pastor in accordance with each of the chapters of this book. I have given you sixteen challenges, one in each chapter of this book. I know it is daunting and overwhelming, but with good measure great things await you if you continue to apply these principles by remembering the promises that are attached to these good works. It is my hope it will give you the courage to keep fighting the good fight. There are many fights in this life, but only ONE good fight. God has called you to fight the good fight of being a pastor and shepherd His people to live as He has called them to live.

Challenge #1: PRACTICE THE DISCIPLINE OF MEDITATING ON GOD'S WORD.

Ezra 7:10, "For Ezra had set his heart to study the Law of the Lord, and to do it, and to teach his statues and rules in Israel."

Promise #1: GOD WILL ACCOMPLISH HIS SUCCESSFUL PURPOSE FOR YOU.

Isaiah 55:11, "So shall my word be that goes out from my mouth; it shall not return to me empty, but it shall accomplish that which I purpose, and shall succeed in the thing for which I sent it."

If you practice the discipline of meditating on God's Word NOTHING will keep you from fulfilling God's purpose for your existence and succeeding in the reason for which He created you.

Challenge #2: PRACTICE THE DISCIPLINE OF CONFESSION.

Acts 24:16, "So I always take pains to have a clear conscience toward both God and men."

Promise #2: GOD WILL REWARD YOU WITH HONORABLE PURPOSES.

2 Timothy 2:22-23 "Therefore, if anyone cleanses himself from what is dishonorable, he will be a vessel for honorable use, set apart as holy, useful to the master of the house, ready for every good work."

If you confess sin, God will set you aside for honorable use. He calls on those who cleanse themselves through confession from dishonorable things. But He exposes the sin of those who refuse to practice this discipline.

Challenge #3: PRACTICE THE DISCIPLINE OF COMMITMENT.

Joshua 11:18 "Joshua made war **a long time** with all those kings."

Promise #3: GOD WILL GIVE YOU A HOPEFUL FUTURE.

Jeremiah 31:16-17 "Thus says the Lord, "Keep your voice from weeping, and your eyes from tears, for there is a reward for your work, declares the Lord, and they shall come back from the land of the enemy. **There is hope for your future**, declares the Lord, and your children shall come back to their own country.

You can't out give God. If you discipline yourself to be committed, you will experience a hope for your future regardless of how bleak your present circumstances are due to your pastorate or your family. Claim this promise and keep pressing on!

Challenge #4: PRACTICE THE DISCIPLINE OF LISTENING.

John 10:27 "My sheep hear my voice, and I know them, and they follow me."

Promise #4: GOD WILL GIVE YOU PEACE TO FIGHT THE ANXIETY.

Philippians 4:6,7, "Do not be anxious about anything, but in everything by prayer and supplication with thanksgiving let your requests be made known to God. And the peace of God, which surpasses all understanding, will guard your hearts and your minds in Christ Jesus."

Why did I say "fight" instead of "overcome"? Because this is a raging battle that gets greater with age. When we are younger, we don't know what to fear, as we age, we figure it out. God wants us to be as courageous at seventy as we were at twenty, maybe even more so, but we need His peace to fight the anxiety that occurs over the long haul of the pastorate.

Challenge #5: DREAM GOD-GIVEN DREAMS.

Psalm 127:1, "Unless the Lord builds the house, those who build it labor in vain. Unless the Lord watches over the city, the watchman stays awake in vain."

Promise #5: GOD WILL ALWAYS BE WITH YOU IN HIS DREAMS.

1 Chronicles 28:20, "Then David said to Solomon his son, 'Be strong and courageous and do it. Do not be afraid and do not be dismayed, for the Lord God, even my God, is with you. **He will not leave you or forsake you, until all the work for the service of the house of the Lord is finished.'"**

Nothing can thwart God's purpose for your life, and nothing can keep God from being with you in it, even when it feels like you have been abandoned. If the dream is from Him, it will happen, in His time and in His way. Be sure and stay with Him and make His presence your focus and not the fulfillment of the dream. He will take care of that in His time.

Challenge #6: DREAM GOD-REALIZED DREAMS.

Exodus 33:15,16, "And he said to him, 'If your presence will not go with me, do not bring us up from here. For how shall it be known that I have found favor in your sight, I and your people? **Is it not in your going with us, so that we are distinct, I and your people**, from every other people on the face of the earth?'"

If we are dreaming God-given dreams, we need proof from Him to know they are from Him. Moses asked for this. It is reasonable for us to do the same so we know if they are from Him. Then they will be realized by Him, through us, because His presence is with us and has led us.

Promise #6: GOD ESTABLISHES HIS DREAMS THROUGH YOU.

> **Psalm 90:16,17,** "Let your work be shown to your servants, and your glorious power to their children. Let the favor of the Lord our God be upon us, and establish the work of our hands upon us; yes, establish the work of our hands!"

I have always been amazed that Jesus went back to heaven and sent the Holy Spirit for us to do the work, honestly, He was better at. God always establishes His dreams through people. Your dream coming true is up to you, but God's realized dream for your life is up to Him.

Challenge #7: DREAM GOD-ALTERED DREAMS.

> **Acts 7:5** "Yet he (God) gave him (Abraham) no inheritance in it, not even a foot's length, but promised to give it to him as a possession and to his offspring after him, though he had no child."

Promise #7: GOD CREATES ODDS ONLY HE CAN FULFILL THROUGH YOU.

Daniel 4:35, "All the inhabitants of the earth are accounted as nothing, and he does according to his will among the host of heaven and among the inhabitants of the earth; and none can stay his hand or say to him, 'What have you done?'"

Challenge #8: DREAM GOD-RESTORED DREAMS.

Genesis 22:1-3, "After these things God tested Abraham and said to him, 'Abraham!' And he said, 'Here I am.' He said, 'Take your son, your **only** son Isaac, whom you love, and go to the land of Moriah, and offer him there as a burnt offering on one of the mountains of which I shall tell you.' So Abraham arose . . . and went to the place which God had told him."

Promise #8: GOD REQUIRES YOU TO SACRIFICE IT BEFORE HE RESTORES IT.

Genesis 22:9,10,12-14, "When they came to the place of which God had told him, Abraham built the altar there and laid the wood in order and bound Isaac his son and laid him on the altar, on top of the wood. Then Abraham reached out his hand and **took the knife to slaughter his son.** But the angel of the Lord called to him from heaven and said, 'Abraham, Abraham!' And he said, 'Here

I am.' He said, 'Do not lay your hand on the boy or do anything to him, for now I know that you fear God, seeing you have not withheld your son, your only son, from me.' And Abraham lifted up his eyes and looked, and behold, behind him was a ram, caught in a thicket by his horns. So Abraham called the name of that place, **'The Lord will provide'."**

You can't cling to God and hold on to the dream He has for your life. You have to sacrifice the dream and trust the Giver of the dream to restore it in His timing. Easier said than done.

Challenge #9: DETERMINE TO PASTOR THROUGH REJECTION AND BETRAYAL.

John 6:66,67, "After this many of his disciples turned back and no longer walked with him. So Jesus said to the twelve, 'Do you want to go away as well?'"

Promise #9: REJECTION AND BETRAYAL CAN'T STOP YOU FROM PASTORING.

Nehemiah 6:1-4, "Now when Sanballat and Tobiah and Geshem the Arab and the rest of our enemies heard that I had built the wall and that there was no breach left in it, Sanballat and Geshem sent to me, saying, 'Come and let us meet together at Hakkephirim in the plain of Ono.' **But they intended to do me harm.** And

I sent messengers to them, saying, 'I am doing a great work and I cannot come down. **Why should the work stop while I leave it and come down to you?'** And **they sent to me four times** in this way, and **I answered them in the same manner.**"

You can't choose how people treat you, but you can choose your response.

Challenge #10: DETERMINE TO PASTOR THROUGH HARDSHIPS AND DISAPPOINTMENTS.

2 Timothy 4:16,17, "At my first defense no one came to stand by me, but **all deserted me. May it not be charged against them! But the Lord stood by me and strengthened me,** so that through me the message might be fully proclaimed . . . So I was **rescued from the lion's mouth.**"

Promise #10: TOMORROW'S BLESSINGS CAN'T BE STOPPED BY TODAY'S DISAPPOINTMENTS.

John 16:33a, "In the world you will have tribulation. But take heart; I have overcome the world."

Don't let one loss today become two losses tomorrow.

Challenge #11: DETERMINE TO PASTOR THROUGH LEADERSHIP FAILURES.

2 Chronicles 25:7-10, "But a man of God came to him and said, 'O king, do not let the army of Israel go with you, for the Lord is not with Israel, with all these Ephraimites. But go, act, and be strong for the battle. Why should you suppose that God will cast you down before the enemy? For God has power to help or to cast down.' And Amaziah said to the man of God, 'But what shall we do about the hundred talents that I have given to the army of Israel?' The man of God answered, 'The Lord is able to give you much more than this.' Then Amaziah discharged the army that had come to him from Ephraim to go home again. And they became **very angry** with Judah and returned home in **fierce anger.**"

Promise #11: GOD'S SOVEREIGN GRACE EXCEEDS OUR PAST FAILURES.

2 Chronicles 25:11, "But Amaziah took courage and led out his people and went to the Valley of Salt and struck down 10,000 men of Seir."

Don't let regret define your future. Allow forgiveness to lead you to a new opportunity that you seize with courage, again.

Challenge #12: DETERMINE TO PASTOR THROUGH TEMPTATION.

Luke 17:1, "And he (Jesus) said to his disciples, 'Temptations to sin are sure to come,'"

Promise #12: SUBMISSION TO GOD GUARANTEES VICTORY OVER TEMPTATION.

James 4:7,10, "Submit yourselves therefore to God. Resist the devil, and he will flee from you. Humble yourselves before the Lord, and he will exalt you."

Don't let your temptations define you. Rather, allow your trust in God's power to dictate your new identity, which is victor over the grave.

Challenge #13: DEPEND ON GOD THROUGH ACCOUNTABILITY.

Proverbs 15:22, "Without counsel plans fail, but with **many** advisers they succeed."

Promise #13: ACCOUNTABILITY PROTECTS YOU FROM YOU.

Proverbs 11:14, "Where there is no guidance, a people fall, but in an abundance of counselors there is **safety**."

Challenge #14: DEPEND ON GOD THROUGH BOUNDARIES.

1 Corinthians 9:27, "But I discipline my body and keep it under control, lest after preaching to others I myself should be disqualified."

Promise #14: BOUNDARIES PROMOTE ORDER AND UNDIVIDED DEVOTION TO GOD.

1 Corinthians 7:33-35, "But the married man is anxious about worldly things, how to please his wife, and **his interests are divided**. And the unmarried or betrothed woman is anxious about the things of the Lord, how to be holy in body and spirit. But the married woman is anxious about worldly things, **how to please her husband**. I say this for your own benefit, not to lay any restraint upon you, but **to promote good order** and to secure your undivided devotion to the Lord."

I am convinced that without good boundaries, I would not still be a husband or a pastor. The battle to be a good pastor, husband, father, and friend are won in the margins of life.

Challenge #15: DEPEND ON GOD THROUGH REST AND RECREATION.

Hebrews 4:7-10, "Today, if you hear his voice, do not harden your hearts. So then there *remains* a Sabbath rest for the people of God (including pastors), for whoever has entered God's rest has also rested from his works as God did from his."

Promise #15: REST AND RECREATION REPLENISHS YOUR MORAL COMPASS.

Hebrews 4:11, "Let us therefore *strive* to enter that rest, so that no one may *fall* by the same sort of disobedience."

Rest is the hardest work with the greatest reward. We see and experience God differently in rest than in work. Both are necessary and important to a real relationship with Jesus.

Challenge #16: DEPEND ON GOD THROUGH TRUSTING HIS PROMISES.

Joshua 23:14 "And now I am about to go the way of all the earth, and you know in your hearts and souls, all of you, that not one word has failed of all the good things[a] that the Lord your God promised concerning you."

Promise #16: GOD WILL DO ALL HE SAID HE WOULD DO FOR YOU.

Joshua 23:14a,15,16, "All (the promises) have come to pass for you; not one of them has failed. But just as all the good things that the LORD your God promised concerning you have been fulfilled for you, so the LORD will bring upon you all the evil things, until he has destroyed you from off this good land that the LORD your God has given you, if you transgress the covenant of the LORD your God, which he commanded you, and go and serve other gods and bow down to them. Then the anger of the LORD will be kindled against you, and you shall perish quickly from off the good land that he has given to you."

Just before I wrote the final chapter of this book, I watched the movie, "Silence." It is about Portuguese missionaries who went to Japan in the 1600s to find a priest who had disappeared. They eventually rediscovered one another, but instead of the movie inspiring you to hold on to your faith in Jesus and risk everything for the cause of Christ, they were fed three meals a day and shown torture of their followers that could end if they recanted their faith and served the Japanese government by eradicating Christianity from their country.

The movie ends with the priest dying with his "secret" faith while serving publicly the gods of the Japanese Buddhism. It is not outlandish to think that we in the Western World are not far from something of this magnitude. Christianity is losing its influence in the Western World more and more every day, as the morals of our faith continue to be questioned and the veracity of the authenticity of Christianity continues to be scrutinized due to pastoral leaders falling seemingly almost every week somewhere in Christendom. We as shepherds have a great responsibility to represent the authenticity of the Gospel in our day-to-day lives and in the relationships of our lives that exist in proximity to where we live most of our lives.

Jesus said to His disciples, "If you deny me before other men, I will deny you before my Father." There are many ways to deny our faith. We can outright deny our faith like the Portuguese missionaries in order to spare our miserable, pathetic existence or we can even (like many I know) deny our need to live by the D's mentioned in this book. It is easy in ministry to lose sight of your disciplines, to grow bitter without any desire to dream, to give up on being determined to fight through the challenges of the pastorate by choosing not to depend on God through accountability or strong boundaries, and not trusting the promises He has made to us.

The pain of the pastorate will at some point cause you to question everything. The silence of God in these moments will not be His absence from your life or lack of real faith, but instead His respect for your sacrifice.

Jesus believed in you enough to die for you, and then called you to shepherd those He died for. He knows this task is not easy. He has walked this road before you. He has shed His own blood for you and for those He now asks you to sacrifice for. He knows the pain you feel right now and will not walk away from you. It is easy to doubt in the darkness what God has revealed to you in the light. It is easy to quit when it gets difficult. It is easy to give up on God when you can't feel Him in the seasons of sorrow in your life.

But I always like to say, "You can always quit tomorrow."

I invite you to trust Jesus and His promises. His life is worthy of emulation and the Enemy knows that if he can get the shepherds to give up on the Savior, eventually he can scatter the sheep like he did the disciples in the darkest hour of Jesus's ministry.

Yes, the sheep will disappoint you and at times they may even bite like Peter did when he denied Jesus in His darkest hour, but don't let that deter you.

The Good Pastor doesn't live to convenience him or herself. They live to please the Savior who died and gave Himself for us. I don't know what season you are in right now for your pastoral ministry, but the Apostle Paul gave his final charge to a pastor, Timothy. I find His words still ring true today, even 2000 years later... let these words flood over you and remind you of why you do what you do, Good Pastor.

> **1 Timothy 6:11-21,** "But as for you, O man of God, flee these things. Pursue righteousness, godliness, faith, love, steadfastness, gentleness. Fight the good fight of the faith. Take hold of the eternal life to which you were called and about which you made the good confession in the presence of many witnesses. I charge you in the presence of God, who gives life to all things, and of Christ Jesus, who in his testimony before Pontius Pilate made the good confession, to keep the commandment unstained and free from reproach until the appearing of our Lord Jesus Christ, which he will display at the proper time— he who is the blessed and only Sovereign, the King of kings and Lord of lords, who alone has immortality, who dwells in unapproachable light, whom no one has ever seen or can see. To him be honor and eternal dominion. Amen.

"As for the rich in this present age, charge
them not to be haughty, nor to set their hopes
on the uncertainty of riches, but on God, who
richly provides us with everything to enjoy. They
are to do good, to be rich in good works, to be
generous and ready to share, thus storing up
treasure for themselves as a good foundation for
the future, so that they may take hold of that
which is truly life.

"O Timothy, guard the deposit entrusted
to you. Avoid the irreverent babble and
contradictions of what is falsely called
'knowledge,' for by professing it some have
swerved from the faith.

Grace be with you."

Fight the good fight, Pastor. It will ALL be worth it in the end.

We can only imagine now, but one day we will see Him
with our own eyes face to face, and we will hear Him
speak just to us with our own ears.

Close your eyes and imagine what that moment will be like.

He tells us, "I will wipe away every tear one day."

The tears coming down your cheeks right now represent
the measure of your love for what your faith in Jesus has
cost you thus far. I don't know what the remaining cost to
follow Him in your pastorate will be for you, but what I do
know is, whatever the cost, these words will one day be
worth the sacrifice.

When you cross the threshold of this life to the next, the only thing that will matter is what you did for Jesus.

Live with the promise of the end in mind, now.

When you cross from this life to the next, the first words you will hear from Jesus on that day will be:

> **Matthew 25:21,** "Well done, good and faithful servant. You have been faithful over a little; I will set you over much."

With a smile, Jesus will say to you:

"Enter into the joy of your master.' (Matthew 25:21a).

Your tears will be translated into His eternal treasure.

Remember ole faithful Joshua?

> **Joshua 24:29,30,** "After these things Joshua the son of Nun, the servant of the Lord, died, being 110 years old. And they buried him in his own inheritance at Timnath-serah, which is in the hill country of Ephraim, north of the mountain of Gaash."

At forty, he was denied the promised land because of the ten other fearful naysayers who saw obstacles greater than their God, but not Joshua. Seventy-years later his faithfulness proved invaluable to himself and more importantly to those he led and influenced.

What became of Joshua's legacy because of his unwillingness to give up on God in spite of the naysayers around him?

Joshua 24:31 tells us: **"Israel served the Lord all the days of Joshua."**

Did you catch that? Israel served the Lord ALL the days of Joshua, 110 years! That's a lot of days! That is OVER 40,000 days. Can you imagine?

His spiritual leadership mattered to a generation, a whole nation for over 40,000 days! That's legacy!

Your pastorate doesn't just matter to your faith. It also matters to the generations of people who have watched your life and sought to emulate the faith you have lived out before them. I heard recently that there are a little over two million pastors in the world to influence 7.5 billion people. You may influence a whole nation like Joshua, or it may be a small town, for over 40,000 days, but whatever your reach, it will matter to others that you remained faithful to the calling Jesus has on your life and didn't quit and didn't fornicate.

Keep that in mind as you journey toward the end of your life like Joshua.

Now, you may say, "But Kelly, I did quit. I did fornicate. I blew it."

Okay, are you willing to share with those who haven't how to avoid that painful reality? Are you willing to encourage others to stay strong and stay called to Jesus? Are you willing to let the grace of God drown the pride of your flesh enough that you look for a younger pastor to pour into? Who can learn from you what you learned the hard way? God is not finished with any of us regardless of our story, but He does expect holiness to be valued above success by His pastors both in their lives and in their churches. We must call sin SIN in our own lives and in His church, otherwise His bride will not be ready when He returns for her. Regardless of your failings as a pastor, you can help others avoid these pitfalls in their future if you choose to humbly let go of "success" and embrace the true purpose of ALL our existences. We are to use whatever influence God gives us to shout from the rooftops His holiness and His "set-apartness" while still proclaiming that His grace is sufficient in our weaknesses and failings. We all have a story, and regardless of your fornications or quittings in the pastorate, don't stop living yours.

When I was a little boy, my Pa Ralph, my dad's dad would take me for "lickins," that was ice cream. And without fail, every time we got in the car, he would start humming a tune that seemed to lift his spirits and create a mood of joy and lightheartedness in the car for both of us. I know my grandfather was not a very good man to my dad when he was a kid and didn't become a believer in Jesus until much later in his life. His dad prayed that one of his sons would be a pastor. Pa Ralph was anything but. However, through my great-grandfather Minnis Williams's prayers, and through the song of his son, Ralph (my grandfather), and through my father who became a pastor, and my cousin, Steve, who became a pastor, they have encouraged me in my faith. And in moments like this, it brings me back to the simplicity of what faithfulness to Jesus means not just for this life, but forever.

As I age, Elmer Cole's song, "Ten Thousand Years," reminds me of why I am a pastor and why I follow Jesus.

Maybe you can join me in humming along … maybe you will pass it on to generations to come like Joshua and my great-grandfather, Minnis.

Soon I'll come to the end of my journey
And I'll meet the One who gave His life for me
And I will thank Him for the love that He gave me
And ten thousand years or more I'll reign with Him

We will just begin to sing loves sweet story
And it's a song that the angels they just could not sing
And I've been redeemed by the blood of my Savior
And ten thousand years or more I'll praise His name

For the battle … is over and the victory's … been won...

...Ten thousand years and we've just begun.

Ten thousand years... And we've just begun!

Good Pastor, these D's are good enough to live our lives for the party Jesus is throwing in heaven right now.

Let's live every day with that eternal party in mind!

Some days will be harder than others, be sure and live EVERYDAY until then as if it is your last and ONE DAY, Good Pastor, you will be right!

Until then, remember the Apostle Paul's words to us:

> **Romans 8:18,** "For we consider that the sufferings of this present time are not worth comparing with the glory that is to be revealed to us."

Can't wait!

How about you good pastor?

Do you want to be great for Jesus?

Though the world forsake you, Jesus NEVER will!

Keep Pressing On, Good Pastor, until He calls you home!

ABOUT THE PASTOR/ AUTHOR

Kelly grew up on a dairy farm in Kentucky. He is a graduate of Liberty University (B.S. 1993) and Dallas Theological Seminary (ThM 1996)

After completing seminary, Kelly and his wife, Tosha, became qualified as church planter apprentices with the Home Mission Board of the Southern Baptist Convention. They moved to Colorado Springs and started Vanguard Church in 1997. Vanguard quickly raised local media attention as well as national attention in media outlets such as *Time, The 700 Club, Christianity Today, The New York Times*, and *ABC World News Tonight*. It is now one of the largest SBC churches in the state of Colorado.

Kelly has now served as the Senior Pastor of Vanguard for 25 years. Vanguard has multiple locations in the Colorado Springs/Palmer Lake area. They have seen 3317 people follow Christ in believer's baptism and have partnered to help plant 73 other churches through the Frontline Church Planting Center. The SBC declared Vanguard in 2014 to be one of the top 30 SBC churches in its size range regarding conversion rate.

Along the way, Kelly has spoken for the Billy Graham Evangelistic Association. He published *real marriage: where fantasy meets reality* with his wife Tosha in 2008.

Kelly has authored three other books as well, *Friend of Sinners: Taking Risks To Reach The Lost*, *The Mystery of 23: God Speaks*, and this his latest book *The Good Pastor*. You can learn more about his books at his amazon author page at amazon.com/author/pastorkelly

Kelly writes regularly for *Patheos, The Christian Post*, and *Outreach Magazine*.

In addition to being the husband of Tosha, and the Senior Pastor of Vanguard Church, Kelly is the proud father of five children: Anastasha, Christianna, Joshua, Annalarie, and Journey Grace. Their family lives on a small beef farm in Colorado Springs. Having grown up in Kentucky, Kelly still loves Kentucky Wildcats Basketball.

If you would like to contact the author, you can reach out to him at kelly@vanguardchurch.org. If you would like to follow his Facebook author page, you can reach him at https://www.facebook.com/PastorKelly23

CPSIA information can be obtained
at www.ICGtesting.com
Printed in the USA
JSHW042156171022
31775JS00001B/5